NICK MALGIERI'S
PASTRY

PASTRY
perfection

Foolproof Recipes for the Home Cook

Nick Malgieri

Photography by Romulo Yanes

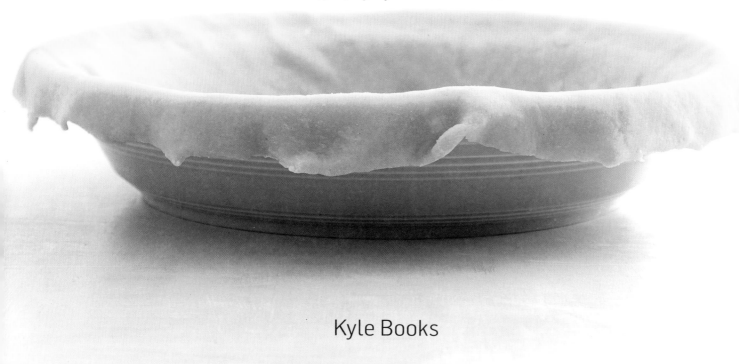

Kyle Books

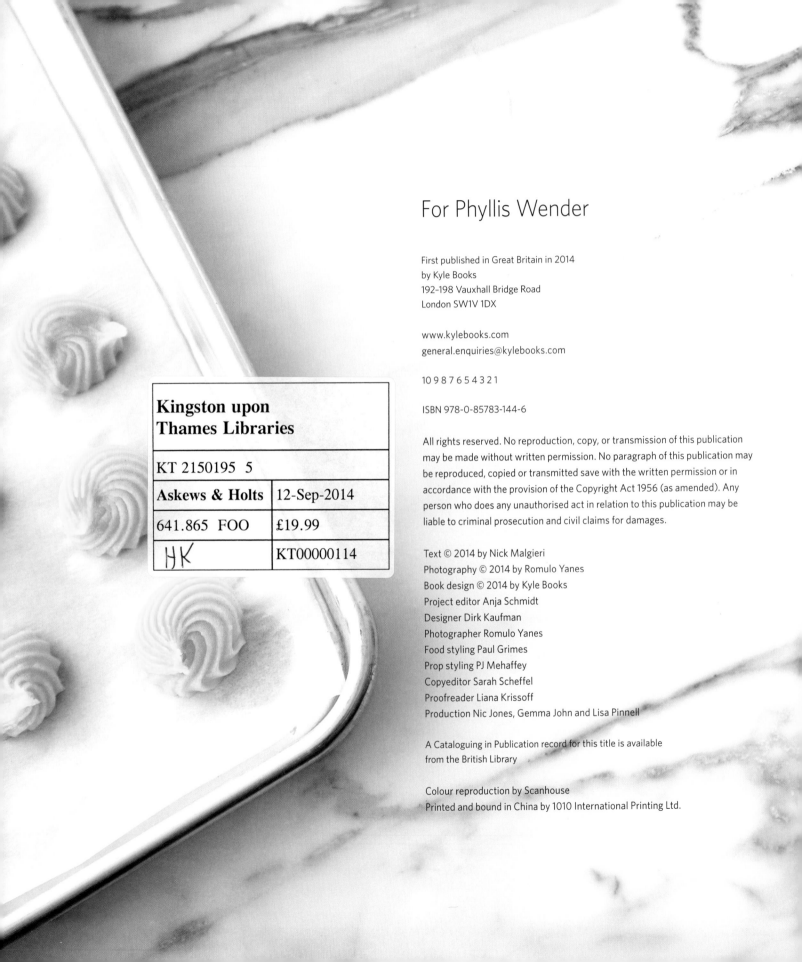

For Phyllis Wender

First published in Great Britain in 2014
by Kyle Books
192–198 Vauxhall Bridge Road
London SW1V 1DX

www.kylebooks.com
general.enquiries@kylebooks.com

10 9 8 7 6 5 4 3 2 1

ISBN 978-0-85783-144-6

Text © 2014 by Nick Malgieri
Photography © 2014 by Romulo Yanes
Book design © 2014 by Kyle Books
Project editor Anja Schmidt
Designer Dirk Kaufman
Photographer Romulo Yanes
Food styling Paul Grimes
Prop styling PJ Mehaffey
Copyeditor Sarah Scheffel
Proofreader Liana Krissoff
Production Nic Jones, Gemma John and Lisa Pinnell

A Cataloguing in Publication record for this title is available
from the British Library

Colour reproduction by Scanhouse
Printed and bound in China by 1010 International Printing Ltd.

CONTENTS

INTRODUCTION

Baking is all I've ever wanted to do. I was a pretty good student at school, but I preferred dreaming about becoming a pastry chef. As a teenager, though, despite my passion for the craft, there were two things I steadfastly refused to do: whisk egg whites and roll out dough.

Looking back, I understand my lack of success with the former – our home kitchen was equipped with plastic mixing bowls that always held slight films of grease. Any attempt to whisk egg whites failed because they just won't foam up in the presence of fat. Rolling dough was a different story: my Italian grandmother, who lived with us, was a whiz at doughs – for pasta, pastry or pizza – but she became ill before I could learn them from her. The first few times I tried working with dough on my own were dismal failures. Any recipe I followed only had the instruction to 'roll the dough'. Well, roll I did: the dough stuck to the surface, the rolling pin, or both. Or it tore or cracked. If I managed to get it into a pie tin in one piece, it usually shrank in the oven. I happily baked cakes and cookies and an occasional fancy dessert, but no whisked egg whites and definitely no dough.

I softened towards the egg whites first. After watching Julia Child whisking egg whites in a copper bowl, I went to the *Bazar Français* in New York City. The copper bowls were way beyond my budget but the friendly owner, Mr Ruegger, showed me a stainless steel bowl and then picked out a large balloon whisk. I still use that bowl often, though I did eventually buy a copper one.

Next came the dough. I watched my aunt, the official American baker in our family, roll her pie dough made with vegetable fat between two sheets of greaseproof paper and gave it a try. My crust for a lemon meringue pie turned out pretty well, but my parents commented on the awful taste the fat imparted. My grandmother had always used lard for her pastry, as is still the custom in southern Italy, so I tried making the crust with butter. It was a little more work, but the crust tasted a lot better and eventually, because I practised a lot, even rolling became easier.

Over the years, I've shared many pastry dough recipes, from ridiculously easy to quite elaborate. In this book I've given you a range of doughs, as well as step-by-step photos, showing you how to prepare, roll, shape and bake them. If you have a bad case of pastry-phobia or a fear of rolling, I can't guarantee a magic cure, but I can promise that if you follow the simple instructions here, you'll be able to tackle any pastry project you like.

CHAPTER 1

INGREDIENTS & EQUIPMENT

While keeping calm and practising often are the keys to mastering pastry doughs, it's still important to use the correct ingredients and equipment if you want the recipes you try to turn out well. The building blocks of pastry doughs are flour, butter (or occasionally oil or lard) and liquids that might be water, eggs or even sour cream. Sugar, flavouring and yeast also play an important part in many doughs and the following brief descriptions of commonly used ingredients can guide you in purchasing the correct ones to use.

Equipment falls into two categories: the first covers equipment needed to prepare doughs and work with them; while the second, and equally important, pertains to the tins used for baking pastries. Flan dishes and cake tins, large and small, flat baking tins for individual free-standing pastries and alternative moulds, such as muffin tins and gratin dishes, fall into the second category.

Good ingredients are often only as far away as a local supermarket, basic equipment is available inexpensively in a hardware or cookware shop and so to prepare all the recipes in this book successfully, the only additional thing you will need is a steady hand.

INGREDIENTS

Flours

A wheat berry consists of three parts: a starchy endosperm, used to make white flour; an outer covering or bran and an oily germ. Flour is made when wheat berries are milled and then sifted and and the type of flour produced (either soft or hard) depends on the wheat kernel's density. Hard wheat contains a high proportion of the proteins that will eventually form strong gluten in a dough and for this reason, flours made from hard wheat are referred to as strong flours. Soft wheat has a lower percentage of gluten-forming proteins and is used to make weak flour. Bread flour is a strong flour; cake flour, a weak one and plain flour falls between the two.

All-purpose flour: This is the standard white flour used in the US and is a mixture of strong and weak flours that has a 10.5–11.5% protein content. As its name implies, it's suitable for almost all uses and may be bleached or unbleached. Stored at room temperature in an airtight container, all-purpose flour will keep for at least one year.

Unbleached plain flour: This has a lower protein content than American all-purpose flour, though it functions well in recipes for pastry doughs and cake and cookie batters.

Pastry flour: Pastry flour has a low protein content and a high starch content and is similar to the unbleached plain flour milled in the UK.

Bread flour: Bread flour is high in protein, around 12%, which is desirable when making bread, other yeast doughs and some doughs that are stretched or rolled paper-thin, like strudel. Bread flour develops strong gluten, trapping gases formed during fermentation in bread and providing much-needed structure in paper-thin doughs.

High-gluten flour: As its name indicates, this has a very high protein content (about 14%) and therefore produces doughs with very strong gluten. In this book it's used for *yufka* and *baklava* doughs.

Sugars

To make sugar, sugar cane is ground, then pressed to release its juice. This liquid is then heated and centrifuged to produce sugar and molasses. The sugar is redissolved and purified with granular carbon, which is then filtered out along with the impurities it traps. Once purified, the sugar is processed to form crystals. The crystals are dried to remove any remaining moisture. Finally, the sugar is passed through a succession of sieves to separate the coarse crystals from the fine ones.

If sugar is stored in an airtight container, it will last indefinitely. However, as it absorbs water from the air, if not properly stored, it will harden into a solid chunk.

Caster sugar: All recipes in this book use caster sugar – regular white sugar – unless otherwise specified. Caster sugar is added gradually to most preparations, especially egg mixtures. Unbeaten egg yolks to which sugar is added quickly may lump and 'burn', meaning the sugar absorbs so much of the yolk liquid on initial contact that the remaining yolk components harden, preventing the sugar from dissolving completely. Also, when you whisk egg whites with sugar, a large quantity of sugar falling on the egg whites at one time can force air out of them.

Brown sugar: Brown sugar is made by blending refined sugar in its liquid form with molasses. The amount of molasses determines whether the sugar is light brown or dark brown. Brown sugar can dry out and harden into a block if left uncovered. Once you open the package, store it tightly covered, preferably in a plastic bag, in the refrigerator. If it hardens, you can place it in the microwave for a few seconds to soften it.

Icing sugar: Also known as powdered sugar or 10X sugar (because it is ten times finer than granulated sugar), icing sugar is made from granulated sugar that has been ground to a powder. Always sift it after measuring to eliminate lumps.

Salt

I prefer fine sea salt and I use it when baking. For coarse salt, I use additive-free kosher salt, or a speciality salt such as French *fleur de sel* or English Maldon sea salt flakes. Check the side panel of any salt you buy: it should list only salt as an ingredient; anticaking agents impart a bitter taste and should be avoided.

Leaveners

Leaveners cause a dough or batter to rise by creating carbon dioxide. Below are the most common leaveners used in baking.

Baking powder: A chemical leavener, this is a mixture of bicarbonate of soda and an acid element. In the past, tartrate baking powder included cream of tartar, a powerful acid although today most baking powder utilises phosphate elements as the acid component. Starch, usually cornflour, is also mixed in to stabilise the powder, as well as to absorb the excess moisture in the air, which would cause caking and lack of potency. Almost all baking powder available today is double-acting, meaning that it creates two chemical reactions that promote rising: first when combined with liquid; and second when exposed to heat. Keep baking powder in a dry spot and replace every six months. When I open a tin, I write the date on the lid with a permanent marker.

Bicarbonate of soda: Bicarbonate of soda, or baking soda, is an alkali, so it needs an acid to begin the leavening process in a dough. Such acids include buttermilk, yogurt, sour cream, molasses, honey, cocoa powder, chocolate and cream of tartar. Always use only the amount of bicarbonate of soda called for in the recipe, sift it over the other dry ingredients and stir it in well to avoid pockets of undissolved bicarbonate of soda, which will form lumps with an unpleasant chemical aftertaste. Any batter made with bicarbonate of soda needs to be placed in a preheated oven fairly quickly, because it reacts on contact with moisture and immediately begins producing the carbon dioxide that will leaven what you're making. Wait too long and you won't get nearly the impact you expect. Keep bicarbonate of soda in a cool, dry spot and replace every six months. Bicarbonate of soda also absorbs odours, so seal it tightly.

Yeast: A fungal leavener, yeast is suited to elastic, gluten-forming doughs that accommodate its slow development of carbon dioxide. Most recipes call for active dried yeast, which is granulated and comes in bulk packages, small containers or individual sachets, which contain 2¼ teaspoons (or 7g). Yeast is also available in small moist cakes and in instant form, which is faster-acting because of its finer granulation. All packaged yeast has an expiration date and should be kept in the refrigerator or freezer.

Fats

Fats have a bad reputation in our society, but there are few pleasing baked items without at least some fat in them. The choice of fat affects both the flavour and the texture of the finished product.

Butter: When it comes to butter, freshness is key. To test a stick of butter for freshness, scratch the surface with the tip of a table knife. Butter that has oxidised will be lighter on the inside than on the outside, and whatever you bake with it will taste stale. Store butter in the freezer and for long-term storage, keep it in its wrapper, sealed in clingfilm and then aluminium foil. Always use unsalted butter for baking.

Oils: Oils are used in baked items in place of or in addition to butter and frequently to coat tins. When vegetable oil is called for, sunflower, peanut and rapeseed oils will all work. Look for 'cold-pressed' oil, which means the oil was not brought to a high temperature during processing. You will also see oils labelled 'expeller-pressed', which means they have been expressed without chemical agents but does not necessarily mean the oil was not processed at a high temperature. (It can also make the oil resistant to high heat, desirable at times for cooking but rarely for baking.) Experiment a little, find a brand you like and use it.

Several recipes call for olive oil. It's fine to use whatever olive oil you habitually have on hand, whether it is extra-virgin or not.

Lard: Good-quality lard is a lot better tasting and more healthful than chemically rendered oils and solid vegetable fats. The best lard to use for baking is rendered from leaf lard, a layer of hard fat from the belly area of a pig. An old-fashioned butcher shop or a farmers' market vendor who sells pork products are the only places you'll find leaf lard. Most lard you find in the supermarket is rendered from pork fat in general and is softer than leaf lard.

Liquids

Liquids are an essential part of most pastry doughs; water being the most common.

Water: Today we don't give much thought to water, but it does have a taste, and the water used in baked goods does impart flavour and affect the results. If you live in an area with particularly hard water, meaning it has a high mineral content, you may want to consider using bottled water for baking. Unless otherwise specified, water added to pastry dough should always be chilled.

Milk and other dairy products: Cow's milk and its derivatives – butter (see page 9), milk, cream, sour cream, yogurt and cheese – make up the baker's dairy ingredients. For baking, choose whole (full-fat) milk; this goes for other dairy products as well. Throughout the Western world, the milk sold in shops is pasteurised to kill bacteria. Most milk is also homogenised to keep the cream from separating to the top and, while convenient, this does remove some of the flavour.

Buttermilk: Low in fat yet rich in texture, buttermilk lends moisture and tenderness. Originally, buttermilk was the liquid left over after slightly fermented cream was churned into butter; the ferments in the cream imparted a tangy flavour to the buttermilk. Now buttermilk is created by combining low-fat milk with cultures similar to those used in yogurt.

Cream: Whipping cream has a fat content of at least 35%, which is why it whips to a silky and luxurious consistency. Double cream (48% butterfat), whips the most easily and to the thickest consistency. Single cream, when called for, contains 18% butterfat.

Sour cream: Again, use only full-fat sour cream. Non-fat versions will not yield the same results.

Eggs

Eggs are the workhorses of the pastry kitchen. With few exceptions, it would be almost impossible to bake classic pastries without them. Sometimes the whole egg is used and sometimes just the yolks or whites. No matter how eggs are used, they bind other ingredients like flour, sugar and butter, act as leaveners, enrich and moisten, thicken mixtures, emulsify liquids and glaze pastries and doughs.

The egg white, or albumen, makes up about two-thirds of the total weight of the egg, providing over half the protein. When whisked, the white will increase in volume six to eight times. The yolk accounts for the remaining third of the total weight of the egg and contains all the fat and a bit less than half the protein.

Eggs are categorised by grade and size. Grade is based on the inner and outer quality of the egg, while size is determined by the average weight per dozen. A dozen eggs graded UK medium weighs 636–756 grams. However, within the dozen there may be variations. Some recipes, notably those for certain meringues, call for heating egg whites without completely cooking them. If you are concerned about eating uncooked eggs, substitute pasteurised egg whites.

Buy eggs with clean, uncracked shells. (There is no difference in quality or nutrition between brown and white eggs.) Store eggs large end up in their cartons and use them before their expiration date. Also, eggs absorb odours, so keep them away from strong-flavoured foods. Extra egg whites can be kept covered in the refrigerator for up to ten days. To store yolks, sprinkle them lightly with water, press clingfilm on the surface and refrigerate for no longer than two days.

A final note: crack your eggs one at a time into a small cup before adding them to the other ingredients. Encountering a rotten egg is fairly rare (and you'll recognise one immediately when it turns up), but if one egg is bad and you've cracked it into the main bowl, you'll have to toss the entire mixture.

EQUIPMENT

Tins

Tart tins: Tart tins have removable bottoms and fluted sides; sometimes these are labelled 'French tart tins'. They will be of various diameters, but the sides should be 2.5cm high.

Pie dishes: I always prefer a Pyrex pie dish, because the glass makes it easier to see the degree of doneness on the bottom crust, and glass heats better than metal, ensuring a well-baked pastry. If you're going to buy only one, choose a 23cm dish with sloping sides.

Individual and tartlet tins: This is one place where you can substitute. Ramekins and muffin tins can stand in for these smaller-sized tins.

Baking tins: Baking tin size might seem flexible, but in most cases it's not. A smaller tin may not hold all the dough and filling to be baked and a larger one will cause it to be spread too thin. Sandwich tins are round tins that are 3.75–5cm deep, sometimes slightly shallower. For rectangular tins, I use 33 x 22.5 x 5cm baking tins, 38 x 25 x 2.5cm Swiss roll tins and 36 x 28 x 2.5cm baking sheets.

In addition to baking biscuits and cookies, flat unrimmed baking trays are useful for moving dough and cake layers and for chilling pieces of dough.

If you find your oven gives off strong heat from the bottom, insulated baking sheets are worth the expense (but use them only on that bottom shelf). You can also stack two tins for a similar effect.

Tools

Rolling pins: I prefer the dowel type of rolling pin without handles – it's basically a straight cylinder of wood, about 40cm long and 5cm in diameter. Nylon rolling pins can also be useful, because dough won't stick to them as easily. For rolling *yufka* and *baklava* dough, I use a 22mm diameter dowel that is 60cm long (dowels are usually 120cm in length, so one dowel will make two rolling pins). An 8mm diameter dowel is used for forming one of the *baklava* pastries.

Scrapers: A dough scraper is a rectangular stainless steel blade – usually about 7.5 x 12.5cm – set in a handle. It is used for keeping the work surface free of stuck dough and for cutting dough into pieces. A silicone bowl scraper is a useful tool for cleaning out the inside of a mixing bowl, filling a pastry bag, or smoothing a batter or filling with a flat edge.

Cutters: Cutters are used to punch regularly shaped pieces out of rolled doughs. Though they may not seem dangerous, biscuit cutters are just as sharp as knives, so work with them carefully. They are usually made from tinned steel or good-quality hard plastic. Sets of graduated sizes of round cutters come in plain and fluted styles.

Pizza wheels: Pizza wheels are useful for cutting various doughs. They come with either straight or serrated wheels, and some are two-in-one, meaning they have a wheel of each type on either end of the handle.

CHAPTER 2

A WHOLE NEW GENERATION OF DOUGHS

For this book, I've developed new doughs alongside some of my old favourites that are as easy to prepare as they are to use. Whether you do this by hand or use a stand mixer or food processor, these doughs are ready quickly. And while most of them benefit from a short rest in the refrigerator before being rolled and formed into a crust, some can be rolled out immediately after mixing.

I like to categorise doughs in two ways: those that have a visible internal structure and those that are merely smooth pastes. The former are the flaky doughs that have tiny pieces of fat randomly sprinkled throughout; when the dough is rolled, the pieces of fat become irregular layers that fill with steam and puff slightly in the oven. The latter are the doughs based on liquid fats or in which solid fat is smoothly mixed with the rest of the ingredients, as for sweetened doughs.

All simple pastry doughs, whether flaky or smooth, should be tender after baking. A large part of that tenderness is due to the proportions of the ingredients, but it is also important to handle the dough minimally during mixing and allow the rolled-out crusts to chill before baking.

If you've had difficulties with pastry doughs in the past, try these recipes; I know you'll be successful with them.

OLIVE OIL DOUGH

Makes enough for one large tart or single-crusted pie (double the quantities for a double crust), or 8 or 9 individual 11.5cm tarts

200g unbleached plain flour

1 teaspoon fine sea salt

1 teaspoon caster sugar

1 teaspoon baking powder

60ml olive oil

2 medium eggs

PLANNING AHEAD

This dough keeps well in the refrigerator for up to 3 days.

VARIATIONS

Use a mild vegetable oil such as organic, cold-pressed sunflower oil for a milder flavour. Double all the ingredients for a two-crust pie.

This is my new favourite dough for savoury tarts and pies and is a perfect example of the fact that baking doesn't have to be complicated to be good. It is easy to prepare, rolls out like a dream, bakes to a tender texture and there's just enough olive oil flavour to complement the filling it surrounds. You can substitute this dough for Flaky Buttery Dough in any of the savoury tart or pie recipes.

1. Use a fork to stir together the flour, salt, sugar and baking powder in a medium bowl.

2. Make a well in the centre of the dry ingredients and add the oil and eggs. Use the fork to beat the eggs and oil together, then gradually draw in the dry ingredients a little at a time until the dough starts to hold together.

3. Scrape the contents of the bowl onto a lightly floured work surface (it's okay if there are still some dry bits) and fold the dough over on itself 4 or 5 times, gently kneading it smooth. Kneading too much might make the oil separate from the dough.

4. Wrap the dough in clingfilm and keep at a cool room temperature if you're using within a few hours; refrigerate for longer storage.

FLAKY BUTTERY DOUGH

Makes enough for two single-crusted pies or one double-crusted pie

315g unbleached plain flour

½ teaspoon fine sea salt

1 teaspoon baking powder

225g unsalted butter, chilled and cut into 1.25cm pieces

2 medium eggs

PLANNING AHEAD

This dough keeps well in the refrigerator for up to 3 days.

To get as much delicate buttery flavour as possible into a dough and to maximise flakiness, you need to use enough butter. However, to keep from melting the butter and creating an excessively soft dough, I recommend you mix this one in a food processor. If you then remember to chill the dough after mixing it and again after rolling it, you'll enjoy both a superior texture and flavour.

1. Combine the flour, salt and baking powder in the bowl of a food processor; pulse several times at 1-second intervals to mix.

2. Add the butter and pulse again 3 or 4 times. Use a metal spatula to scrape the side of the bowl and mix the butter pieces throughout the flour.

3. Pulse again 3 or 4 times.

4. Using a fork, beat the eggs to break them up and add to the bowl. Pulse again until the dough almost forms a ball; avoid pulsing too much, or the pieces of butter needed to make the dough flaky will become too small.

5. Invert the dough onto a lightly floured work surface, carefully remove the blade, and quickly press the dough together.

6. Divide the dough into 2 pieces, form into thick disks and wrap each in clingfilm. Chill for a couple of hours before rolling.

FLAKY DOUGH USING LARD

Since I grew up on southern Italian food that used lard in both cooking and baking, I've never had an aversion to it. And while I support anyone's desire to avoid pork products for religious reasons, I don't quite understand the general aversion to lard. It certainly tastes better and is much healthier than chemically rendered solid vegetable fat with or without trans fats. Even if you only have access to lard from the supermarket, try this recipe for a savoury tart or pie or something simple and rustic like an apple pie, and you'll see why many people swear by lard for pie dough. This dough is best mixed by hand and you can substitute it for Flaky Buttery Dough in any savoury recipe. It also works well in some less delicate sweet tarts and pies, such as the Apple & Cheddar Pie on page 88.

Makes enough for two single-crusted pies or one double-crusted pie

270g unbleached plain flour

½ teaspoon fine sea salt

1 teaspoon baking powder

75ml ice water

170g lard, chilled and cut into 1.25cm pieces

1. Use a fork to stir together the flour, salt and baking powder in a medium bowl.

2. Pour the water into a small bowl or cup, and then transfer 60ml to another bowl or cup, leaving the remainder in the original bowl. Set both aside.

3. Add the lard to the dry ingredients and, keeping your fingers apart, use both hands to reach to the bottom of the bowl and lift upwards through the pieces of lard ① so that they're all coated with flour and evenly distributed throughout.

4. Gently rub the pieces of lard into the flour using your fingertips, occasionally repeating the motion in step 3, until the lard is reduced to 0.5cm pieces ②.

5. Pour the 60ml of water all over the surface of the flour and lard mixture ③, then use the fork to toss upwards from the bottom of the bowl, until the water is evenly mixed through ④. If there are a lot of dry bits in the dough, use some of the remaining water a little at a time, repeating the tossing motion with the fork, until the dough starts holding together easily ⑤.

6. Invert the dough onto a lightly floured work surface and quickly press it together.

7. Divide the dough into 2 pieces and wrap each in clingfilm. Chill for 2 hours before rolling.

VARIATION

FLAKY DOUGH MADE WITH LARD AND BUTTER: For a milder flavour, replace half the lard with an equal amount of butter, adding the butter first and rubbing it in a little before adding the lard.

PASTY DOUGH

Makes enough for six large or twelve small pasties

500g strong bread flour

1½ teaspoons fine sea salt

140g unsalted butter, cold, cut into 0.5cm cubes

200ml cold water

This unusual dough is reserved exclusively for making Cornish-style pasties on page 125. While most of the recipes that pasty makers have revealed call for solid vegetable fat, I was bent on using only butter, but I was afraid that butter might not survive the vigorous mixing that the dough requires. Fortunately, butter held its own, resulting in a dough with both the right degree of elasticity for making pasties as well as excellent flavour.

1. Stir the flour and salt together in the bowl of an electric mixer. Stir in the butter and place the bowl on the mixer fitted with the paddle attachment. Mix on the lowest speed for 3–4 minutes until the butter is finely worked into the flour, .

2. Scrape the bowl and beater and attach the dough hook. Start mixing on the lowest speed and pour in the water in a stream. Mix until the dough is evenly moistened and masses around the hook. If some dry bits remain unmoistened at the bottom of the bowl, add up to a tablespoon more water, a little at a time, until no dry flour remains.

3. Increase the speed to medium-low and beat for a further 2–3 minutes until smooth and elastic.

4. Transfer the dough to a floured work surface and knead by hand for a minute or two. Divide the dough into 6 x 140g pieces or 12 x 70g pieces and round them smoothly. Wrap individually in clingfilm, place in a bowl and chill for several hours before rolling.

SOUR CREAM DOUGH

Makes enough for the top crust of a large savoury pie or sweet cobbler or eight empanadas

270g unbleached plain flour

½ teaspoon fine sea salt

225g unsalted butter, chilled and cut into 20 pieces

150ml sour cream

My dear late friend Sheri Portwood ran a Dallas catering business for years and was constantly trying to perfect her recipe for *rugelach*, which uses this dough. I've included recipes for *rugelach* in several other books, but I love this dough as the top of a deep-dish savoury pie, a cobbler (especially when it's cut into separate overlapping disks for the top crust), or for any top-crust-only pie. It's flaky, extremely tender and delicate; almost like puff pastry. A food processor does the best job of mixing this.

1. Combine the flour and salt in the bowl of a food processor and pulse several times at 1-second intervals to mix.

2. Add the butter and pulse until it's finely mixed into the flour and no visible pieces remain.

3. Spread the sour cream all over the top of the flour and butter mixture (rather than adding it all in one spot). Pulse 3–4 times; if the dough is already starting to form a ball, stop pulsing; if not, pulse a few more times but don't overmix or the flaky quality of the dough will be lost.

4. Invert the dough onto a lightly floured work surface. Shape into a disk and wrap in clingfilm.

5. Chill the dough for 2–3 hours or overnight before using.

YEAST-RISEN DOUGH FOR EMPANADAS

This dough is similar to that used for the Spanish pie or *Empanada Gallega* in my *BREAD* book. Although the empanada in the original recipe is a large pie, this also works very well for turnover-type empanadas (you can use this dough for any of the empanada recipes). A half recipe of this dough can also make an excellent single crust for a savoury pie or tart.

1. Mix the flour with the sugar and salt and set aside.

2. Whisk the water and yeast together by hand in the bowl of an electric mixer, then whisk in the oil and egg. Use a large rubber spatula to stir in the flour mixture.

3. Place the bowl on the mixer fitted with the dough hook and beat on the lowest speed for about 2 minutes until fairly smooth. Remove the dough from the mixer and knead for a minute.

4. Place the dough in a lightly oiled bowl and turn it so that the top is oiled. Cover the bowl with clingfilm and let the dough ferment for 30–45 minutes until it doubles in bulk.

5. Divide the dough into 12 x 60g pieces. Form into even disks, place on a floured tin, cover with clingfilm and chill for about 1 hour until they are firm enough to roll.

Makes about 675g, enough for about twelve empanadas

400g unbleached plain flour

1½ teaspoons caster sugar

1½ teaspoons fine sea salt

180ml room-temperature (about 24°C) tap water

7g sachet fine granulated active dried yeast or instant yeast

120ml olive oil, plus more for brushing

1 medium egg

POLENTA DOUGH

Makes enough for one large tart or single-crusted pie

90g unbleached plain flour

110g stoneground polenta

1 teaspoon fine sea salt

1 teaspoon caster sugar

1 teaspoon baking powder

110g unsalted butter, chilled and cut into 12 pieces

1 medium egg

PLANNING AHEAD

This dough keeps well in the refrigerator for up to 3 days.

The slightly sweet and nutty flavour of polenta pairs well with many savoury or sweet fillings (it's especially good as a cobbler topping). I also love this dough because it bakes to a slightly crunchy but tender texture. Please be sure to use stoneground polenta for this; it's more finely milled and has much more corn flavour than the typical degerminated polenta available in the supermarket. You can substitute this dough for Flaky Buttery Dough in any of the savoury tart or pie recipes.

1. Combine the flour, polenta, salt, sugar and baking powder in the bowl of a food processor and pulse several times at 1-second intervals to mix.

2. Add the butter and pulse again repeatedly until it is finely mixed into the dry ingredients.

3. Add the egg and pulse again until the dough just starts to form a ball.

4. Invert the dough onto a lightly floured surface and quickly press it together.

5. Form the dough into a disk shape and wrap in clingfilm. Refrigerate until needed.

VARIATION

POLENTA DOUGH WITH CHEESE OR HERBS: Add 55g coarsely grated Gruyère or Cheddar cheese and/or 1 tablespoon chopped flat-leaf parsley, coriander or finely snipped chives along with the butter.

SWEET PASTRY DOUGH MADE WITH OIL

Makes enough for one large tart or single-crusted pie

170g unbleached plain flour

2 tablespoons caster sugar

½ teaspoon baking powder

¼ teaspoon fine sea salt

3 tablespoons expeller-pressed sunflower or rapeseed oil, preferably organic

2 tablespoons water

1 medium egg

PLANNING AHEAD

This dough keeps well in the refrigerator for up to 3 days.

This dough is a fraternal twin to both the unsweetened olive oil dough (page 14) and the butter-based sweet pastry dough opposite. It has the advantage of being really easy to prepare and to roll and is ready to go immediately after it's mixed. I always use an organic expeller-pressed sunflower oil to make this. Other easily available oils, especially ones that have fat chemically extracted from seeds or nuts, give an off taste to a delicate dough like this. I experimented with using nut oils, but since the nut flavour almost entirely dissipates while the dough is baking, I couldn't justify the added expense involved in using them. You can substitute this dough for the Sweet Pastry Dough made with butter that follows.

1. Use a fork to stir together the flour, sugar, baking powder and salt in a medium bowl.

2. Make a well in the centre of the dry ingredients and add the oil, water and egg. Use the fork to beat the liquids together, then begin to draw in the dry ingredients a little at a time until the dough starts to hold together.

3. Scrape the contents of the bowl (it's okay if there are still some dry bits) onto a lightly floured work surface and fold the dough over on itself 4 or 5 times, gently kneading it smooth. Kneading too much might make the oil separate from the dough.

4. Wrap the dough in clingfilm and keep at a cool room temperature if you're using it within a few hours, or refrigerate for longer storage.

SWEET PASTRY DOUGH

This is the same recipe as my Sweet Pastry Dough from *BAKE!* and several other books that I've been using successfully for over thirty years and have taught to thousands of people. I thought of doing something different just for the sake of having something new, but then decided that the ease of preparation and handling, plus the tender quality of this dough after baking, can't be improved upon. Below are the food processor instructions, and after the recipe, you'll find instructions for working by hand and for using a stand mixer.

1. Combine the flour, sugar, baking powder and salt in the bowl of a food processor; pulse several times at 1-second intervals to mix.

2. Add the butter and pulse again until the butter is finely mixed through the dry ingredients and no visible pieces remain.

3. Use a fork to beat the eggs enough to break them up, and add to the bowl. Pulse again until the dough almost forms a ball; avoid pulsing too much or the dough might become too soft.

4. Invert the dough onto a lightly floured work surface and gently knead together 3 or 4 times to make it smooth.

5. Divide the dough into 2 pieces, form them into disks, and wrap each in clingfilm. Chill for a couple of hours before rolling.

6. Place the dough on a floured surface and gently knead until smooth and malleable. Form into disks again before beginning to roll.

VARIATIONS

To mix the dough by hand, stir the dry ingredients together in a medium mixing bowl. Add the butter and use your fingertips to rub the butter into the dry ingredients, occasionally using your hands to scrape the bottom of the bowl and incorporate any unmixed flour. Once the butter is finely mixed through and no visible pieces remain, use a fork to beat the eggs to break them up; add them to the bowl. Use the fork to scrape up from the bottom of the bowl and incorporate the eggs. You can also stir with the fork while using the other hand to move the bowl back and forth on the work surface. Once the dough starts holding together, continue with step 4.

To mix the dough in a stand mixer, combine the dry ingredients in the mixer bowl and place on the mixer fitted with the paddle attachment. Mix on the lowest speed for a few seconds, then add the butter and mix for about 30 seconds until it begins to break down into smaller pieces. Stop and scrape the bowl and beater, then repeat 30 seconds of mixing, followed by stopping and scraping, until the butter is finely worked into the dry ingredients and no visible pieces remain. Whisk the eggs to break them up; add to the bowl and mix again on the lowest speed until the dough begins to hold together, then continue with step 4.

Makes about 500g dough, enough for two single-crusted pies or tarts or one double-crusted pie

260g unbleached plain flour

75g caster sugar

½ teaspoon baking powder

¼ teaspoon fine sea salt

110g unsalted butter, chilled and cut into 12 pieces

2 medium eggs

PLANNING AHEAD
This dough keeps well in the refrigerator for up to 3 days.

FRENCH-STYLE COOKIE DOUGH (PÂTE SABLÉE)

Makes enough for two large tarts or twelve individual 11.5cm tarts

225g unsalted butter, slightly softened

110g icing sugar, sifted

2 teaspoons vanilla extract

½ teaspoon lemon extract, optional

2 medium egg yolks

340g unbleached plain flour

PLANNING AHEAD
This dough keeps well in the refrigerator for up to 3 days.

There's nothing better for a tart assembled in a fully baked sweet crust than this type of cookie dough. It's sweet, slightly crumbly and perfectly complements the filling – usually tangy citrus curd or velvety pastry cream topped with delicate fruit and berries. Good cookie dough is soft; it's not so easy to work with, but provides a crisp and delicate crust for many sweet tarts both large and small.

1. Beat the butter and icing sugar on the lowest speed in a stand mixer fitted with the paddle attachment until well-mixed, then increase the speed to medium and beat for about 3 minutes until lightened.

2. Add the extracts, then the egg yolks, one at a time, beating after each addition until the mixture is smooth.

3. Use a rubber spatula to scrape down the bowl and beater and beat in the flour on the lowest speed.

4. Scrape the dough onto a lightly floured work surface and gently knead it together 3 or 4 times to make it smooth.

5. Divide the dough into 2 pieces, form them into disks and wrap each one in clingfilm. Chill the dough for a couple of hours before rolling.

ALMOND COOKIE DOUGH

Makes enough for two large tarts

270g unbleached plain flour

110g finely ground blanched almonds, sifted

170g unsalted butter, slightly softened

110g icing sugar, sifted

2 teaspoons vanilla extract

½ teaspoon lemon extract, optional

2 medium egg yolks

PLANNING AHEAD
This dough keeps well in the refrigerator for up to 3 days.

Most cookie doughs enhanced with ground nuts don't have enough added to make much of a difference to the dough's taste or texture. This dough is loaded with ground almonds, so it has great flavour and a crumbly quality that sets it apart. While any ground nuts would work, blanched almonds are my choice for the delicate flavour and texture they impart.

1. Stir the flour and ground almonds together and set them aside.

2. Beat the butter and icing sugar on the lowest speed in a stand mixer fitted with the paddle attachment until well-mixed, then increase the speed to medium and beat for about 3 minutes until lightened.

3. Add the extracts, then the egg yolks, one at a time, beating after each addition until the mixture is smooth.

4. Use a rubber spatula to scrape down the bowl and beater and beat in the flour mixture on the lowest speed.

5. Scrape the dough onto a lightly floured work surface and gently knead it together 3 or 4 times to make it smooth.

6. Divide the dough into 2 pieces, form them into disks and wrap each one in clingfilm. Chill the dough for a couple of hours before rolling.

SWEET COCOA DOUGH

This is a slight variation on my favourite, Sweet Pastry Dough (page 19), and is just as easy to prepare and use. I like alkalised (Dutch-process) cocoa powder best for this because it has a more chocolatey colour and delicate flavour than natural cocoa. Follow the instructions in the Sweet Pastry Dough recipe if you want to mix by hand or in a stand mixer.

1. Combine the flour, cocoa powder, sugar, baking powder and salt in the bowl of a food processor; pulse several times at 1-second intervals to mix.

2. Add the butter and pulse again until the butter is finely mixed through the dry ingredients and no visible pieces remain.

3. Use a fork to beat the egg enough to break it up, then add it to the bowl. Pulse again until the dough almost forms a ball; avoid pulsing too much or the dough might become too soft.

4. Invert the dough onto a lightly floured work surface and gently knead it together 3 or 4 times to make it smooth.

5. Form the dough into a disk and wrap it in clingfilm. Chill it for a couple of hours before rolling.

6. Place the dough on a floured surface and gently knead until smooth and malleable. Form into a disk again before beginning to roll.

Makes enough for one large tart or single-crusted pie

135g unbleached plain flour

3 tablespoons alkalised (Dutch-process) cocoa powder, sifted after measuring

3 tablespoons caster sugar

½ teaspoon baking powder

¼ teaspoon fine sea salt

70g unsalted butter, chilled and cut into 8 pieces

1 medium egg

PLANNING AHEAD

This dough keeps well in the refrigerator for up to 3 days.

CHOCOLATE COOKIE DOUGH

This dough has real chocolate flavour and an extremely delicate texture after baking, making it particularly well suited to individual and miniature tarts. Use the best quality chocolate you can get, but if it has more than 60% cocoa solids, it might make the dough too bitter.

1. Stir the flour and icing sugar together and set aside.

2. Place the butter in a bowl and use a large rubber spatula to beat it smooth. Scrape in the chocolate and stir it into the butter (if the chocolate is still warm, the butter will melt and the dough will be ruined).

3. Add the flour mixture and stir it in to form a soft dough.

4. Scrape the dough out onto a piece of clingfilm and cover it with more clingfilm. Press the dough with the palm of your hand to make it about 1.25cm thick. Slide the dough onto a plate or baking tray and refrigerate for 1–2 hours until it is firm.

5. As this dough becomes very hard when chilled, soften it for 20–30 minutes at room temperature, then knead it together until malleable.

NOTE

The butter has to be softened to the consistency of mayonnaise – if it's firmer, it won't mix evenly with the cooled chocolate. If you forgot to soften the butter, cut it into small cubes and microwave it for no more than 3 seconds at a time until it is very soft. Don't let the butter melt, or the dough won't have the right texture.

Makes enough for two large tarts or single-crusted pies or twelve individual 11.5cm tarts or at least thirty-six tartlets or barquettes

340g unbleached plain flour

60g icing sugar, sifted

225g unsalted butter, very soft (see Note)

170g dark chocolate (no more than 60% cocoa solids), melted and cooled to room temperature

PLANNING AHEAD

This dough keeps well in the refrigerator for up to 3 days.

NUT BISCUIT BATTER (FOR COOKIE DOUGH CRUSTS)

2 tablespoons unbleached plain flour

2 tablespoons caster sugar

1 medium egg

Pinch of salt

½ teaspoon vanilla extract

30g ground nuts

30g unsalted butter, melted

This buttery batter is spread on the bottom of a cookie dough tart crust before it's baked. It adds richness, a note of flavour and, most of all, prevents the crust from softening by absorbing any liquid draining from fruit or other filling in the tart.

1. Whisk the flour and sugar together in a medium bowl; add the egg and whisk smooth.

2. Whisk in the salt and vanilla extract, then use a small rubber spatula to fold in the nuts and butter.

3. Follow steps 1-3 in Baking an Empty Crust for a Tart or Pie (page 37), using the cookie crust and tart tin of your choice. Spread the nut biscuit batter into the crust. Do not line the crust with paper and beans; instead, skip to step 6 and bake the crust for 20-25 minutes until it is completely baked through.

Using Scraps of Dough

While all the pastry dough recipes in the previous pages are calculated to provide the right amount of dough for the tin size required, you may still accumulate some dough scraps after trimming a crust when it's safely in its baking tin. If you have just a couple of tablespoons of dough scraps, you can reroll them and use a round or decorative cutter to make a few decorations for the top of a double-crusted pie. However, if you have a handful of scraps, use one of the procedures below to make some little treats from them.

USING SCRAPS OF UNSWEETENED DOUGH: These may be treated the same way as the sweet dough scraps below or used to make a savoury snack. Form the scraps into a square and wrap and chill if the dough has become soft. Place the square of dough on a floured surface and flour it; roll it to a rectangle twice as long as it is wide. Spray or brush the dough with water and sprinkle on some grated dry cheese, fresh or dried herbs, or even some coarse salt and freshly ground pepper on the bottom half of the dough. Fold the top half of the dough down to enclose the seasonings and press well. Roll again to almost the original size and use a pizza wheel to cut the dough into 0.5cm-wide strips. Transfer them to a parchment-covered tin and bake them at 180°F/gas mark 4 until golden and dry, about 15 minutes.

USING SCRAPS OF SWEETENED DOUGH: Proceed as above, rolling the dough to a rectangle and spraying with water. Use some cinnamon sugar with or without the addition of ground nuts to cover half the dough. Fold, roll, cut and bake as above.

Gluten-Free Doughs

These recipes were both shared by Michelle Tampakis, our gluten-free baking expert at the Institute of Culinary Education and a friend and colleague for more than 30 years. After discovering her gluten allergy, she plunged wholeheartedly into working with alternative flours and has developed delicious recipes in every category of baked goods – her rice flour pasta and her gluten-free brioche are both outstanding. She now owns and operates *Whipped Pastry Boutique*, a gluten-free bakery.

Chances are that if you have wheat sensitivities of any kind, you won't be reading this book, but many readers might be inspired to prepare a pie or tart for someone who is gluten intolerant. There are quite a few pie and tart fillings that contain no flour, which would pair well with these doughs. Please remember though, that if you decide to bake for someone who can't have wheat, you'll have to scrupulously clean all your vessels, utensils and work areas; even a minuscule amount of flour could cause a life-threatening reaction in someone with a severe allergy.

Both the following doughs bake up crisp and flavourful. The unsweetened dough is best when fully baked and finished with a filling that needs little or no subsequent baking. The sweet cookie dough is similar, but because of its particularly inelastic nature, is best suited for individual or miniature tarts. With these limitations in mind, substitute these doughs in any recipes that have gluten-free fillings.

UNSWEETENED GLUTEN-FREE DOUGH

Makes enough for one large tart or single-crusted pie

75g brown rice flour

40g potato flour

15g white rice flour

15g tapioca flour

1 tablespoon caster sugar

1 teaspoon fine sea salt

110g unsalted butter, chilled and cut into 12 pieces

3 tablespoons ice water

1 teaspoon distilled white vinegar

1. Combine all the dry ingredients in the bowl of a food processor and pulse several times at 1-second intervals to mix.

2. Add the butter and pulse again until the ingredients are finely blended but still mealy.

3. Mix the water and vinegar together and add the liquid to the bowl. Pulse again until the dough forms a ball.

4. Invert the dough onto the work surface. Mould the dough into a disk, wrap it in clingfilm, and chill for about 1 hour until firm.

PLANNING AHEAD
This dough keeps well in the refrigerator for up to 3 days.

GLUTEN-FREE COOKIE DOUGH

Since this dough is sweetened with icing sugar, be sure to read the ingredients on the packaging as some icing sugars might contain wheat starch and therefore not be entirely gluten-free.

Makes enough for two large tarts or ten to twelve individual tarts

170g sorghum flour

85g brown rice flour

30g tapioca flour

2 tablespoons (15g) potato flour

50g caster sugar

25g icing sugar, sifted

½ teaspoon fine sea salt

170g unsalted butter, chilled and cut into 20 pieces

1 medium egg

1 medium egg yolk

1 teaspoon vanilla extract

1. Combine all the dry ingredients in the bowl of a food processor and pulse several times at 1-second intervals to mix.

2. Add the butter and pulse again until the ingredients are finely blended but still mealy.

3. Mix the egg, egg yolk and vanilla extract together and add them to the bowl. Pulse again until the dough forms a ball.

4. Invert the dough onto the work surface. Mould the dough into a disk, wrap it in clingfilm and chill for about 1 hour until firm.

ROLLING GLUTEN-FREE DOUGHS & FORMING TART CRUSTS

BAKING GLUTEN-FREE TART CRUSTS

See the instructions for blind-baking tart crusts on page 37. Be careful not to overbake a gluten-free crust, or it will become very hard.

Unlike most pastries, you can't dust the surface of gluten-free doughs with any sort of flour for rolling – the sticky nature of these doughs only makes them absorb more and more of it as you roll. Because of this, they have to be rolled between pieces of parchment or wax paper and chilled before being transferred to the baking tin.

1. Have 2 large squares of parchment paper and a thin baking tray or flexible cutting board ready before beginning to roll.

2. Place one of the squares of paper on your work surface and centre the chilled dough on it. Cover it with the second piece of paper ①.

3. Press gently with your rolling pin in successive strikes that are parallel to each other and to the edge of the work surface. Turn the whole package of dough and paper 30 degrees and repeat.

4. After the dough has softened slightly, roll it as for any other dough ②, from 6 o'clock to 12 o'clock and back again without rolling over the edges and rotating the dough 30 degrees after every set of rolls.

5. Once the dough is large enough for your tin ③, slide the package of dough and papers onto your baking tray and chill for 15–20 minutes until it is firm.

6. Once the dough has chilled, spray your tart tin with vegetable cooking spray. Carefully peel off the top paper and quickly invert the dough ④, centring it over the tin.

7. Peel away the second paper and gently ease the dough into the bottom and against the sides of the tin all around ⑤, allowing any extra to hang over the top edge.

8. Roll over the top of the tin with your rolling pin to remove any excess dough ⑥. Finish off the top edge of the crust by pressing against the side of the dough with your thumb and down from the top at the same time.

9. For individual tart crusts, roll the dough to a square, then use scissors to cut it into squares large enough to cover the bottom and sides of your tins. Follow steps 6–8 with the individual squares of dough.

ROLLING SIMPLE PASTRY DOUGHS

Rolling dough is easy; millions – probably billions – of people can do it, and so can you. Over the years, I've developed some specific methods for teaching people how to do it successfully and they are listed here.

1. Always start with chilled dough; the only exception is dough that's made with oil.

2. Flaky doughs and cookie doughs need to soften briefly at room temperature before being rolled, but be careful not to wait too long if the room is warm.

3. Sweet doughs have to be floured and kneaded briefly until malleable.

4. Before rolling any dough, ease it into the shape needed for the tin. For a round tin, form it into a rough disk shape ①; for a square or rectangular tin, form it into a square. Only press in on the sides of your piece of dough; don't fold it over on itself or roll it into a ball. The only exception is the sweet dough.

5. Once you have the shape you need, flour the work surface with pinches of flour and place the dough on it, then flour the top of the dough. Using pinches of flour means that you are much less likely to add too much flour while you're rolling. Never use handfuls of flour on the surface or the dough.

6. Before beginning to roll, flatten your piece of dough by pressing it with the rolling pin in a series of lines parallel to the edge of the work surface. Turn a round piece of dough 30° or a square piece 90° and repeat. You'll see that the dough starts getting slightly softer and thinner but keeps the shape you've eased it into. Remember to renew the pinches of flour under and on top of the dough even as you're pressing it out.

7. When you roll, imagine that the dough is the face of a clock and roll from 6 o'clock to 12 o'clock and back again, stopping short of rolling over the edges in both directions ②.

8. Turn a round piece of dough 30° or a square 90° ③ and repeat ④, remembering to flour the surface and the dough.

9. Repeat steps 7 and 8 until the dough is the correct size for your tin. Have your tin nearby so that you can compare the size of the dough to it. For a tart tin, the diameter of the dough should be the diameter of the tin plus twice its depth plus 2.5cm. For a pie dish, the size should be 7.5cm wider than the top of the tin.

①

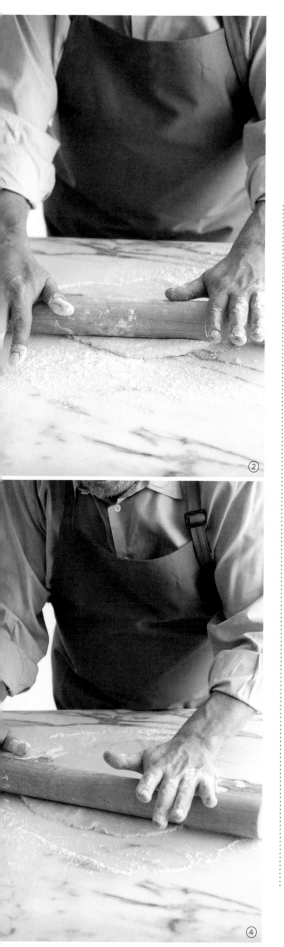

PRE-ROLLED TART OR PIECRUSTS

Having rolled crusts ready in the refrigerator or freezer takes little time and makes assembling tarts and pies a snap.

1. Follow the directions for rolling on page 26.

2. Calculate the diameter of your pre-rolled crust; it should be several centimetres larger than the tin you'll eventually bake it in.

3. Cut a pattern from stiff cardboard or use a cake board to trim the first piece of dough to the required size.

4. Transfer the dough to a baking tray covered with clingfilm.

5. Cover the dough round with clingfilm and stack the next crust you roll on top of it, continuing for however many crusts you're making.

6. Wrap and refrigerate the baking tray and use the pre-rolled crusts within a day or two.

7. Alternatively, you can freeze the crusts: let them rest in the refrigerator overnight first. Then place the baking tray in the freezer until the crusts are frozen solid, slide them from the tray to a piece of cardboard, and wrap them well in clingfilm. They will keep for a month or two.

8. To use your pre-rolled crust, whether refrigerated or frozen, slide it to the work surface still on its base of clingfilm. While the dough is still relatively stiff, slide your hands between the crust and plastic, palms up, and centre it on the tin you're using. Let the dough soften slightly so that there is no danger of tearing it.

9. Form the tart or pie crust according to the instructions on pages 28 and 29.

LINING A TIN FOR A TART OR PIE

1. For a tart tin, once the dough is in the tin, lift the edges and ease the dough into place from the edge inward. Never stretch dough to conform to the shape of the tin, or it will shrink back while baking.

2. Press the dough against the bottom of the tin and then gently press with a fingertip into the angle where the side meets the bottom of the tin.

3. Gently press the dough against the side of the tin and let the excess hang over the rim of the tin.

4. For sweet doughs and cookie doughs, roll over the top of the tin with a rolling pin to remove the excess dough.

5. For flaky doughs, use scissors, a dough scraper, or the back of a paring knife to trim all but 1.25cm of the excess dough ①. Fold this dough back into and against the side of the tin to reinforce it and to provide a little extra dough to make up for eventual shrinkage ②.

6. If you are making a tart with any type of dough or a pie with a cookie crust, even off the top edge of the crust by pressing it in against the side of the crust with your thumb and down with your index finger at the same time ③.

7. For a pie, unfold the flaky or sweet dough into the tin and press well against the bottom and sides of the tin. If you are making a single-crust pie, see the instructions on page 36 for finishing the edge. For a double-crusted pie, you do not need to do anything more to the bottom crust; see pages 32–34 for instructions on forming the top crust.

8. Chill the crust until firm. If you're going to keep it refrigerated for more than a few hours (overnight is best, especially with a flaky dough), wrap the chilled crust in clingfilm.

FORMING INDIVIDUAL TART CRUSTS

The tins I use for individual tarts are 11.5cm in diameter. They make a generous individual serving, whether savoury or sweet. If you know you're going to be making individual tarts, the process starts right after mixing the dough.

1. Once your dough is mixed, shape it into a fat cylinder, wrap it and chill it. This makes it easy to cut round slices of dough for lining the tins. The Sweet, Cocoa and Chocolate doughs are the exception, since they have to be kneaded to make them malleable enough for rolling before being shaped into a cylinder.

2. Weigh your dough and calculate how many tarts you can make with it – you'll need a 60g piece of dough for each tin. Mark the dough into the corresponding number of equal-sized pieces. Once it is marked, use a dough scraper to cut the dough.

3. Roll and form the small pieces of dough in exactly the way described for a tart crust on page 26 and on the left of this page.

4. Arrange the tart tins on a Swiss roll tin and chill them before baking. If you're going to keep the crusts chilled until the next day, wrap them in clingfilm once they're firm.

FORMING MINI ROUND TART CRUSTS

The tins I use for these are slope-sided and 6cm in diameter at the top. If you have new ones, wash them well and dry them, then bake them at 190°C/gas mark 5 for 30 minutes and allow them to cool. Heating them seasons the surface, much as you might do with a new omelette pan. Coat the tins with vegetable cooking spray the first few times you use them; after that, it will no longer be necessary. Once you start baking with the tins, only wipe them well after each use; don't wash them in soapy water, or dough might stick in them. Be especially careful not to overfill the tarts, especially with anything custardy that might overflow and glue the crust to the tin.

1. Divide the dough you're using for miniature tarts into 3 or 4 pieces and work with one piece at a time, keeping the remainder wrapped and chilled.

2. Roll as appropriate for the specific dough you're using, keeping it about 3mm thick.

3. Use a plain or fluted round cutter that's slightly larger in diameter than the top of your tins to cut the dough. As each disk of dough is cut, centre it in one of the tins and gently press it into place, making sure that the edge of the dough reaches the top of the little tin all around.

4. Arrange the miniature tins on a Swiss roll tin and chill them before baking.

5. Before you roll out the next piece of dough, incorporate the scraps from the previous piece under it so as to avoid having a large pile of scraps too soft to re-roll when you're finished rolling the chilled dough.

LINING A MUFFIN TIN

Make sure to prepare the cavities of your muffin tin with a heavy coat of soft butter or vegetable cooking spray ①.

1. Follow steps 1 through 3 in Forming Individual Tart Crusts, opposite.

2. After rolling, each piece of dough should be a little more than 12.5cm in diameter (the cavities in a standard muffin tin are about 5cm in diameter at the base and about 4cm deep).

3. Gently fold the piece of dough in half and slightly curve the folded edge upward on each side. Open out the piece of dough and let the centre of the disk fall into the bottom centre of the cavity in the tin ②.

4. Use your fingertips to press it in place against the bottom and sides of the cavity, then use the point of a paring knife to trim the edge of the dough even with the top of the cavity ③.

FORMING MINIATURE RECTANGULAR, SQUARE OR BARQUETTE CRUSTS

Miniature tins that come in other than round shapes are easy to line with dough.

1. Start with steps 1 and 2 as for Forming Miniature Round Crusts (page 29) and slide the dough to a lightly floured flexible cutting board or baking tray.

2. Cut off a scrap of excess dough and use it to make a little tool for pressing the dough into the tins: Form the dough into a ball and flour it well. Pinch the top to make a little upright handle ① press it into an extra one of the tins ② and pull the dough from the tin ③.

3. Arrange the tins on the work surface in approximately the same shape as the piece of dough, but keep the arrangement of tins an inch or two smaller in all directions. Coat the tins with vegetable cooking spray.

4. Slide an inch of the dough off the far end of the baking tray, tilt the tray at about a 45° angle to the work surface and, beginning with the arrangement of tins furthest from you, slide the dough onto the tins ④. If the dough fails to cover all the tins, slide the ones that are only partially covered out from under the dough.

5. Gently press with a fingertip in the centre of each little tin to begin moulding the dough to the shape of the tin. Use the dough tool to press the rolled dough into each tin ⑤.

6. Lightly flour the top of the dough and run your rolling pin over the surface to cut off the excess ⑥.

7. Arrange the lined tins on a Swiss roll tin; chill them before baking.

8. Incorporate the scraps into the next piece of dough to be rolled and continue until all the tins are lined.

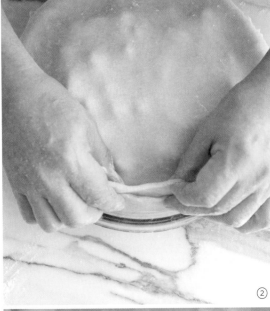

TOP CRUSTS FOR DOUBLE-CRUSTED PIES

A whole top crust is made from a disk of dough a little larger than the top of the pie dish or other tin to allow for some dough to be turned under the edge of the bottom crust to prevent juices from leaking out. Top crusts are pierced or slashed in several places so steam can escape during baking; otherwise, the steam will burst through the weakest place on the side of the pie, causing a leak.

Lattice crusts are made from strips of dough that are arranged in a diagonal or perpendicular pattern over the filling. In general, roll the dough for lattice crusts a little thinner than you would for a whole top crust, since the strips tend to sink a little into juicy fillings and thicker strips, once they get soaked with juice, do not bake through well.

Before making the top crust, prepare the bottom crust as described in Lining a Tin for a Tart or Pie on page 28, and fill the pie as directed in your recipe.

FULL TOP FOR A PIE

1. Roll the dough for the top crust about 4cm larger in diameter than the top of the pie.

2. Brush the edge of the bottom crust with water.

3. Fold the dough for the top crust in half, line up the fold with the diameter of the tin and unfold it to cover the filling ①.

4. Gently press the edge so that the top and bottom crusts adhere to each other ②.

5. Trim away all but 1.25cm of excess dough from the top of the pie.

6. Use the blunt edge of a table knife to lift a piece of the bottom crust and fold the edge of the top crust under it so that it is even with the rim of the tin ③; repeat all around the pie.

7. Flute the edge of the pie as in the instructions on page 36.

DIAGONAL LATTICE TOP FOR A PIE

1. Roll the dough for the top crust into a square a little longer than the diameter of the tin's top.

2. Use a sharp pastry wheel, plain or serrated, to cut the square into strips 1.25cm wide.

3. Arrange one of the strips across the centre of the filled pie ①.

4. Place more strips parallel to the first one and equidistant from each other on both sides of the centre strip ②.

5. Turn the pie 45° and arrange another strip across the diameter, at an angle to the first strips ③.

6. Repeat step 4.

7. Use a dough scraper or the back of a knife to sever the strips at the edge of the tin.

8. Use your thumb to press the ends of the strips securely against the edge of the bottom crust, then use a dough scraper or the back of a knife to even up the rim.

9. Flute the edge of the pie as described on page 36 if you wish; I think it looks better when left plain.

PERPENDICULAR LATTICE

In step 5, give the pie a quarter turn so that the second set of strips is laid at a 90° angle to the first.

①

②

③

WOVEN LATTICES

I make perpendicular woven lattices both open, with spaces between the strips, and closed, with the strips next to each other. The procedure is the same for both.

1. Lightly dust with flour a cardboard round or a tart tin base a couple of inches wider in diameter than the top of your pie.

2. Follow steps 1 and 2 in the diagonal lattice on page 33, arranging parallel strips on the cardboard, instead of the pie. If you want an open lattice, space the strips 1–2 inches apart; for a closed lattice, use twice as many strips and place them right next to one another.

3. Fold back every other strip at its midpoint ①.

4. Insert a perpendicular strip up against the folds.

5. Unfold the strips so that they cross over the perpendicular strip.

6. Fold back the strips that are underneath the perpendicular strip, positioning the folds 2.5–5cm from the perpendicular for an open lattice ② or leaving no space for a closed lattice.

7. Insert another perpendicular strip and unfold the strips to cross over it.

8. Repeat steps 6 and 7, until you reach the edge of the cardboard.

9. Turn the cardboard 180° and repeat steps 3–8 ③.

10. Chill the lattice for a couple of minutes. Brush the edge of the bottom crust with water, then slide the lattice off the cardboard round or tart tin base onto the top of the filled pie ④. Trim the strips at the edge of the tin and use your thumb to press the ends of the strips securely against the edge of the bottom crust. Use the dough scraper or the back of a knife to even up the rim.

11. Flute the edge of the pie as described on page 36 if you wish; I like it better left plain.

① ② ③ ④

FINISHING A PIECRUST (FOR A SINGLE-CRUST PIE)

Preparing a single pie crust requires finishing the edge (when preparing the same crust for a double-crusted pie, the edge is simply trimmed even with the top edge of the tin). Fluting is easy to do, especially if you follow my method of shaping the edge and then going back over the pattern to make it more distinct.

1. Follow steps 1 through 3 on page 28 to line the tin for a single-crusted pie ①.

2. For a single-crust pie, use scissors or the back of a knife to trim away all but 1.25cm of dough at the top edge of the tin ②.

3. Evenly fold the extra dough under at the edge of the tin.

4. Lightly flour your fingertips; position the thumb and index finger of one hand together on the outside of the crust's edge.

5. Gently pinch while using the index finger of the other hand to push from inside the crust ③.

6. Continue all around the crust.

7. Flour your fingertips again and repeat.

8. Chill the crust before baking.

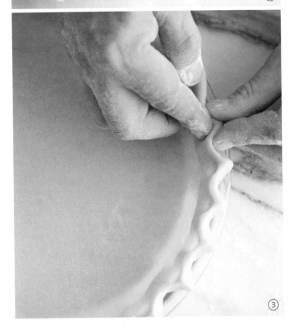

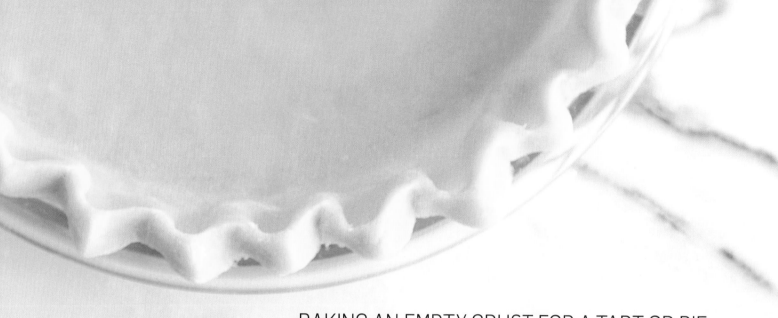

BAKING AN EMPTY CRUST FOR A TART OR PIE

Baking a tart or pie crust 'blind', or unfilled provides a crisp crust and is often done for pies that will have a creamy filling. It's easy, but requires a little advance planning, because your crust should be baked and cooled before you proceed with the remaining steps of the recipe.

1. Chill your crust – ideally, overnight – before you start the process.

2. When you're ready to bake, set a rack at the middle level in the oven and preheat to 190°C/ gas mark 5.

3. For a large pie or tart, pierce the dough at 2.5cm intervals all over with the tines of a fork.

4. Line the dough with a disk of parchment paper or lightweight foil. If you use foil, spray the surface that will come in contact with the dough to avoid any possibility of sticking. Never use heavy-duty foil – a fold in the foil can easily cut through the dough.

5. Fill the lined pastry shell with dried beans. You'll need about 350g of beans for a large pie or tart, or about 60g per 11.5cm pastry shell. For small individual tartlet crusts about 6.5cm in diameter, you can cut down cupcake paper liners to line the tins; alternatively, if you have enough extra little tins, spray the backs of some and use them inside the dough-lined ones. Set individual tarts or tartlets on a Swiss roll tin.

6. Place the tart, pie or loaded Swiss roll tin in the oven and decrease the temperature to 180°C/gas mark 4.

7. For large tart or pie crusts, bake until the dough is set and is no longer shiny and raw looking when you lift the paper to look, about 15 minutes. Carefully remove the paper and beans and continue baking for about 15 minutes longer until golden.

8. Individual and miniature crusts take much less time to bake and might be completely done in less than 15 minutes. Begin checking them after 8-10 minutes.

CHAPTER 3

SWEET TARTS & TARTLETS

While it's possible to argue the differences between tarts and pies, I like a simple definition of a tart or tartlet: a large tart is straight-sided, single-crusted, and served unmoulded from its baking tin. Individual tarts are the same, but may also be slope-sided. That's it. You can add a top crust to a tart, but in this book I've confined top crusts to sweet or savoury pies baked in pie dishes or sandwich tins.

This chapter starts with recipes that don't require blind-baking the crusts; perhaps the easiest and quickest way to make a tart. Each has specific instructions about placement in the oven and the temperatures to use to make sure both crust and filling bake to perfection. If you follow them exactly, you'll have excellent results.

Tarts in blind-baked crusts follow; there are several ways to keep the crust from becoming soggy after filling in this type of tart and they all work well. Remember, though, that a tart like this is always best on the day it's assembled.

Individual tarts and tartlets round out the chapter. I use specific-sized moulds for both, though a lot of variation in size is possible.

ORANGE & ALMOND TART

Makes one 25cm tart, 8-10 servings

One 25cm tart crust made from Sweet Pastry Dough (page 19)

TART FILLING

4 large navel oranges, about 680g

60ml water

85g caster sugar

170g marzipan

1 medium egg

85g unsalted butter, very soft

1 medium egg yolk

1 teaspoon vanilla extract

35g unbleached plain flour

¼ teaspoon baking powder

FINISHING

220g apricot jam, heated and strained before measuring

20g lightly toasted flaked almonds

VARIATIONS

The upper tart in the photo is made with red-fleshed Cara Cara oranges. Blood oranges would be a flavourful and visually striking choice too. A couple of small and very sweet white or pink grapefruit would also make a lovely tart, but don't use the zest, which is too bitter.

Flavourful oranges are available all year long, but this tart is especially welcome in early winter, when there is little fresh fruit besides imports available. Lightly poaching the oranges controls the amount of juice that exudes from them during baking and makes for a neater and more intensely flavoured tart. Almost any fruit can be adapted to this type of filling and crust – see Variations for suggestions.

1. Finely grate enough zest from the oranges to make 2 teaspoons, and set it aside for the almond filling. Use a sharp paring knife to remove the skin and white pith completely from the oranges, and then halve them from stem to blossom end. Cut the oranges into 0.5cm thick slices and set them aside.

2. Bring the water and 4 tablespoons sugar to the boil in a non-reactive sauté pan large enough to hold the orange slices in a shallow layer; remove the pan from the heat and add the slices.

3. Bring the oranges to the boil over a medium heat, then let them cool in the syrup. When you're ready to assemble the tart, transfer the orange slices to a pan lined with kitchen towels and reserve the syrup.

4. Set a rack at the lowest level in the oven and preheat to 180°C/gas mark 4.

5. Beat the marzipan and remaining 3 tablespoons sugar on a low speed in the bowl of a stand mixer fitted with the paddle attachment until reduced to fine crumbs. Add the whole egg and beat for 1-2 minutes until the mixture is completely smooth. Beat in the butter until smooth, then stop and scrape the bowl and beater. Beat in the reserved orange zest, egg yolk and vanilla. Quickly mix the flour and baking powder together and fold them into the filling using a rubber spatula.

6. Spread the filling in the prepared crust and smooth the top. Arrange the orange slices, overlapping, in concentric rows over the almond filling. Gently press the oranges into the filling.

7. Bake the tart for 30-40 minutes until the crust is baked through and golden and the almond filling is set.

8. While the tart is baking, bring the syrup to the boil and allow it to reduce for 4-5 minutes until slightly thickened; don't reduce it too much or it will solidify. Let it cool.

9. For the apricot glaze, combine 4 tablespoons of the reduced syrup with the apricot jam. Bring to the boil, reduce the heat to a simmer and cook for about 5 minutes until thickened.

10. Cool the baked tart on a rack and unmould it. Slide the tart onto a serving plate. Lightly brush the oranges with the apricot glaze, reheating it first if necessary, immediately before serving; sprinkle the edge of the tart with the sliced almonds.

APPLE & CALVADOS CREAM TART

Makes one 25cm tart, 8-10 servings

One 25cm tart crust made from Sweet Pastry Dough (page 19)

APPLE FILLING

30g unsalted butter

3 tart apples such as Granny Smith, about 680g, peeled, halved, cored and cut into 1.25cm dice

3 tablespoons demerara or light brown sugar

¼ teaspoon ground cinnamon

CALVADOS CREAM

50g caster sugar

2 tablespoons unbleached plain flour

2 medium eggs

120ml double cream

1½ tablespoons Calvados

Icing sugar for finishing

Apples and custard cream make a rich and satisfying tart filling, especially when flavoured with Calvados, French apple brandy.

1. For the apple filling, melt the butter in a wide sauté pan over a medium heat and add the diced apples. Sprinkle with the demerara sugar and cinnamon and toss. Reduce the heat to low and cook the apples until they exude water; raise the heat to high and, stirring frequently, let the excess juices reduce. Test the apples for doneness: if they still seem hard, turn the heat down and cook for up to 5 minutes more until tender. Scrape the filling onto a plate to cool. The filling can be prepared in advance, covered and refrigerated for a day or two.

2. Set a rack at the lowest level in the oven and preheat to 180°C/gas mark 4.

3. For the Calvados cream, combine the sugar and flour in a medium bowl and whisk them thoroughly together. Add the eggs and whisk smooth before whisking in the cream and Calvados.

4. Spoon the cooled apple filling into the crust without pressing it. Set the tart on the hob or close to the oven to avoid spills when moving it and gently pour in the Calvados cream, filling the crust only to within 0.5cm of the top. If the crust is too full, the custard cream will overflow while the tart is baking.

5. Carefully transfer the tart to the oven. Bake for 30-40 minutes until the crust is baked through and the custard cream has set.

6. Cool the tart on a rack. Lightly dust the edge with icing sugar. Unmould the tart and slide it onto a serving plate; serve the tart on the day it's baked.

VARIATIONS

APPLE CREAM TART: Omit the Calvados and substitute 2 teaspoons vanilla extract.

PEAR TART: Substitute well-drained diced poached pears for the sautéed apples. Omit the butter, demerara sugar and cinnamon. Sprinkle the pears with a few pinches of nutmeg after arranging them in the tart crust. Instead of using Calvados, flavour the custard cream with vanilla or substitute Poire William.

PEACH TART WITH ROSE GLAZE: Instead of making the apple filling, use 900g-1.15kg ripe peaches, peeled, stoned and cut into quarters or sixths, depending on their size. Arrange the peach wedges in the crust peeled side down and perpendicular to the edge of the tart. Flavour the custard cream with vanilla extract only and fill and bake the tart as above. Brush the cooled tart with a glaze made from 95g apricot jam, 95g Turkish rose petal jam and 2 tablespoons water, brought to the boil, reduced slightly, and strained.

APPENZELL HAZELNUT TART (APPENZELLER HASSELNUSSFLADE)

The town of Appenzell and its surrounding two half cantons are a land of dairy farms, excellent cheese and traditional pastries and honey cakes. This hazelnut tart is more like a breakfast cake than a dessert tart, but it's delicious nonetheless. The best way to 'chop' hazelnuts is to place them on a Swiss roll tin and rock a small saucepan back and forth over them to crush them.

1. Set a rack at the lowest level in the oven and preheat to 180°C/gas mark 4.

2. Put the whole hazelnuts and sugar in the bowl of a food processor and pulse repeatedly at 1-second intervals until the nuts are finely ground.

3. Add the flour, baking powder, spices, eggs, egg yolks and butter to the work bowl and pulse again (about 10–12 1-second pulses) until the mixture is smooth.

4. Use a thin-bladed metal spatula to scrape down the side of the bowl; add the milk and pulse again until smooth.

5. Remove the blade and scrape the filling into the prepared crust. Sprinkle the chopped hazelnuts on top.

6. Bake the tart for 30–40 minutes until the crust is baked through and the filling has set.

7. Cool the tart on a rack. Unmould it to a serving plate and dust icing sugar over the top immediately before serving.

Makes one 25cm tart, 8–10 servings

One 25cm tart crust made from Sweet Pastry Dough (page 19)

HAZELNUT FILLING

115g whole natural hazelnuts, plus 3 tablespoons coarsely chopped hazelnuts

150g caster sugar

100g unbleached plain flour

½ teaspoon baking powder

½ teaspoon ground cinnamon

½ teaspoon freshly grated nutmeg

Large pinch of ground cloves

2 medium eggs

2 medium egg yolks

115g unsalted butter, very soft

75ml whole milk

Icing sugar for finishing

VARIATION

APPENZELLER ZIMTFLADE (CINNAMON TART): Reduce the hazelnuts (or substitute the same amount of walnuts or almonds) to 80g. Increase the cinnamon to 1 teaspoon, the nutmeg to 1 teaspoon and the cloves to ¼ teaspoon. Omit the chopped nuts on top.

PINEAPPLE & COCONUT TART

I love pineapple, but supermarket pineapples are frequently disappointing, so I developed a pineapple confit to sweeten and concentrate the fruit for this tart. The confit takes some time to prepare, but it's worth the extra effort.

1. Set a rack at the lowest level in the oven and preheat to 180°C/gas mark 4.

2. Combine the sugar and flour in a medium bowl and whisk them thoroughly together. Add the eggs and whisk smooth before whisking in the coconut cream and vanilla extract.

3. Cut the wedges of pineapple confit into 0.5cm thick slices and arrange them, overlapping, on the prepared crust.

4. Gently pour in the coconut cream, filling the crust only to within 0.5cm of the top. If the crust is too full, the coconut cream will overflow while the tart is baking. Sprinkle the top of the tart with the shredded coconut.

5. Carefully transfer the tart to the oven. Bake for 30-40 minutes until the crust is baked through and the coconut cream has set.

6. Cool the tart on a rack. Unmould the tart and slide it onto a plate; serve it on the day it's baked.

Pineapple Confit

If you live in Hawaii or Puerto Rico, you can buy a perfectly ripe, sweet pineapple, but most of us have to make do with ones that are underripe and lacking in sweetness. Several years ago, I experimented successfully with roasting pineapple before using it in a *tarte tatin*; this recipe takes the process a step further and adds some butter and sugar to enhance the pineapple's flavour with excellent results.

1. Set a rack at the middle level in the oven and preheat to 150°C/gas mark 2; if you have a convection setting, preheat to 135°C/gas mark 1.

2. Trim the top and bottom from the pineapple and halve it lengthways. Cut each half into 4 long wedges, then trim the core and peel from each, being careful to cut away any eyes that remain on the skin side.

3. Sprinkle the bottom of a small roasting pan with a third of the butter and a third of the sugar and arrange the pineapple wedges on it peeled-side down. Sprinkle with the remaining butter and sugar.

4. Bake the pineapple for about 1½ hours until it softens and starts to colour a little. Use tongs to turn the wedges every half hour.

5. Increase the temperature to 220°C/gas mark 7 (200°C/gas mark 6 convection) and continue baking the pineapple until the sugar caramelises. Watch carefully to be sure the sugar doesn't darken too much.

6. Allow the pineapple to cool for a few minutes, then use tongs to transfer it to a shallow bowl.

7. Place the roasting pan over a low heat and let the sugar start to melt. Add the water and use a silicone spatula to scrape up any caramel stuck to the pan. Let the juices reduce slightly and pour them over the pineapple.

8. Cool the pineapple completely. For the best flavour, refrigerate it before using.

Makes one 25cm tart, 8-10 servings

One 25cm tart crust made from Sweet Pastry Dough (page 19)

COCONUT CREAM FILLING

50g caster sugar

2 tablespoons unbleached plain flour

2 medium eggs

120ml coconut cream

1 teaspoon vanilla extract

Pineapple Confit (recipe follows)

40g sweetened shredded coconut (can be sourced online)

PINEAPPLE CONFIT

Makes about 500g, enough for one large tart

1 large pineapple, about 900g

60g unsalted butter, melted

150g caster sugar

60ml water

VARIATIONS

Substitute light brown sugar or demerara sugar for one-third of the caster sugar.

One 25cm tart crust made from Sweet Pastry Dough (page 19)

FILLING

4 medium eggs

1 recipe McIntosh Applesauce (recipe follows) (see Note below)

1 teaspoon finely grated lemon zest

1 tablespoon lemon juice, strained before measuring

150ml double cream

65g caster sugar

70g demerara or light brown sugar

½ teaspoon ground cinnamon, plus more for sprinkling

Lightly sweetened whipped cream for serving, optional

MCINTOSH APPLESAUCE

Makes about 500g

1.15kg McIntosh apples (see note below), peeled, halved, cored and sliced

120ml water

OLD-FASHIONED APPLESAUCE TART

My dear friend Ann Amendolara Nurse shared this recipe that she used to make every autumn when McIntosh apples are in season (see note below). The original calls for sweetened condensed milk, but I've changed it to use a combination of cream and both white and brown sugars.

1. Set racks in the lowest level and upper third of the oven and preheat to 180°C/gas mark 4.

2. For the filling, whisk the eggs in a bowl until frothy, then whisk in the applesauce.

3. Whisk in the lemon zest, juice, cream, sugars and cinnamon.

4. Pour the filling into the prepared crust and sprinkle with several pinches of cinnamon.

5. Bake the tart on the bottom rack for about 30 minutes until the crust is baked through and the filling is set. Move the tart to the upper rack for a further 15 minutes until the filling is fully set and slightly puffed.

6. Cool the tart on a rack and unmould it to a serving plate. Serve with whipped cream if you wish.

McIntosh Applesauce

1. Combine the apples and water in a non-reactive saucepan over a medium heat; bring to the boil.

2. Decrease the heat to maintain a simmer and cook for 15–20 minutes until the apples are reduced to a chunky purée and most of the water has evaporated. If the apples remain firm, add 60ml more water and continue cooking until they soften.

3. Use a potato masher to smooth out the applesauce - it's not necessary to purée it in a blender or food processor.

4. Scrape the applesauce into a container, cool it and store it covered in the refrigerator for up to 3 days.

5. Bring the applesauce to room temperature before using it in the recipe above.

Note: British cooks can either use Bramley apples or a favourite dessert apple for this recipe.

SWISS EASTER RICE TART (OSTERFLADE)

More a pastry shop speciality than a dessert prepared by home cooks, this rice tart – a sort of rice pudding baked in a crust – is popular throughout Switzerland. The key to getting the right consistency for the filling is to overcook the rice from the outset. It needs to be smooth and creamy to purée well later on. The ground almonds add richness and flavour.

1. For the rice filling, bring a large pot of water to the boil and add the rice. Stir occasionally until the water returns to a full rolling boil. Reduce the heat to maintain a low boil and cook the rice for about 15 minutes – the grains should be split at the ends when the rice is properly cooked. Drain the rice, but do not rinse it.

2. Combine the cooked rice with the milk, sugar, butter and salt in a large, heavy saucepan. Bring the mixture to the boil over a medium heat. Decrease the heat to low and cook for about 20 minutes until it is reduced and thickened. Cool the mixture, then purée it in a food processor.

3. Pour the puréed rice into a bowl and stir in the lemon zest. Mix the ground almonds and flour, then stir them into the rice. Add the eggs one at a time, stirring until smooth after each addition.

4. Set a rack at the lowest level in the oven and preheat to 180°C/gas mark 4.

5. Pour the rice filling into the prepared crust and smooth the top.

6. Bake for 30-40 minutes until the crust is baked through and the filling is set and golden.

7. Cool the tart on a rack. Unmould and slide it onto a serving plate. Sprinkle lightly with icing sugar right before serving.

Makes one 25cm tart, 8-10 servings

One 25cm tart crust made from Sweet Pastry Dough (page 19)

RICE FILLING

90g long-grain rice

720ml whole milk

100g caster sugar

15g unsalted butter

¼ teaspoon salt

2 teaspoons finely grated lemon zest

55g blanched almonds, finely ground in a food processor

1 tablespoon unbleached plain flour

3 medium eggs

Icing sugar for finishing

One 25cm tart crust made from French-Style Cookie Dough spread with 1 batch Nut Biscuit Batter (pages 20 and 22), fully baked

LEMON CREAM

240ml whole milk

65g caster sugar

2 tablespoons cornflour

60ml lemon juice, strained before measuring

2 medium egg yolks

275g Lemon Curd (recipe follows)

MERINGUE

4 medium egg whites

150g caster sugar

Pinch of salt

LEMON CURD

120g unsalted butter

5 medium egg yolks

200g caster sugar

75ml lemon juice, strained before measuring

2 teaspoons finely grated lemon zest

FRENCH LEMON MERINGUE TART (TARTE AU CITRON MERINGUÉE)

This is based on a similar tart made by Philippe Conticini at his *Pâtisserie des Rêves* shop in Paris. I was struck by a photo of the tart topped with a wave of meringue. Fortunately M. Conticini was forthcoming with his method of achieving this unique effect.

1. For the lemon cream, whisk the milk and sugar together in a small saucepan and bring to the boil over a low heat. Meanwhile, whisk the cornflour, lemon juice and egg yolks smooth in a small bowl. When the milk boils, whisk it into the lemon mixture, then strain this back into the pan and cook over a low heat, whisking constantly, until it thickens and boils for 2 minutes. Scrape into a small bowl, press clingfilm directly against the surface and chill thoroughly. This can be prepared up to 3 days ahead.

2. To assemble the tart, pipe the lemon curd in a spiral on the hazelnut biscuit. Cover with the lemon cream, filling the crust to the top; use a metal spatula to spread the top smooth and flat. Cover and freeze the tart solid.

3. Finish the tart at least 6 hours before serving. Set a rack at the middle level in the oven and preheat to 190°C/gas mark 5.

4. For the meringue, combine the ingredients in a mixer bowl and set it over a pan of boiling water; whisk until all the sugar has dissolved. Whisk on medium-high speed until the egg whites have risen in volume but are still creamy and not dry.

5. Scrape the meringue onto a baking tray, forming a 25cm disk. Invert the frozen tart into the meringue and gently press to adhere. Pull the tart away sideways, leaving a tall point at one side. Bake for 7–8 minutes until the meringue is golden, then keep the tart at room temperature until fully defrosted.

6. Unmould and slide the tart onto a serving plate. Use a thin, sharp knife to cut it and wipe with a wet cloth between cuts.

Lemon Curd

This makes more than you need for the lemon tart, but it keeps for weeks if tightly covered and refrigerated (use it for the Traditional Vanilla Mille-Feuille variation on page 161). An enamelled small casserole is perfect for preparing it.

1. Melt the butter in a medium non-reactive saucepan. Off the heat, whisk in the egg yolks, sugar, lemon juice and lemon zest.

2. Set the pan over a medium heat and whisk until the curd gets hot and steam starts to emerge. Decrease the heat to low and continue whisking until the curd thickens. Take care not to let the curd come to a boil; move the pan on and off the heat as needed.

3. Strain into a stainless steel bowl or clean plastic container; press clingfilm directly against the surface and chill until cold.

STRAWBERRY & RASPBERRY TART WITH MINT

While I hate the indiscriminate use of mint leaves as a decoration for desserts in general, the flavour of mint in moderation is wonderful with berries. Right before serving this tart, I like to scatter over tiny mint leaves, then lightly dust it with icing sugar. If you only have large mint leaves, then stack them and cut them into fine ribbons.

1. For the pastry cream, combine the milk, cream and half of the sugar in a small saucepan and whisk. Place the pan over a low heat and bring it to the full boil. Meanwhile, in a bowl, whisk the egg yolks and then whisk in the remaining sugar. Sift the flour over the egg yolk mixture and whisk it in.

2. When the milk mixture boils, whisk it into the egg yolk mixture, then strain it back into the pan and place it over a medium heat. Use a small, pointed-end whisk to stir constantly, being sure to reach into the corners of the pan, until the cream comes to the full boil and thickens. Continue to cook, whisking constantly, for 30 seconds. Remove the pan from the heat and whisk in the vanilla extract.

3. Scrape the cream into a glass or stainless-steel bowl and press clingfilm directly against the surface. Chill thoroughly.

4. No more than 4 hours before you intend to serve the tart, unmould the cooled, baked tart crust and slide it onto a serving plate. Spread the cold pastry cream into the crust.

5. Randomly scatter the strawberries and raspberries on the pastry cream or arrange in concentric rings, gently pressing them so they adhere, and covering the cream completely.

6. Immediately before serving, sprinkle the tart with the mint leaves, followed by a light dusting of icing sugar.

Makes one 25cm tart, 8–10 servings

One 25cm tart crust made from French-Style Cookie Dough spread with (almond) Nut Biscuit Batter (pages 20 and 22), fully baked

PASTRY CREAM

180ml whole milk

60ml double cream

50g caster sugar

3 medium egg yolks

2 tablespoons unbleached plain flour

1 teaspoon vanilla extract

340g tiny height-of-season strawberries, rinsed and hulled

340g fresh raspberries, picked over but not washed

3 tablespoons tiny mint leaves or larger leaves stacked and cut into thin ribbons

Icing sugar for finishing

NOTE
The 23cm square tin in the photo has approximately the same volume as a 25cm round tin.

SOUR CHERRY TART WITH ALMOND MERINGUE

Makes one 25cm tart, 8-10 servings

One 25cm tart crust made from French-Style Cookie Dough spread with a double batch of (almond) Nut Biscuit Batter (pages 20 and 22), fully baked

CHERRY FILLING

900g sour cherries, rinsed, stemmed, and stoned

65g sugar

¼ teaspoon almond extract

2 tablespoons cornflour

2 tablespoons water

ALMOND MERINGUE

3 medium egg whites

Pinch of salt

100g caster sugar

85g flaked almonds

VARIATIONS

Substitute a 675g jar of sour cherries packed in water. Drain the cherries over a bowl and reserve the juice. In a non-reactive saucepan, whisk 120ml of the cherry juice with the sugar and cornflour. Set over a low to medium heat and whisk until it thickens and comes to the boil. Off the heat, fold in the drained cherries and the almond extract. Resume the recipe at step 3.

Cherries and almonds are an easy flavour combination; they're botanically related, though distant cousins, and the perfume of almonds is a perfect complement to the tartness of sour cherries. Where I live in New York City, sour cherries are available for only a few weeks in mid- to late July; out of season I like to use sour cherries that come packed in water in a 675g jar. See Variations at the end of the recipe for using these.

When baking the cookie dough crust, don't let the nut biscuit get more than lightly golden as the tart needs to bake again to crisp the meringue topping.

1. For the cherry filling, combine the cherries, any accumulated juices, the sugar and almond extract in a non-reactive saucepan and bring the mixture to the boil over a medium heat. Mix the cornflour and water and stir in 120ml of the hot cherry juices. Remove the pan from the heat, then stir the cornflour mixture into the filling.

2. Return the pan to a medium-low heat and cook, stirring, for about 2 minutes until the filling thickens, comes to the boil and turns clear.

3. Scrape the filling into a bowl, press clingfilm directly against the surface and cool it to room temperature. For advance preparation you can chill the filling for up to 2 days, but bring it to room temperature before using it.

4. Set a rack at the middle level in the oven and preheat to 160°C/gas mark 3.

5. For the almond meringue, half-fill a medium saucepan with water and bring it to the boil over a medium heat. Meanwhile, whisk the egg whites, salt and sugar together by hand in the bowl of an electric mixer. Place the mixer bowl over the pan of boiling water and whisk gently but constantly for about 2-3 minutes until the egg whites are hot (60°C) and the sugar has dissolved.

6. Using an electric mixer fitted with the whisk attachment, whisk the meringue on medium-high speed until the egg whites have risen in volume but are still creamy. Overwhisking will make the meringue dry and grainy.

7. While the meringue is whisking, spread the cooled cherry filling into the tart crust.

8. Once the meringue is whisked, fold in all but a tablespoon of the sliced almonds. Spread the meringue over the cherry filling, making sure the meringue makes contact with the side of the tart crust all around. Sprinkle with the reserved almonds.

9. Bake the tart for 20-30 minutes until the meringue is crisp.

10. Cool the tart on a rack, unmould it and slide it onto a serving plate to serve.

MANGO LASSI TART

This light and delicate tart filling is based on the popular Indian drink that's not unlike a mango smoothie. In India, mango lassi is sometimes perfumed with a few pinches of ground cardamom. If you'd like to try that combination, just sprinkle a little on the tart right before serving or pass round some ground cardamom in a tiny bowl for the guests to add on their own if desired.

1. Use a fork to stir the gelatine and water together in a small heatproof bowl. Let the mixture stand for 3–4 minutes while you half-fill a small sauté pan with water and bring it to the boil. Once the gelatine has softened and absorbed all the water, set the bowl in the hot water off the heat and wait another 5 minutes for the gelatine to melt.

2. Combine the yogurt, mangoes and sugar in a blender jar and purée it. Once the gelatine has melted completely, add it to the blender jar and purée again.

3. Pour the mango purée into a mixing bowl. Re-whip the whipped cream if it has gone liquid during chilling, then quickly fold the cream into the mango mixture.

4. Pour the filling into the tart crust and refrigerate for at least 3 hours until it sets.

5. Unmould the tart and slide it onto a serving plate to serve. Sprinkle it very lightly with the cardamom if you like.

Makes one 25cm tart, 8-10 servings

One 25cm tart crust made from French-Style Cookie Dough spread with (almond) Nut Biscuit Batter (pages 20 and 22), fully baked

1 tablespoon unflavoured powdered gelatine

60ml cold water

240g Greek yogurt, any fat content you like

340g peeled mangoes (about 3 large Indian mangoes or 4–5 Mexican ones), cut into 1.25cm pieces

50g caster sugar

240ml double cream, whipped to soft peaks and chilled

Ground cardamom for dusting, optional

NOTE
Large, round Indian mangoes are perfect for this; smaller, yellow, flat Mexican mangoes are also very flavourful.

CHOCOLATE RASPBERRY TART

Makes one 25cm tart, 8-10 servings

1 x 25cm tart crust made from French-Style Cookie Dough or Chocolate Cookie Dough (pages 20 or 21), fully baked

GANACHE FILLING

240ml whipping or double cream

2 tablespoons light corn syrup or golden syrup

280g dark chocolate (60% cocoa solids), melted and cooled

55g unsalted butter, very soft

350-500g fresh raspberries, picked over but not washed

Icing sugar for finishing

Cocoa powder for finishing

I used to make this tart with an elaborate chocolate mousse filling. Now I prefer it with a simple and flavourful ganache under the berries. Be sure to use premium chocolate, since there's nothing to camouflage its flavour.

1. For the ganache filling, whisk the cream and corn syrup together in a small saucepan. Bring to a slight simmer over a low heat, then pour it into a bowl and cool to room temperature.

2. Pour the cream mixture over the chocolate and vigorously whisk them together. Whisk in the butter and immediately pour the ganache into the baked tart crust. Be careful: if the butter isn't as soft as mayonnaise, it won't mix easily with the chocolate and cream and might leave lumps.

3. Arrange the raspberries on the ganache, either symmetrically or in a generous-looking pile.

4. Just before serving, dust the raspberries with icing sugar and a bit of cocoa powder.

NOTE

This tart can sit for several hours before serving; just don't refrigerate it, or both the crust and filling will harden.

Individual Tarts

Individual removable-base tart tins are 11.5cm in diameter, 2.25cm deep and hold about 180ml. Once lined with dough, the capacity will decrease to around 120ml, depending on the dough's thickness. If you don't want to invest in them, you could substitute individual aluminium foil tins, but they're usually a lot deeper.

If you want to convert one of the large tart recipes to individual tart tins, as a general rule, the dough and filling of the large tart should be enough for 6–8 individual tins.

Small slope-sided tartlet tins are about 6.5cm in diameter and 1.25cm deep. Too small for one to be an individual dessert, these are best served with tea or coffee in the afternoon or alongside a simple dessert such as a fruit salad.

Mini muffin tins can substitute for small tartlet tins, especially when the filling is baked in the crust. Just be careful to brush them with soft butter and then coat the buttered surface with vegetable cooking spray so that they unmould successfully.

INDIVIDUAL APPLE TARTS WITH ALMOND CRUNCH

The crisp topping on these tarts – almonds, sugar and butter caramelised together while the tarts are baking – is delicious and a welcome change from crumb topping.

1. For the apple filling, melt the butter in a wide sauté pan over a medium heat and add the apples. Sprinkle with the demerara sugar and cinnamon and toss to combine. Decrease the heat to low and let the apples cook until they exude some water; increase the heat to high and, stirring frequently, let the excess juices reduce. Test the apples for doneness: if they still seem hard, decrease the heat and cook for up to 5 minutes longer until tender. Scrape the filling onto a plate to cool. The filling can be prepared in advance and covered and refrigerated for a day or two.

2. When you're ready to bake the tarts, set a rack at the lowest level in the oven and preheat to 200°C/gas mark 6. Arrange the tart tins on a Swiss roll tin.

3. For the topping, butter or spray a 2-litre heatproof bowl and set it aside. Melt the butter in a small saucepan and stir in the honey and sugar. Bring the mixture to a full rolling boil over a low heat, then remove it from the heat and stir in the almonds. Scrape the topping into the prepared bowl and let it cool slightly.

4. Spoon the cooled apple filling into the crusts without pressing it. Spoon some of the cooled topping onto each tart, distributing it in as even a layer as possible.

5. Place the tarts in the oven and decrease the temperature to 180°C/gas mark 4. Bake for about 30 minutes until the crusts are baked through and the topping has caramelised.

6. Cool the tarts on a rack. Unmould the tarts and serve them on individual dessert plates.

Makes six individual tarts

Six 11.5cm tart crusts made from Sweet Pastry Dough (page 19)

APPLE FILLING

30g unsalted butter

4 tart apples, such as Granny Smith, about 900g, peeled, halved, cored and cut into 1.25cm dice

50g demerara sugar or light brown sugar

¼ teaspoon ground cinnamon

ALMOND CRUNCH TOPPING

85g unsalted butter

85g honey, light corn syrup or golden syrup

50g caster sugar

85g blanched sliced almonds

SALTED CASHEW CARAMEL CHOCOLATE TARTLETS

Makes about 12-18 tartlets

Twelve 6.5cm tartlet crusts made from Flaky Buttery Dough or French-Style Cookie Dough, (page 14 or 20), fully baked. It's best to chill the tartlet crusts overnight before baking to reduce shrinkage.

CARAMEL CASHEW FILLING

2 tablespoons water

130g caster sugar

1 tablespoon honey

80ml double cream

70g roasted, salted cashews, rubbed in a kitchen towel to remove excess salt, chopped into 0.5cm pieces

CHOCOLATE TOPPING

85g dark chocolate (60% cocoa solids), melted and cooled

120ml double cream

1 tablespoon light corn syrup or golden syrup

Coarse salt such as *fleur de sel* or crushed Maldon salt for finishing, optional

Salty nuts and caramel are a delicious combination – and when you add a chocolate topping, you get a candy bar in a tart crust. By the way, roasted and salted cashew halves are much less expensive than whole ones – in the recipe they're chopped anyway. Roasted salted almonds are also delicious in these tartlets.

1. For the filling, combine the water and sugar in a medium saucepan and stir to mix. Cook the mixture over a medium heat and stir occasionally until the syrup turns to a deep amber caramel.

2. Meanwhile, stir the honey into the cream in a small saucepan and bring it to a slight simmer over a low heat; cover and set aside.

3. When the sugar mixture is ready, remove the pan from the heat and begin pouring in the hot cream and honey mixture, a little at a time, to avoid having the caramel boil over. If the caramel hardens, return the pan to the heat and cook, stirring for no more than a few seconds until the caramel is smooth. Stir in the cashews.

4. Evenly divide the filling among the baked tartlet crusts filling them with about a tablespoon of the cashew caramel, to within 0.5cm of the top.

5. For the chocolate topping, place the chocolate in a mixing bowl and bring the cream and corn syrup to a simmer in a saucepan. Pour the cream over the chocolate and whisk smooth.

6. Spoon some of the topping onto each of the tartlets, using an offset spatula to spread it smooth and flat if necessary.

7. Let the glaze set at a cool room temperature. If you like, sprinkle each tartlet with a tiny pinch of salt before serving.

INDIVIDUAL RASPBERRY & PISTACHIO TARTS

Makes eight individual tarts

Eight 11.5cm tart crusts made from Sweet Pastry Dough (page 19)

3 medium egg whites

Pinch of salt

130g caster sugar

85g unsalted butter, melted

1 tablespoon kirsch or white rum

1 teaspoon vanilla extract

70g very green pistachios, skins removed (see Note), finely ground in a food processor

100g unbleached plain flour

340g fresh raspberries, picked over but not rinsed

Icing sugar for finishing

The pistachio filling in these tarts is very much like the small French cake known as a *financier*. Less rich and more flavourful than the typical nut-based tart filling called frangipane, it creates a moist and subtle background for the berries. A spoonful of lightly sweetened whipped cream would be good with these.

1. Set a rack at the lowest level in the oven and preheat to 200°C/gas mark 6. Arrange the tart tins on a Swiss roll tin.

2. Whisk the egg whites and salt by hand in a mixing bowl and whisk in the sugar.

3. Whisk in the butter, followed by the rum and vanilla extract.

4. Use a rubber spatula to fold the pistachios and flour in at the same time.

5. Pour a scant 60ml of the batter into each of the tart crusts. Arrange the raspberries in a couple of concentric circles on each tart, keeping them about 0.5cm apart. Gently press so that the raspberry bases are embedded about 0.5cm deep in the filling.

6. Place in the oven and decrease the temperature to 180°C/gas mark 4. Bake for 30–35 minutes until the crust is baked through and the filling has set. Cool the tarts on a rack, then unmould them. Dust lightly with icing sugar before serving.

NOTE

To remove the skins from pistachios, cover them with water in a saucepan and bring to a rolling boil. Drain, then rub the pistachios in a towel to loosen the skins. If you're not using straight away, place the nuts on a Swiss roll tin and dry them out in a 150°C/gas mark 2 oven for 10 minutes. After they cool, store in the freezer.

MORAVIAN CITRON TARTLETS

Don't get scared – these aren't made with crystallised citron. Here the word is a corruption of *zitrone*, the German word for lemon, used by the nineteenth-century German-speaking Moravian settlers of the Winston-Salem area in North Carolina. I learned about these years ago from Beth Tartan, the pen name of Elizabeth Hedgecock Sparks, who was for many years the food editor of the Winston-Salem newspaper and an expert on the cooking of the region. This is adapted from her book *North Carolina and Old Salem Cookery*, a classic of American culinary literature. Though similar to the lemon-scented chess pies also popular in the area, the filling for citron tartlets is distinguished by the fact that the ingredients are chopped together, not beaten smooth.

1. Set a rack at the lowest level in the oven and preheat to 190°C/gas mark 5. Arrange the tartlet tins on a Swiss roll tin.

2. Combine the egg yolks, butter, brown sugar, lemon zest and juice in the bowl of a food processor fitted with the metal blade. Pulse repeatedly at 1-second intervals until the butter is broken down into 3mm pieces. Don't try to make a smooth mixture.

3. Pour the filling into a bowl; pour a tablespoon of the filling into each tartlet crust, stirring up the filling as you do to maintain an even distribution of the ingredients.

4. Bake the tartlets for 20–25 minutes until the crust is baked through and the filling is set. Don't overbake or the filling will start to simmer, overflow and cause the tartlets to stick to their tins.

5. Cool the tarts on a rack and serve them the day they are baked.

Makes 12 tartlets

Twelve 6.5cm tartlet crusts made from Sweet Pastry Dough (page 19), see Note

3 medium egg yolks

30g unsalted butter, cut into 20 pieces and chilled for 5 minutes in the freezer

100g light brown sugar

Finely grated zest of 1 medium lemon

1 tablespoon lemon juice, strained before measuring

NOTE

Normally Sweet Pastry Dough is rolled about 3mm thick. For these tartlets, roll the dough thinner because they bake so quickly. Use your thumb to press the dough firmly against the side of each little tin to raise the crust about 3mm above the rim to allow for shrinkage and to prevent the filling from coming in direct contact with the tin or it will stick there.

LESLEY'S INDIVIDUAL DOUBLE CHOCOLATE TARTS

Makes eight individual tarts

Eight 11.5cm tart crusts made from French-Style Cookie Dough (page 20), fully baked

CHOCOLATE CUSTARD FILLING

120ml whole milk

315ml double cream

100g caster sugar

4 medium eggs

85g dark chocolate (60% cocoa solids), cut into 0.5cm pieces

GANACHE GLAZE

170g dark chocolate (60% cocoa solids), cut into 0.5cm pieces

240ml double cream

These ethereal chocolate tarts come from my friend Lesley Chesterman, restaurant critic and food writer at the *Montreal Globe*, Quebec's premier English-language newspaper. Her recipe originally produced a single large tart, but I like this as an individual dessert.

1. Set a rack at the middle level in the oven and preheat to 180°C/gas mark 4. Arrange the tart tins on a Swiss roll tin.

2. For the custard filling, whisk the milk, cream and half of the sugar together in a saucepan and bring the mixture to the boil over a medium heat.

3. Whisk the eggs with the remaining sugar. Place the chocolate in a separate bowl.

4. Once the cream mixture boils, pour a quarter of it over the chocolate and whisk until smooth and melted. Whisk in the remaining cream mixture, then whisk the chocolate and cream mixture into the eggs. Pass the filling through a fine mesh sieve.

5. Fill the tart crusts to within 0.5cm of the top with the chocolate cream. Carefully place the tarts in the oven and decrease the temperature to 160°C/gas mark 3. Bake for about 20 minutes until the chocolate cream has set.

6. Cool the tarts on a rack.

7. For the ganache glaze, place the chocolate in a mixing bowl and bring the cream to a simmer in a saucepan. Pour the cream over the chocolate and whisk smooth.

8. Pour one-eighth of the ganache on one of the tarts and tilt it to cover the surface evenly and entirely with ganache. Repeat with the remaining tarts. Let the glaze set at a cool room temperature and serve the tarts the day they are baked.

MEXICAN CHEESE TARTLETS (TARTAS DE REQUESÓN)

In Mexico these tarts are both sold and consumed with *panes dulces*, Mexican sweetened breads that are eaten for breakfast and later in the day for *merenda*, the late afternoon meal. The cheese used in Mexico is *requesón*, which is very similar to Italian ricotta, as it is made from whey rather than milk. However, it's usually clotted at a higher temperature, making the curds harder, and it has a higher salt content. Part-skim milk ricotta is a perfect substitute but ordinary ricotta will also work.

1. Set a rack at the lowest level in the oven and preheat to 180°C/gas mark 4.

2. If the ricotta is very coarse, press it through a sieve into a bowl. Stir in the salt and sugar.

3. Beat in the vanilla extract, then the egg and egg whites, one at a time.

4. Spoon the mixture into the prepared muffin tin, filling each crust only to within 0.5cm of the top to allow for expansion. Sprinkle the filling with a pinch or two of cinnamon.

5. Bake for 30–35 minutes until the filling is set and slightly puffed.

6. Cool the tarts in the tin. To unmould them, invert a Swiss roll tin on the muffin tin and flip the whole stack. Lift off the muffin tin and turn the tarts right-side up. If it's cool in the kitchen and you've used soft butter for greasing the tin, it will be easier to unmould the tarts if you place the tin in a hot oven for a minute or two to melt the butter.

Makes twelve 7.5cm tarts

One 12-cavity muffin tin lined with Sweet Pastry Dough (page 19)

675g ricotta cheese

¼ teaspoon salt

100g caster sugar

1 teaspoon vanilla extract

1 medium egg

2 medium egg whites

¼ teaspoon ground Mexican cinnamon (see Note)

NOTE

Mexican cinnamon, also known as Ceylon cinnamon or 'true cinnamon', is sweeter and less intense than other varieties and is used liberally in Mexican sweet baking. It can be ordered online in the UK.

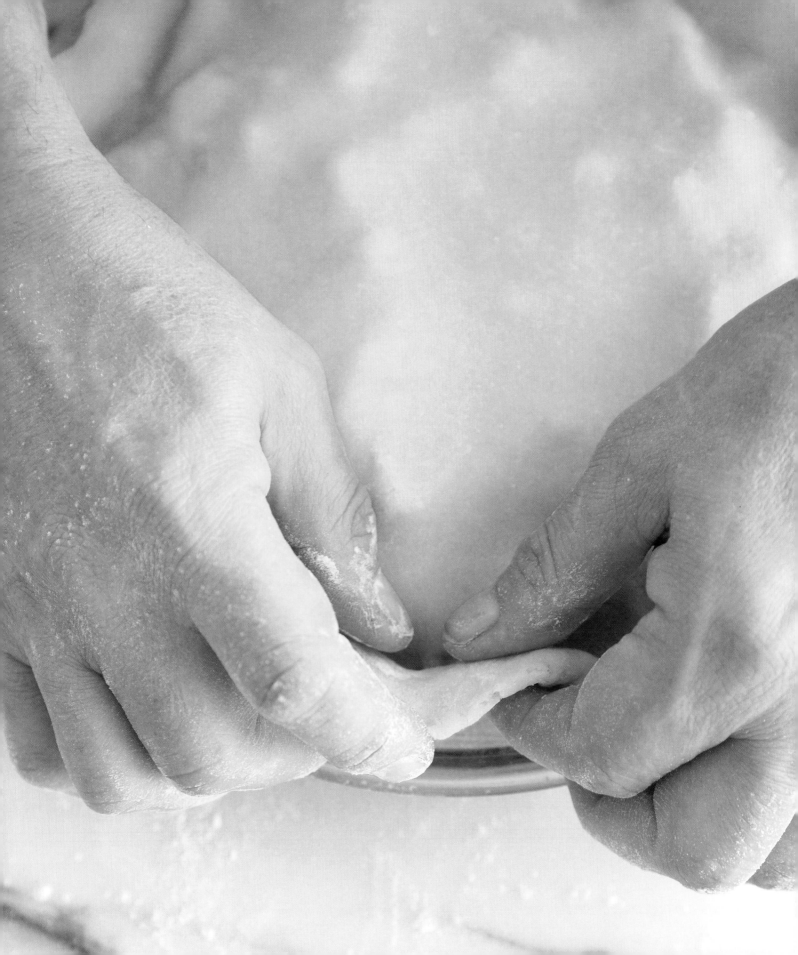

CHAPTER 4

SWEET PIES, COBBLERS & CRISPS

Cakes, cookies and other simple sweets can create pleasurable memories of home-baked treats, but nothing connotes home baking better than a juicy homemade pie. Whether piled high with fruit or loaded with rich, creamy filling, pies – and cobblers and crisps, their close relatives – are perfect for simple meals and family gatherings.

All the pies in this chapter are baked in a standard slope-sided Pyrex glass pie dish. For readers outside the United States, this pan fortunately has approximately the same volume as a 25cm round French tart tin with 2.5cm-high sides and it can easily be substituted.

Cobblers and crisps are easy to prepare in almost any baking dish, but my preference runs to dishes no more than 5cm deep. A deeper baking dish provides proportionately less surface area for the topping, and the filling takes longer to bake.

Pies and cobblers may be topped in a variety of imaginative ways; use the photographs of top crusts in chapter 2 as a guide.

CRANBERRY PECAN PIE

Makes one 23cm pie, about 8 servings

One 23cm pie crust made from Sweet Pastry Dough (page 19)

675g fresh cranberries, rinsed, picked over and drained

65g caster sugar

130g demerara or light brown sugar

1 tablespoon finely grated peeled fresh ginger

Finely grated zest of 1 large orange

120ml fresh orange juice, strained before measuring

60g unsalted butter, cut into 5 or 6 pieces

½ teaspoon ground cinnamon

¼ teaspoon ground ginger

115g coarsely chopped pecan pieces

VARIATIONS

Substitute walnuts for the pecans. Or use the crumb topping on page 85 instead of just the nuts (you can stir those into the crumb topping before you sprinkle it on).

Warning: this pie has a tart and tangy filling that might not be sweet enough for some people. That said, I love the tangy quality and wouldn't want it to be any other way. By the way, since the filling is cooked before the pie is baked, you can taste it and add a little more sugar if you want. My late friend Joseph Viggiani shared this recipe years ago; I have no idea where he might have found it.

1. Combine the cranberries with the rest of the ingredients except the pecans in a large non-reactive saucepan. Bring the mixture to a simmer, stirring often, and cook for about 5 minutes at an active simmer until slightly thickened. Don't overcook or the filling will be hard after the pie is baked. Let cool.

2. Set a rack at the lowest level in the oven and preheat to 190°C/gas mark 5.

3. Stir half of the pecans into the filling and pour it into the prepared pie crust. Smooth the surface and scatter the remaining pecans on top.

4. Place the tin in the oven and decrease the temperature to 180°C/gas mark 4. Bake for 35–40 minutes until the crust is baked through and the pecans are toasted.

5. Cool the pie on a rack and serve it at room temperature.

Makes one 23cm pie, about 8 servings

One 23cm pie crust made from Sweet Pastry Dough (page 19)

165g mild molasses

60ml water

200g caster sugar

60g unsalted butter

4 medium eggs

¼ teaspoon fine sea salt

2 tablespoons bourbon whiskey, optional

225g pecan halves, or a mixture of halves and pieces

Lightly sweetened whipped cream for serving

VARIATION

TRADITIONAL PECAN PIE: Substitute 330g dark corn syrup or golden syrup and 130g caster sugar for the molasses, water and sugar; use 3 eggs instead of 4. Everything else is exactly the same.

MOLASSES PECAN PIE

Molasses lends an old-fashioned flavour to a rich pecan pie, in addition to cutting back on the intense sweetness that the typically used corn syrup brings. For traditionalists, see the Variation for my Traditional Pecan Pie recipe.

1. Set a rack at the lowest level in the oven and preheat to 200°C/gas mark 6.

2. Stir the molasses, water and sugar together in a saucepan and bring the mixture to the boil over a medium heat. Remove from the heat, add the butter and let it melt into the hot syrup.

3. In a medium bowl, whisk the eggs with the salt and bourbon, if using. Stir the butter and syrup mixture and slowly pour it into the egg mixture while whisking.

4. Let the filling stand for 10-15 minutes, then skim any foam from the surface.

5. Stir in the pecans and pour the filling into the prepared crust.

6. Place the pie in the oven and decrease the temperature to 180°C/gas mark 4. Bake for 45-50 minutes until the crust is baked through and the filling is set and slightly puffed.

7. Cool on a rack and serve at room temperature with some whipped cream.

OSGOOD PIE

I first heard of this pie when Bennie Sue Dupy, a native of Mart, Texas, near Waco, shared its recipe, suggesting that it would also make a good bar cookie. I did adapt the recipe for my cookie book – and now here it is in its original form. Many versions of this pie – also referred to as Raisin Pecan Chess Pie – have vinegar as a flavouring. I've decided to use gentler lemon juice instead and it certainly brightens the flavour of this quite sweet filling.

1. Set a rack at the lowest level in the oven and preheat to 200°C/gas mark 6.

2. Beat the butter and sugars together by hand using a rubber spatula. Add the egg yolks one at a time, beating smooth after each addition.

3. Stir in the lemon juice, pecans and raisins.

4. Whisk the egg whites and salt in a stand mixer on a medium-high speed using the whisk attachment. Continue whisking until the egg whites hold a soft peak – don't overwhisk.

5. Use a rubber spatula to fold the egg whites into the filling.

6. Scrape the filling into the prepared crust and place the pie in the oven. Immediately decrease the heat to 180°C/gas mark 4.

7. Bake the pie for 45–50 minutes until the crust is baked through and the filling has set and taken on a deep golden colour.

8. Cool the pie on a rack and serve it on the day it's baked.

Makes one 23cm pie, about 8 servings

One 23cm pie crust made from Flaky Buttery Dough (page 14)

55g unsalted butter, softened

65g caster sugar

65g demerara or light brown sugar

2 medium eggs, separated

1 tablespoon lemon juice, strained before measuring

55g pecan pieces, coarsely chopped

55g raisins, coarsely chopped

¼ teaspoon fine sea salt

VARIATION

Though not traditional, chopped dried cranberries are wonderful in this pie; their tartness perfectly offsets the sweet filling.

COCONUT CREAM PIE

An old-fashioned American bakery and diner favourite, coconut cream pie has all but disappeared from retail bakeries and menus. This version intensifies the coconut flavour with coconut cream added to the filling.

1. For the filling, whisk 360ml of the milk, the coconut cream and sugar in a non-reactive saucepan and bring the mixture to a simmer over a low heat.

2. Meanwhile, whisk the remaining 120ml milk with the cornflour and egg yolks. Sprinkle the gelatine on the water in a small bowl and set it aside.

3. When the milk mixture comes to the boil, whisk about a third of it into the egg yolk mixture. Return the remaining milk mixture to a low heat and bring it back to the boil. When it starts to boil, begin whisking, then whisk in the yolk mixture. Continue whisking constantly for about 2 minutes until the cream thickens and returns to the boil.

4. Off the heat, whisk in the softened gelatine and the vanilla extract. Press clingfilm directly against the surface of the filling and refrigerate for 30 minutes, then continue cooling it at room temperature (if left in the refrigerator, it will set solid before the whipped cream is added). Once the filling has cooled, re-whip the cream if it has become liquid, then quickly fold it into the filling. Scrape the filling into the cooled pie crust, doming it slightly in the centre. Chill the pie to completely set the filling. After an hour or so, cover the pie with clingfilm if you're not finishing it straight away.

5. For the topping, whip the cream with the vanilla extract and sugar to a soft peak and spread it evenly over the filling. Generously sprinkle the cream with the toasted coconut.

Makes one 23cm pie, about 8 servings

One 23cm pie crust made from Flaky Buttery Dough (page 14), fully baked

COCONUT CREAM FILLING

480ml whole milk

240ml coconut cream

100g caster sugar

2 tablespoons cornflour

4 medium egg yolks

7g unflavoured powdered gelatine

60ml water

2 teaspoons vanilla extract

240ml double cream, whipped to a soft peak

TOPPING

240ml double cream

1 teaspoon vanilla extract

2 tablespoons sugar

75g sweetened, shredded coconut, lightly toasted (can be sourced online)

VARIATIONS

BANANA CREAM PIE: Replace the coconut cream with milk. When filling the pie, spread half the filling in the pie crust, then top it with a layer of sliced bananas – about 2 medium – and spread the rest of the filling over them. Top the pie with whipped cream but no coconut.

COTTAGE CHEESE PIE

A Pennsylvania Dutch standard, this cheese pie was popular because cottage cheese was easily made in farm kitchens and always available as an ingredient. Some more recent versions of this pie filling dress it up by adding cream cheese, but this one is a little more lean and uses a combination of milk and cream for slight added richness.

Makes one 23cm pie, about 8 servings

One 23cm pie crust made from Sweet Pastry Dough (page 19)

225g full-fat, small curd cottage cheese, drained in a fine sieve for 2–3 hours

100g caster sugar

2 tablespoons unbleached plain flour

¼ teaspoon ground cinnamon, plus more for sprinkling

Large pinch of freshly grated nutmeg

Large pinch of fine sea salt

2 teaspoons finely grated lemon zest

3 medium eggs

120ml whole milk

120ml single cream

VARIATION

Add 1 tablespoon lemon juice.

1. Set a rack at the lowest level in the oven and preheat to 180°C/gas mark 4.

2. Pulse the cottage cheese in a food processor to make it smoother. Set aside.

3. Combine the sugar, flour, spices and salt in a medium bowl and whisk them together.

4. Stir in the cottage cheese, then the lemon zest, eggs, milk and cream.

5. Scrape the filling into the prepared pie crust and sprinkle with cinnamon.

6. Bake the pie for 45–50 minutes until the crust is baked through and the filling is set and has turned a deep golden colour.

7. Cool the pie on a rack and serve it on the day it's baked.

MISSISSIPPI CHESS PIE

Chess pies are a classic dessert of the American South, though they have nothing to do with the board game that goes by the same name. Chess may be a corruption of 'cheese', since in the distant past, any kind of a mixture that jelled or coagulated was considered a type of cheese. This version comes from my friend Ben Mims, formerly the baking expert of the *Saveur* magazine test kitchen. Recipes for chess pie often contain a little polenta. As it's not really enough to thicken the filling, or is it detectable as a flavour, I've omitted it. This cries out for a little whipped cream, even though that's not traditional.

1. Set a rack at the lowest level in the oven and preheat to 180°C/gas mark 4.

2. Whisk the eggs and egg yolks by hand in a large bowl, then whisk in the sugar, nutmeg and salt just to blend. Avoid overwhisking, which will make the top of the filling crusty after baking.

3. Use a rubber spatula to stir in the butter, buttermilk and lemon juice.

4. Pour the mixture into the prepared pie crust. Set the tin in the oven and decrease the temperature to 160°C/gas mark 3. Bake for 45–50 minutes until the crust is baked through and golden and the filling is set. When you remove it from the oven, there should be still be a soft area in the centre about 2.5cm in diameter.

5. Cool the pie on a rack and serve it on the day it's baked.

Makes one 25cm pie, about 8 servings

One 25cm pie crust made from Sweet Pastry Dough (page 19)

3 medium eggs

2 medium egg yolks

200g caster sugar

½ teaspoon freshly grated nutmeg

¼ teaspoon fine sea salt

55g unsalted butter, melted

240ml buttermilk

2 tablespoons lemon juice, strained before measuring

BUTTERSCOTCH CUSTARD PIE

Makes one 23cm pie, about 8 servings

One 23cm pie crust made from Sweet Pastry Dough (page 19)

BUTTERSCOTCH FILLING

120g best-quality salted butter

480ml whole milk

100g demerara sugar

1 vanilla pod, split lengthways

45g unbleached plain flour

4 medium eggs

FINISHING

240ml double cream

2 tablespoons caster sugar

1 teaspoon vanilla extract

1 teaspoon demerara sugar

That elusive flavour butterscotch is a combination of equal parts butter and caramel coupled with a strong hint of salt. For this pie filling, I decided to let some salted butter colour until deep golden brown and to use demerara sugar instead of standard brown sugar and the results are as butterscotch as you can get.

1. For the filling, melt the butter over a medium heat in a saucepan. Cook, watching the butter closely, until it turns a deep golden brown. Immediately pour the butter into a cool, dry stainless steel bowl to stop the cooking and reduce the temperature.

2. Set a rack at the lowest level in the oven and preheat to 190°C/gas mark 5.

3. In the same saucepan, whisk the milk and half the demerara sugar together. Add the split vanilla pod and bring the mixture to a simmer. Whisk well, then remove the vanilla pod.

4. Whisk the remaining sugar and the flour together, then whisk in the eggs until the mixture is smooth. Whisk in the milk mixture and finally the cooled brown butter.

5. Pour the filling into the prepared pie crust and set in the oven. Immediately decrease the temperature to 180°C/gas mark 4 and bake for about 45 minutes until the crust is baked through and the filling is set.

6. Cool the pie on a rack and chill it, loosely covered, before finishing.

7. To finish the pie, whip the cream with the sugar and vanilla extract to a soft peak. Spread the whipped cream over the chilled pie and sprinkle it with the demerara sugar.

8. Keep at a cool room temperature until serving; cover and chill leftovers for up to 2 days.

RASPBERRY CREAM PIE

After a few experiments with an all-raspberry pie filling that turned into a watery mess, I decided to use these berries to their best advantage: some slightly cooked and thickened, with the remainder added uncooked. I then layered the fruit between a light pastry cream and a whipped cream topping. Blueberries and blackberries are just as good, and a combination of berries would work well too.

1. For the raspberry filling, combine a third of the berries and the sugar in a non-reactive saucepan and mash together. Place over a low heat and bring to a simmer. Meanwhile, whisk the water and cornflour together. When the raspberries begin to boil, stir a third of the hot juices into the cornflour mixture. Return the raspberry mixture to the boil over a low heat and quickly stir in the cornflour mixture. Continue stirring until the juices thicken, return to the boil, and become clear. Stir in the lemon zest off the heat, then scrape the thickened raspberry mixture into a bowl. Press clingfilm directly against the surface and let the mixture cool.

2. For the pastry cream, combine the milk, cream and half the sugar in a small saucepan and whisk to combine. Place over a low heat and bring to the full boil. Meanwhile, in a bowl, whisk the egg yolks and then add the remaining sugar. Sift the flour over the mixture and whisk it in.

3. When the milk mixture boils, whisk it into the yolk mixture. Strain the pastry cream back into the pan and place it over a medium heat. Use a small, pointed-end whisk to stir constantly, being sure to reach into the corners of the pan, until the cream comes to a full boil and thickens. Continue to cook, whisking constantly, for 30 seconds, then take off the heat and whisk in the vanilla extract.

4. Scrape the pastry cream into a glass or stainless-steel bowl and press clingfilm directly against the surface. Chill until cold.

5. To finish the pie, whip the cream with the sugar and vanilla extract to a soft peak.

6. Evenly spread the cooled pastry cream in the bottom of the pie crust. Fold the fresh raspberries into the cooled, thickened cooked berries and spread the fruit on top of the pastry cream. Re-whip the cream if necessary and spread it, swirling it with a metal spatula or the back of a large spoon, over the raspberries.

7. Keep the pie at a cool room temperature until serving time. Refrigerate any leftovers.

Makes one 23cm pie, about 8 servings

One 23cm pie crust made from Flaky Buttery Dough (page 14), fully baked

RASPBERRY FILLING

500g fresh raspberries, picked over, but not rinsed

65g caster sugar

60ml water

2 tablespoons cornflour

2 teaspoons finely grated lemon zest

PASTRY CREAM

180ml whole milk

60ml double cream

50g caster sugar

3 medium egg yolks

2 tablespoons unbleached plain flour

1 teaspoon vanilla extract

FINISHING

240ml double cream

2 tablespoons caster sugar

1 teaspoon vanilla extract

OLD-FASHIONED SWEET POTATO PIE

Makes one 23cm pie, about 8 servings

One 23cm pie crust made from Sweet Pastry Dough (page 19)

2 medium sweet potatoes

65g caster sugar

50g demerara or light brown sugar

1 teaspoon ground cinnamon

½ teaspoon ground ginger

½ teaspoon freshly grated nutmeg

¼ teaspoon fine sea salt

3 medium eggs

150ml each milk and double cream or 300ml single cream

VARIATION

Use acorn or butternut squash instead of sweet potatoes. To prepare the squash, halve it and scrape out the seeds and filaments. Loosely cover with aluminium foil to keep the flesh from drying out and bake, cut-side up, as for the sweet potatoes. Cool, scrape the squash from the skin and mash. If the squash is very fibrous, purée it in the food processor.

Though I love pumpkin pie, I have to admit that lately I've just got tired of using tasteless tinned pumpkin. A couple of years ago, I tried substituting baked, mashed sweet potatoes for the pumpkin in my favourite recipe and I was more than happy with the results. Baked winter squash, such as butternut or acorn, works just as well. Serve with lightly sweetened whipped cream.

1. Set a rack at the middle level in the oven and preheat to 190°C/gas mark 5. Place the sweet potatoes on a small ovenproof tin and bake for 50–60 minutes until tender. Cool, peel and mash the potatoes – you should have about 450g purée. Prepare the purée several days in advance if you wish and keep it covered in the refrigerator, but bring to room temperature before using.

2. Move the rack to the lowest level in the oven and and preheat to 190°C/gas mark 5.

3. Whisk together the sweet potatoes, sugars, spices and salt, then whisk in the eggs, followed by the milk and cream.

4. Pour the filling into the prepared crust. Place in the oven and decrease the temperature to 180°C/gas mark 4. Bake the pie for 50–60 minutes until the crust is baked through and the filling is set.

5. Cool the pie on a rack.

Two-Crust Pie Tips and Tricks

Adding a top crust to a pie protects the filling from becoming dry while the pie is baking and reveals the filling with a little flourish as the pie is cut. Each of the pies that follow has a specific top crust in the recipe, but you can pretty much interchange them as you wish. See the variety of pie tops described and illustrated in chapter 2. Another possibility for covering a pie is the crumb topping on page 85.

Thickening Fruit Pie Fillings

Most fruit pie fillings need some thickening. For simple ones like apple and peach pies, I'm happy to use a little flour. It thickens the juices slightly so they aren't watery but doesn't make the filling overly dense.

For juicier pies, I like to use cornflour, but I always cook it out first with some of the juices in the filling so that it thickens efficiently and no chalky cornflour texture remains (as it would if it were added uncooked to the filling ingredients).

Fruit Pies and Simmering Juices

Before preheating your oven, slide a large sheet of aluminium foil onto the bottom of the oven. When fruit pie fillings start to simmer towards the end of baking, they frequently leak. Lining the bottom of your oven will help to prevent the overflowing juices from remaining there and burning over several hours.

Positioning in the Oven

For any pie or tart that has an unbaked crust, the paramount concern is to make sure that the bottom of the crust bakes through. That's why I always specify placing the pie or tart on the lowest rack in the oven. In the case of two-crust pies, though, we also have to make sure that the top crust colours to an appetising finish. Watch the pie during the last 15 minutes or so of the suggested baking time. If the juices are beginning to simmer but the top crust is still too pale, then move it to the upper third of the oven so it will sufficiently darken while finishing baking.

BLUEBERRY & APPLE PIE

Makes one 23cm pie, about 8 servings

One 23cm pie crust made from Sweet Pastry Dough (page 19), plus dough for a top crust

BLUEBERRY AND APPLE FILLING

570g blueberries, rinsed, dried and picked over

150g caster sugar

4 tablespoons water or apple juice

3 tablespoons cornflour

¼ teaspoon ground cinnamon

¼ teaspoon freshly grated nutmeg

450g Granny Smith apples, peeled, halved, cored and cut into 1cm dice

45g unsalted butter

Milk for brushing

1–2 teaspoons caster sugar

VARIATIONS

Use the crumb topping on page 85, without the almonds, instead of the full top crust. For this pie there's no need to pre-bake the crumbs. For an all-blueberry pie, use 850g blueberries, omit the apples and add 2 teaspoons grated lemon zest to the filling along with the spices.

For a raspberry or blackberry pie, use 790g berries, 200g sugar and 25g cornflour. Mix 2 tablespoons of water with the cornflour and stir into the berries with 2 teaspoons finely grated lemon zest and omit the spices.

Tart apples marry well with sweet, spicy blueberries, even though their seasons are fairly opposite. In early summer when blueberries come into season there are always imported apples available, and when apples come into season it's okay to use frozen blueberries. I find that dicing the apples quite small makes them cook through easily, and their tartness gives a better boost to the blueberry flavour than adding lemon juice or zest.

1. Combine 185g blueberries, the sugar, and 2 tablespoons of the water in a medium saucepan. Set over a low heat and cook, stirring often, until the blueberries have become very juicy and the sugar has dissolved. Mix the cornflour with the remaining water, then stir in about a third of the blueberry juices. Stir the cornflour mixture into the saucepan, return to the heat and cook, stirring constantly, for about 3 minutes until thickened and clear.

2. Remove from the heat, scrape the filling into a medium bowl and stir in the spices. Let cool.

3. Set a rack at the lowest level in the oven and preheat to 190°C/gas mark 5.

4. Fold the remaining blueberries and the diced apples into the cooled filing.

5. Scrape into the pie crust and spread evenly. Dot with the butter and arrange the top crust. Attach, flute and pierce the top crust as on page 32. Brush with milk and sprinkle with the sugar.

6. Place the pie in the oven and decrease the temperature to 180°C/gas mark 4. Bake for about 45 minutes until the crust is baked through and the juices are actively simmering.

7. Cool the pie on a rack and serve warm or at room temperature.

SWEET CHERRY & RHUBARB PIE

One 23cm pie crust made from Flaky Buttery Dough (page 14), plus dough for a lattice top

CHERRY AND RHUBARB FILLING

150g caster sugar

60ml water

450g pink, tender rhubarb, trimmed, rinsed and cut into 5cm lengths

3 tablespoons cornflour

Large pinch of ground cinnamon

Finely grated zest of 1 small orange, about 1 teaspoon

675g sweet black cherries, rinsed, stemmed and stoned

30g unsalted butter

Milk for brushing

1-2 teaspoons caster sugar

Lightly sweetened whipped cream for serving

VARIATION

Substitute 450g strawberries (rinsed, hulled and halved) for the cherries.

While sweet cherries are both abundant and delicious during the summer, they can be a little dull when cooked in a pie filling. Punching up the flavour with some tart rhubarb makes a big difference and rescues the cherries from a bland fate.

1. For the filling, combine the sugar and water in a non-reactive saucepan with a cover. Stir over a medium heat until boiling, then add the rhubarb. Cook until the mixture returns to a simmer, then remove the pan from the heat and cover it. Let the rhubarb remain in the syrup for about 15 minutes until it's tender. Transfer the rhubarb to a bowl and set it aside.

2. Whisk the cornflour into the rhubarb syrup and return the pan to the heat. Cook, stirring constantly, for about 3 minutes until the syrup thickens, comes to the boil and turns clear. Off the heat, stir in the cinnamon and orange zest. Scrape the thickened juices over the rhubarb without stirring them together and let the mixture cool.

3. Set a rack at the lowest level in the oven and preheat to 200°C/gas mark 4.

4. Add the cherries to the cooled rhubarb mixture and gently fold the filling together. Scrape into the pie crust and dot with the butter.

5. Finish the top of the pie with a diagonal or perpendicular lattice (page 33). Brush the lattice strips with milk and sprinkle them with sugar.

6. Place the pie in the oven and decrease the temperature to 190°C/gas mark 5. Bake for about 45 minutes until the crust is baked through and the filling is actively bubbling.

7. Cool the pie on a rack and serve it on the day it's baked with a little whipped cream.

PEACH & GINGER PIE

A tablespoon of grated fresh ginger enlivens the filling of this peach pie. Use only really ripe height-of-summer peaches to make this. Less ripe peaches lack the flavour necessary for a good filling and are also a nightmare to peel. This is a perfect pie for a crumb topping, especially when you use my improved method for applying it: I often noticed that the bottom of the crumbs added in the usual way had a layer of wet and unbaked flour where they had absorbed moisture from the filling. Now I bake the crumbs and the pie separately for a few minutes before bringing them together.

1. Set racks at the middle and lowest levels in the oven and preheat to 200°C/gas mark 6. Line a Swiss roll tin with parchment paper or aluminium foil.

2. For the topping, combine the flour, sugar and nutmeg in a mixing bowl; stir well to mix and stir in the flaked almonds if using. Stir in the butter evenly. Set the mixture aside for 5 minutes, then break it into 0.5–1.5cm crumbs. Scatter the crumbs on the prepared tin.

3. To make the filling, peel the peaches by cutting a cross in the blossom end of each and dropping them three at a time into a pan of boiling water. After 20 or 30 seconds, use a slotted spoon to transfer them to a bowl of ice water. If the peaches are ripe, the skin will slip off easily. If it does not, remove the skin with a sharp stainless steel paring knife. Holding the peaches over a bowl to catch any juices, slice them into wedges by cutting in toward the stone with a paring knife and drop the wedges into the bowl.

4. Add the sugar, flour and ginger to the peaches and stir gently with a rubber spatula to combine. Pour the filling into the prepared pie crust and dot it with the butter.

5. Place the pie on the bottom rack of the oven and the crumbs on the middle rack, decrease the temperature to 180°C/gas mark 4 and bake for 15 minutes.

6. Remove the pie and crumbs from the oven, chop the crumbs with a dough scraper if necessary and scatter them on top of the pie. Return the pie to the bottom rack and bake for a further 30 minutes, or until the crust and the crumb topping are a deep golden colour and the juices are actively bubbling. Cool the pie on a rack and serve warm or at room temperature.

Makes one 23cm pie, about 8 servings

One 23cm pie crust made from Sweet Pastry Dough (page 19)

CRUMB TOPPING

130g unbleached plain flour

3 tablespoons caster sugar

¼ teaspoon freshly grated nutmeg

85g flaked almonds, optional

85g unsalted butter, melted

PEACH FILLING

1.15–1.35kg firm, ripe yellow-fleshed peaches (see Note)

100g caster sugar

3 tablespoons unbleached plain flour

1 tablespoon finely grated peeled fresh ginger

30g unsalted butter

NOTE

Ripe peaches can exude an enormous amount of juice into a pie filling. Don't mound the filling beyond 2.5cm above the side of the crust or it will spill a flood of juice into the oven.

VARIATIONS

For a traditionally flavoured pie, omit the ginger and flavour the filling with ¼ teaspoon each almond extract and freshly grated nutmeg. An open diagonal or perpendicular lattice top (page 33) would also be perfect on this pie.

I don't recommend a full top crust or a closed woven lattice because of the rawness factor mentioned above.

DRIED APRICOT PIE

This pie is directly modelled on old-fashioned recipes for Pennsylvania Dutch Raisin Pie. To my taste, dried apricots are so much more appealing than raisins for an entire pie filling – their flavour has a welcome touch of tartness that raisins lack.

1. Combine the apricots and water in a non-reactive saucepan and bring the mixture to a full boil. Remove the pan from the heat and let the apricots stand for about 2 hours until cooled.

2. Transfer the apricots and liquid to a bowl. Set a sieve over the saucepan in which the apricots soaked and drain the apricots well, letting the liquid fall back into the pan. Return the apricots to the bowl.

3. Combine the sugar and flour and whisk the mixture into the apricot liquid. Place over a low heat and stirring constantly, bring the juices to a full boil; decrease the heat and let simmer for 2 minutes, stirring often. Stir in the lemon zest, butter and almond extract. Pour the juices over the plumped apricots in the bowl and let cool.

4. Set a rack at the lowest level in the oven and preheat to 190°C/gas mark 5.

5. Pour the filling into the pie crust and arrange the lattice top over it (page 33). Brush the lattice with milk and sprinkle with sugar.

6. Place the pie in the oven and decrease the temperature to 180°C/gas mark 4. Bake for about 45 minutes until the crust is baked through and the filling is actively simmering.

7. Cool the pie on a rack and serve slightly warm or at room temperature.

Makes one 23cm pie, about 8 servings

One 23cm pie crust made from Sweet Pastry Dough (page 19), plus dough for a lattice top

450g dried apricots, cut into 1.5cm dice (see Note)

720ml water

150g caster sugar

3 tablespoons unbleached plain flour

2 teaspoons finely grated lemon zest

30g unsalted butter

¼ teaspoon almond extract

Milk for brushing

1–2 teaspoons sugar

NOTE
For ease in cutting the apricots, snip them with lightly oiled scissors or use an oiled knife.

VARIATIONS
Substitute a combination of equal amounts of prunes and dried apricots in the filling. Or if you're a real raisin lover, try a combination of raisins and sultanas instead of the apricots. Omit the almond extract and substitute 1 teaspoon vanilla extract.

APPLE & CHEDDAR PIE

Makes one 23cm pie, about 8 servings

One 23cm pie crust made from Buttery Dough or Flaky Dough Using Lard (pages 14 and 15), plus dough for a top crust

APPLE AND CHEDDAR FILLING

150g caster sugar

3 tablespoons unbleached plain flour

1 teaspoon ground cinnamon

675g Golden Delicious apples and 225g crunchy, tart dessert apples, peeled, halved, cored and cut into 1.5cm dice

140g coarsely grated mature Cheddar cheese

2 teaspoons lemon juice, strained before measuring

30g unsalted butter, chilled and cut into 10 pieces

Milk for brushing

1–2 teaspoons caster sugar

Apple pie served with Cheddar cheese is a New England classic, so why not combine them right in the pie filling? My favourite apples for a pie are Northern Spies, but they're available only in the fall and early winter, and mostly in the northeastern United States. Failing that, I think a combination of two-thirds Golden Delicious and one-third other crunchy tart dessert apples perfectly combines sweet and tart with firm and juicy.

1. Set a rack at the lowest level in the oven and preheat to 200°C/gas mark 6.

2. For the filling, mix the sugar, flour and cinnamon in a large bowl. Add the apples and Cheddar cheese and fold together to evenly coat the apples with the sugar mixture. Scrape the filling into the pie crust, making sure the top is flat and even rather than mounded in the centre.

3. Sprinkle the filling with the lemon juice and dot with the butter.

4. Attach, flute and pierce the top crust as on page 32. Brush with milk and sprinkle with sugar.

5. Bake the pie for 15 minutes, then decrease the temperature to 180°C/gas mark 4. Continue baking for up to 45 minutes longer until the crust is baked through and the juices are actively simmering.

6. Cool the pie on a rack and serve it on the day it's baked.

VARIATIONS

For an apple pie without the Cheddar, increase the apples to 900g Golden Delicious and 450g crunchy, tart dessert apples.

For a change of pace, use half caster sugar and half demerara or light brown sugar.

For a maple flavour, use 100g caster sugar and 75ml maple syrup, adding the syrup along with the lemon juice and butter before topping the pie.

PEAR & CURRANT PIE

Baking a pear pie requires a little advance planning. Sold hard and green in most shops, pears need to ripen in a paper bag at room temperature for a couple of days before you use them. For the best results, they need to be ripe but still firm – when you press your thumb into the bottom of the pear near the blossom end, it should be just slightly springy. Softer than that, and the pear is too ripe – it will turn into a mass of water when cooked. The best pear to use for a pie is a Bartlett, called a Williams outside North America.

1. Set a rack at the lowest level in the oven and preheat to 190°C/gas mark 5.

2. For the filling, thoroughly mix the sugar, flour and nutmeg in a large mixing bowl. Add the pears and half the currants and gently fold them together.

3. Scrape the filling into the pie crust, making sure the top is flat and even rather than mounded in the centre. Sprinkle with the remaining currants and the lemon juice and dot with the butter.

4. Attach, flute and pierce the top crust as on page 32. Brush the top crust with milk and sprinkle with the sugar.

5. Bake the pie for 10 minutes, then decrease the temperature to 180°C/gas mark 4. Continue baking for up to 45 minutes longer until the crust is baked through and the juices are actively simmering.

6. Cool the pie on a rack and serve it on the day it's baked.

Makes one 23cm pie, about 8 servings

One 23cm pie crust made from Sweet Pastry Dough (page 19), plus dough for a top crust

PEAR AND CURRANT FILLING

100g caster sugar

2 tablespoons unbleached plain flour

Pinch of freshly grated nutmeg

1.24kg firm, ripe pears, peeled, halved, cored and sliced 0.5cm thick

65g dried currants

2 tablespoons lemon juice, strained before measuring

30g unsalted butter

Milk for brushing

1 teaspoon sugar

VARIATIONS

Substitute the crumb topping, with or without the almonds (page 85), for the top crust; bake the pie and crumb topping according to the instructions in that recipe.

'FRENCH' APPLE PIE

This was a mainstay of retail bakeries about fifty years ago and has all but disappeared from sight. A cooked apple filling with raisins is baked in a sweet crust in a straight-sided tin. After cooling, the top is spread with a simple sugar icing. I have no idea how or why it acquired the name, but despite the fact that there is no equivalent in France, it has always been one of my favourite bakery treats.

1. For the apple filling, melt the butter in a wide saucepan or casserole with a lid and add the apples, sugar, cinnamon and raisins. Stir well and place over a medium heat. Cook until the apples start to sizzle, then cover the pan and decrease the heat. Cook for 5–10 minutes until the apples have exuded water. Uncover the pan and stir occasionally while the water evaporates. Off the heat, stir in the rum. Spread the filling in a shallow bowl and refrigerate until cooled or up to 2 days before filling the pie.

2. When you are ready to assemble the pie, set a rack at the lowest level in the oven and preheat to 180°C/gas mark 4.

3. Roll out a little more than half of the dough on a floured surface and line the prepared tin, cutting away any excess dough at the rim. Spread the apple filling in the crust. Roll the remaining dough and cut a 20cm disk. Set it atop the filling and fold the dough on the side of the tin onto the disk of dough to seal it.

4. Bake the pie for 35–40 minutes until the crust is baked through. Cool on a rack.

5. Unmould the pie onto a serving plate, keeping the bottom of the pie as the top.

6. For the icing, place the icing sugar and water in a small saucepan and stir well. Heat to lukewarm and quickly spread over the pie. Let the icing set before serving.

Makes one 20cm pie, about 8 servings

One batch Sweet Pastry Dough (page 19)

APPLE FILLING

30g unsalted butter

900g Golden Delicious apples, peeled, halved, cored and cut into 1.5cm dice

100g caster sugar

½ teaspoon ground cinnamon

75g raisins

1 tablespoon dark rum

ICING

105g icing sugar, sifted

1½ tablespoons water

20cm round cake tin, 5cm deep, buttered and the bottom lined with a disk of parchment paper

Cobblers & Crisps

There are probably dozens of regional names for fruit baked in a shallow dish with only a top crust. I'm calling anything a cobbler if it has a full top crust of baking powder scone, pastry dough, or even a poured-on batter; if it has a crumb or other non-dough topping, I consider it a crisp. These are versatile preparations, and you can have fun adding and subtracting ingredients and flavourings at will. If you want more guidance in the way of fillings, any of the fruit pie fillings on pages 82–91 will also make a great cobbler or crisp.

DEEP-DISH BLUEBERRY PIE (WITH CREAM SCONE CRUST)

Makes one large pie, about 8 servings

CREAM SCONE CRUST

400g unbleached plain flour

1 tablespoon baking powder

1 tablespoon caster sugar

1 teaspoon fine sea salt

170g unsalted butter, slightly softened

300ml single cream

FILLING

1 kg fresh blueberries, rinsed and picked over

150g caster sugar

2 teaspoons finely grated lemon zest

½ teaspoon freshly grated nutmeg

½ teaspoon ground cinnamon

40g unsalted butter

Single cream for brushing

1-2 teaspoons caster sugar

Whipped cream or vanilla ice cream for serving

There isn't much difference between this pie and what we normally call a cobbler, except that this has much more fruit in relation to the crust. The blueberries have no thickeners added to mar their natural flavour and juiciness, so the filling is quite soupy.

1. For the crust, place the flour, baking powder, sugar and salt in a bowl and rub in the butter until fine and mealy. Do not allow the mixture to become pasty. Use a fork to stir in the cream – the dough will be very soft. Press the dough together on a floured surface, turn it over on itself several times to make it slightly more elastic, and wrap in clingfilm. Set aside.

2. Preheat the oven to 200°C/gas mark 6 and set a rack in the lower third of the oven.

3. Place the blueberries in a bowl and add all the remaining filling ingredients, except the butter. Toss well and pour into a baking dish. Distribute pieces of the butter evenly amongst the filling.

4. Press the dough out on a floured surface until it is roughly the size of the baking dish. Lift the dough onto the filling using a thin, flexible baking tray, and cut several vent holes in the top. Brush it with some cream and sprinkle it with the sugar.

5. Bake the pie for 25–30 minutes until the crust is deep golden and the filling is bubbling. Cool slightly on a rack and serve warm or at room temperature.

6. To serve the pie, place a portion of the scone crust into a shallow bowl. Pour a couple of large spoonfuls of the filling next to it and add some whipped cream or vanilla ice cream.

PLUM & RASPBERRY CRISP

You could use almost any combination of summer fruits in this, but sweet-tart ripe plums are perfect with tart raspberries. Choose red or green plums; prune plums come into season later in the summer and work beautifully too. Peaches or apricots would stand in well for the plums, and earlier in the season, you could sneak in some rhubarb instead of the raspberries. Baking the topping for a few minutes while the fruit begins to cook makes it much more crisp.

1. Set a rack at the middle level of the oven and preheat to 190°C/gas mark 5. Butter a 1.9–2.4 litre baking dish and cover a Swiss roll tin with aluminium foil.

2. For the crisp topping, stir the flour, sugar, baking powder, cinnamon and nuts, if you're using them, together in a medium mixing bowl. Add the butter and use a rubber spatula to fold it in evenly. Let the crumb mixture stand while preparing the fruit.

3. For the filling, mix the sugars and cinnamon in a bowl then stir in the plums and lemon zest. Pour half the plum filling into the prepared baking dish and scatter on half of the raspberries. Repeat with the remaining plums and raspberries. Dot with the butter.

4. Break the crumb mixture into 0.5–1.25cm crumbs and scatter them on the prepared Swiss roll tin. Bake the crumbs for about 15 minutes until they are set and beginning to colour.

5. Use a dough scraper or metal spatula to break up the crumb topping if it has clumped together. Scatter the pieces on top of the fruit, using a large spoon if the crumbs are still hot.

6. Bake for 45–50 minutes until the fruit is tender and bubbling and the crumbs are a deep golden colour. Cool slightly and serve warm with whipped cream, crème fraîche or vanilla ice cream.

Makes one large crisp, about 8 servings

CRISP TOPPING

180g unbleached plain flour

65g sugar

½ teaspoon baking powder

¼ teaspoon ground cinnamon

60g chopped walnuts or almonds, optional

125g unsalted butter, melted

FILLING

50g caster sugar

50g demerara or light brown sugar

¼ teaspoon ground cinnamon

1.15kg ripe plums, rinsed, halved, stoned and sliced 1.25cm thick

2 teaspoons finely grated lemon zest

340g fresh raspberries, picked over, but not washed

30g unsalted butter

Whipped cream, crème fraîche or vanilla ice cream for serving

APPLE & CRANBERRY GRANOLA CRISP

Makes one large crisp, about 8 servings

APPLE FILLING

65g demerara or light brown sugar

50g caster sugar

2 tablespoons unbleached plain flour

½ teaspoon ground cinnamon

1.35kg Golden Delicious apples, peeled, cored, and cut into thin wedges

90g fresh or dried cranberries

30g unsalted butter, chilled and cut into 10 pieces

GRANOLA TOPPING

125g porridge oats

60g coarsely chopped walnuts, pecans or almonds

65g caster sugar

50g demerara or light brown sugar

85g unsalted butter, melted

Juicy and tart, with a sweet and crunchy granola-type topping, this is as easy to assemble and bake as it is to enjoy. Use old-fashioned porridge oats, not the quick or instant types. The standard crumb topping on page 85, if you bake it for a few minutes first, would also be perfect on this crisp. If you want to serve some cream with this crisp, I prefer liquid double cream or crème fraiche to whipped cream.

1. Set a rack at the middle level of the oven and preheat to 200°C/gas mark 6. Butter a 1.9–2.4 litre baking dish.

2. To make the apple filling, mix the sugars, flour and cinnamon in a bowl and thoroughly fold in the apples and cranberries. Scrape into the prepared dish and level the top; dot with the butter.

3. To make the topping, mix the oats, nuts and sugars together and thoroughly fold in the butter. Scatter the granola mixture on the fruit in the baking dish.

4. Set the dish in the oven and immediately decrease the temperature to 190°C/gas mark 4. Bake for 45–55 minutes until the fruit is tender and bubbling and the topping has become a deep golden colour.

5. Cool the crisp slightly and serve warm or reheat at 180°C/gas mark 4 for about 10 minutes before serving.

MIXED BERRY COBBLER (WITH REVERSIBLE TOPPING)

This has been a popular recipe since my childhood. It's usually made with a prepared scone mix, but that's easy enough to duplicate with fresh ingredients. Feel free to mix up the assortment of berries any way you like; only blueberries or blackberries have enough flavour and texture once baked to be used on their own, though. Don't try to crowd in extra berries or there might not be enough batter to cover them; and please use only a 1.9 litre baking dish or the layer of batter might be too thin or thick to magically rise up and cover the berries.

1. Set a rack at the middle level in the oven and preheat to 200°C/gas mark 6. Grease a 1.9 litre baking dish with vegetable spray.

2. For the topping, stir the flour, sugar, salt, baking powder and spices together in a bowl. Add the milk, 45g of the butter, and the lemon zest and whisk smooth.

3. Pour the last 15g of butter into the baking dish and tilt the dish to evenly coat the bottom. Pour in the batter.

4. Evenly spoon the berries on top of the batter and sprinkle with the 50g sugar.

5. Place in the oven and decrease the temperature to 190°C/gas mark 5. Bake for about 45 minutes until the topping has risen to cover the berries and has turned a deep golden colour.

6. Cool the cobbler on a rack and serve warm or at room temperature with some double cream.

Makes one large cobbler, 8–10 servings

TOPPING

100g unbleached plain flour

130g caster sugar

¼ teaspoon fine sea salt

2 teaspoons baking powder

Large pinch of ground cinnamon

Large pinch of freshly grated nutmeg

240ml whole milk

60g unsalted butter, melted

Finely grated zest of 1 small lemon

BERRIES

350–500g assorted rinsed berries (blackberries, blueberries, raspberries and hulled and sliced strawberries)

50g caster sugar for sprinkling on the berries

Double cream for serving

CHAPTER 5
SAVOURY TARTS & PIES

Savoury baking has always appealed to me – at home my grandmother baked *pizza rustica* filled with dried sausage, prosciutto and mozzarella every year for Carnival and then again for Easter and we had the occasional side dish of rice seasoned with ricotta, eggs and cheese.

Whenever I invite guests for lunch, I panic a few days before, because I haven't decided what to cook. A savoury tart, quiche or pie is often the solution. Add a salad and a fruit dessert and you have a meal. A savoury pie can also be a perfect part of an assortment of hors d'oeuvres for a large party or a first course to be served at the table, especially if the main course is a light dish.

Many nationalities have traditional savoury pies. In France a quiche was pretty much always a Quiche Lorraine until the 'quiche revolution' of the 1960s and 70s added every imaginable savoury ingredient to the filling. Now that the craze is over I think of a quiche as a savoury tart that has a cream and egg custard poured over the solid ingredients before baking. In Italy a *pizza rustica* or a *torta salata* (salted pie) may be made with a single or double crust containing any type of savoury filling, though when I think of *pizza rustica* it's mostly the meat and cheese–filled Easter version. There are quite a few vegetable fillings here, a great choice if you, as I often do, tire of meat and fish-based meals. Aside from pies, there are also some Argentine empanadas and Cornish pasties here. And in chapter 6 you'll find some delicious savoury strudels and other savoury pastries made from Turkish *yufka* dough. Try a few of these, and I'm sure you'll add savoury tarts and pies to your favourite list of recipes.

Quiches & Other Savoury Tarts

These are usually baked in French removable-base tart tins with fluted sides about 2.5cm deep. If you have a similar but deeper tin, bear in mind that you're going to have excess dough at the top of your quiche or tart. Once the filling is added, there will be no danger of the side collapsing.

REAL QUICHE LORRAINE Overleaf, page 102

Makes one 25cm quiche, about 8 servings

One 25cm tart crust made from Flaky Buttery Dough (page 14)

225g slab skinless bacon, sliced 0.5cm thick and cut into 1.25cm strips, or thick-cut sliced bacon, cut into 1.25cm strips

420ml crème fraîche or 300ml double cream plus 120ml sour cream, at room temperature

5 medium eggs, at room temperature

¼ teaspoon fine sea salt

¼ teaspoon freshly ground black pepper

Large pinch of freshly grated nutmeg

Perfect for a fancy breakfast or for brunch, today's Quiche Lorraine has its roots in the rustic baking traditions of northeastern France and southern Germany; due to changes in the political breezes, the area known as the Lorraine has several times been a part of both countries. The word *quiche* is derived from the German *Kuchen*, which can refer to both what we call a pie or tart as well as a simple cake. The crust used to be made from a thinly rolled bread dough, and the mixture of cream and eggs, known as *la migaine* in the Lorraine, has always been part of the preparation, but many authorities say the bacon was added later. No cheese, full stop! Yes, you can make an excellent quiche, tart or pie with bacon, custard and cheese – it's just not Quiche Lorraine. (See the next recipe, and we can break the rules together.) A Quiche Lorraine should be served immediately after it's baked, before the puffy crown of custard has time to sink, so plan accordingly.

1. Set a rack at the lowest level in the oven and preheat to 200°C/gas mark 6.

2. Half-fill a large saucepan with water and bring it to the boil over a medium heat; add the bacon. Once the water returns to the boil, cook the bacon for 3 minutes. Drain.

3. Heat a non-stick sauté pan and add the bacon. Cook over a medium heat for 3–4 minutes until the bacon takes on a little colour. Set it aside to cool, then scatter it over the tart crust.

4. Whisk the crème fraîche and eggs together and season with the salt, pepper and nutmeg.

5. Place the tart tin on the hob or close to the oven to avoid spills when moving it and pour the custard into the crust, filling it to within about 0.5cm of the top.

6. Bake the quiche for about 30 minutes until the crust is baked through and the filling is set.

7. Unmould the quiche and serve it immediately.

LEEK & MUSHROOM QUICHE Overleaf, page 103

The sweet flavour of slow-cooked leeks complements the woodsy scent of mushrooms especially well in the creamy custard of this quiche. Although it might be delicious to use some fancy wild mushrooms in this, I've crafted the recipe with the white cultivated mushrooms available everywhere. I would definitely prepare the leeks and mushrooms the day before to cut down on the last-minute rush. Since they both need to cook slowly for maximum flavour, cooking them simultaneously actually saves you time. This is a perfect starter for an elegant dinner.

1. Melt half the butter in a medium saucepan and add the leeks. Stir to coat them and cook over a medium heat until they start to sizzle. Lower the heat and cook, stirring often, for about 30 minutes until the leeks are reduced and starting to colour.

2. As soon as you have started the leeks, use a separate pan and the remaining butter to start cooking the mushrooms. Season them with salt and pepper and once they begin to exude their juices, cook them slowly for about 30 minutes until the juices evaporate and the mushrooms begin to colour. Mix the mushrooms into the leeks, taste for seasoning and transfer them to a bowl to cool. For advance preparation, cover and refrigerate them for up to a couple of days.

3. When you're ready to bake the quiche, set a rack at the lowest level in the oven and preheat to 200°C/gas mark 6.

4. Whisk the eggs in a large bowl and season them lightly with salt and pepper. Whisk in the cream, cheese if using, and parsley.

5. Spread the leek and mushroom mixture on the tart crust. Pour in the custard mixture, filling only to within 0.5cm of the top of the crust.

6. Carefully set the quiche in the oven. Immediately reduce the temperature to 195°C/gas mark 5. Bake for 35–40 minutes until the crust is baked through and the filling is set and puffed.

7. Cool the quiche briefly on a rack, then unmould and serve it either hot or warm.

Makes one 25cm tart, 8-10 servings

One 25cm tart crust made from Flaky Buttery Dough or Olive Oil Dough (page 14)

60g unsalted butter

450g leeks (about 2 medium), white part and 2.5–5cm of the green part, sliced 0.5cm thick and washed repeatedly to remove all sand

340g white mushrooms, rinsed and thinly sliced (see Note)

Fine sea salt and freshly ground black pepper

3 medium eggs

240ml single cream

40g finely grated Parmesan cheese, optional

2 tablespoons finely chopped fresh flat-leaf parsley

NOTE

If you want to boost the woodsy flavour, soak 7g dried *porcini* mushrooms in 240ml boiling water for 10 minutes; lift them from the soaking water (they might be sandy), chop them finely, and add them to the fresh mushrooms when you start to cook them.

APPLE, BACON & GRUYÈRE QUICHE

Makes one 25cm tart, 8-10 servings

One 25cm tart crust made from Flaky Buttery Dough (page 14)

115g bacon, cut into 1.25cm strips

2 Golden Delicious apples, peeled, cored and cut into 1.25cm dice

170g coarsely grated Swiss Gruyère cheese

1 tablespoon unbleached plain flour

480ml single cream

3 medium eggs

¼ teaspoon salt

2 pinches freshly ground white pepper

The interplay of tart apples with the salty cheese and bacon filling make for a delicious and easy brunch dish.

1. Set a rack at the lowest level in the oven and preheat to 200°C/gas mark 6.

2. Cook the bacon slowly in a non-stick sauté pan over a medium heat until it is browned but not too crisp. Lift it from the fat with a slotted spoon and drain it on kitchen towels. Cool and scatter it over the tart crust.

3. Drain most of the bacon fat from the pan and add the apples. Cook over a medium heat, stirring often, until tender. Cool and scatter them in the crust on top of the bacon.

4. Toss the cheese with the flour and evenly distribute it over the apples. Whisk the remaining ingredients together and pour the mixture over the cheese.

5. Set the tart in the oven and immediately reduce the temperature to 190°C/gas mark 5. Bake for about 30 minutes until the crust is baked through and the filling is set and well-coloured.

6. Cool the quiche in the tin on a rack for a few minutes before serving.

POTATO & CHEDDAR QUICHE

I know this sounds starchy, but give it a try. It is my attempt to combine the goodness of home-fried potatoes with the cheesy richness of a Cheddar custard. It's a great breakfast or brunch dish and is so easy to get ready in advance. If possible, boil the potatoes the day before and let them dry at room temperature.

1. The day before preparing the quiche, place the potatoes in a saucepan and cover them with water. Place them over a medium heat and bring them to the boil for 10 minutes, then cover the pan, remove it from the heat, and let the potatoes sit until they have cooled. Drain the potatoes for a few minutes, then keep them at a cool room temperature until the next day – this helps to evaporate some of the excess moisture the potatoes have absorbed.

2. Peel and trim any blemished areas and cut the potatoes into 1cm dice - you don't need to use a ruler but the texture of the filling is better when the pieces aren't too large. Melt the butter in a non-stick sauté pan and add the onion. Cook over a low heat for about 10 minutes until soft and translucent. Add the potatoes, season generously with salt and pepper, add the thyme (if you're substituting parsley, stir it in after the potatoes have cooled) and toss well. Increase the heat slightly so that the potatoes start to colour. Cook, stirring often, for 10-15 minutes until the potatoes are nicely flecked with brown. Scrape the potatoes onto a plate and let cool.

3. Set a rack at the lowest level in the oven and preheat to 200°C/gas mark 6.

4. Arrange the potato mixture in the tart crust without pressing it down, then toss the cheese and flour together and scatter over the potatoes. Whisk the eggs in a bowl, season lightly with salt, pepper and nutmeg and whisk in the cream.

5. Pour the custard into the quiche, filling only to within 0.5cm of the top of the crust.

6. Set the tin in the oven and immediately reduce the temperature to 190°C/gas mark 5. Bake for 35-40 minutes until the crust is baked through and the filling is set and puffed.

7. Cool the quiche briefly on a rack, then unmould and serve either hot or warm. This doesn't make a great leftover as the filling becomes heavy after the potatoes have cooled. Reheat leftovers at 180°C/gas mark 4 for 15 minutes before serving.

Makes one 25cm tart, 8-10 servings

One 25cm tart crust made from Flaky Buttery Dough (page 14)

450g Maris Piper or other all-rounder or waxy potatoes

45g unsalted butter

55g finely chopped white onions

Fine sea salt and freshly ground black pepper

1 teaspoon finely chopped fresh thyme leaves (substitute 1 tablespoon chopped fresh parsley rather than dried thyme)

115g coarsely grated mature Cheddar cheese

1 tablespoon unbleached plain flour

3 medium eggs

Large pinch of freshly grated nutmeg

240ml single cream

QUICHE OF SALMON & PEAS

Makes one 25cm tart, 8-10 servings

One 25cm tart crust made from Flaky Buttery Dough (page 14)

340g skinless and boneless salmon fillet

Fine sea salt and freshly ground black pepper

170g shelled tiny peas, fresh or frozen

15g unsalted butter

Pinch of caster sugar

1 tablespoon finely chopped fresh flat-leaf parsley

1 tablespoon finely chopped fresh dill

4 medium eggs

150ml single cream

1 teaspoon finely grated lemon zest

For a long time the traditional July Fourth meal in the state of Maine, early peas and salmon, have not been in season so far north at the beginning of July for over a hundred years, according to culinary historians. Oh well, they still taste great together, especially in a creamy quiche. All the elements of the dish are quite at home in a tart crust, and it's also an easy way to serve them all hot at the same time. A great way to use leftover cooked salmon or other firm-fleshed fish, this is also good with diced cooked prawns or even crabmeat.

1. Set one rack at the middle level in the oven and another at the lowest level and preheat to 190°C/gas mark 5. Butter a small baking dish.

2. Season the salmon with salt and pepper and place it in the prepared dish; bake the salmon on the middle oven rack for 15-20 minutes (depending on its thickness) until it just begins to flake easily. Undercooked a little is preferable to the alternative. Transfer the salmon to a plate to cool. Increase the oven temperature to 200°C/gas mark 6.

3. Meanwhile, fill the base of a small saucepan with water and add the peas, butter and sugar. Bring to the boil and cook over a low heat at a slow simmer for about 5 minutes until tender. Cool the peas.

4. Flake the salmon with a fork and scatter evenly over the tart crust. Top with the parsley and dill, then the peas.

5. Whisk the eggs well, season them lightly with salt and pepper, then whisk in the cream and the lemon zest.

6. Pour the custard mixture into the crust, filling only to within 0.5cm of the top.

7. Set the quiche on the bottom rack of the oven and immediately reduce the temperature to 190°C/gas mark 5. Bake for 25-30 minutes until the crust is baked through and the filling is set and puffed.

8. Cool the quiche briefly on a rack, then unmould and serve it either hot or warm.

CURRIED CRABMEAT TART

One 25cm tart crust made from Flaky Buttery Dough (page 14), fully baked

2 tablespoons sunflower or other mild vegetable oil

1 small bunch spring onions (about 35g), rinsed, trimmed, white part and half the green, cut into 1.25cm pieces

340g white crabmeat

30g unsalted butter

1 tablespoon best-quality curry powder

1 teaspoon caster sugar

1 tablespoon *nam prik pao* (Thai chilli paste)

2 teaspoons oyster sauce

120ml chicken stock

2–4 green, red, or a combination of Thai bird's eye chillies, stemmed, rinsed and sliced (see Note)

4 tablespoons coarsely chopped Asian celery leaves (Western celery leaves can do in a pinch)

4 medium eggs

½ teaspoon fine sea salt

½ teaspoon freshly ground white pepper

NOTE

If you don't want a lot of heat from the chillies, stem and halve them, then scrape out the seeds with a sharp pointed spoon or measuring spoon. Mexican serrano chillies are a decent substitute for the Thai ones.

A popular dish at seafood restaurants in Bangkok, curried crab is usually served in the shell, leaving diners in need of an immediate shower after the meal. My friend Chef Somsak, who used to have a restaurant in the northern part of the city before the 2011 autumn floods destroyed it, made his version, using crabmeat, several times when I visited him there. I was surprised at the use of butter in a Thai dish but Chef Somsak assured me that it's an important part of the preparation. Since the dish already calls for several eggs, I knew it would make an excellent tart filling. This is also a great choice as a starter for an important dinner.

Since this only needs to bake long enough to set the eggs in the filling, I'm starting with a completely baked crust.

1. Heat the oil in a wok or sauté pan until medium hot, then add the spring onions. Toss for 30 seconds, then add the crabmeat and butter. Stir-fry quickly, sprinkling on the curry powder and sugar after a few seconds. Stir-fry again very briefly, then take the wok off the heat.

2. Quickly mix the *nam prik pao*, oyster sauce and stock. Return the wok to a high heat, add the liquid and quickly stir-fry. Off the heat, fold in the chillies and celery leaves. Scrape the mixture to a bowl to cool briefly.

3. When you're ready to bake the tart, set a rack at the middle level in the oven and preheat to 200°C/gas mark 6.

4. Whisk the eggs well in a bowl with the salt and white pepper and gently fold in the cooled crab mixture. Scrape the mixture into the prepared crust (still in its tin) and use a fork to evenly distribute the crabmeat.

5. Place the tart in the oven, reduce the temperature to 190°C/gas mark 5 and bake for 15-20 minutes until the eggs are set.

6. Cool the tart slightly on a rack, unmould it onto a serving plate and serve it warm from the oven but not red hot.

COURGETTE & RED PEPPER TART

Courgette's mild flavour reminds me of Brillat-Savarin's comment that chicken is to cooking what a canvas is to painting. In this case we're painting the courgette with some red peppers and a touch of mildly spicy Turkish urfa chilli flakes, both of which enhance but don't drown the mild courgette. Less like a quiche and more like a frittata, this tart has no cream or soft cheese to dilute the eggs in the filling.

1. In a bowl toss the courgette slices with 1-2 teaspoons salt. Scrape into a non-reactive colander and set a small plate on top. Place the colander back in the bowl and add a weight such as a can of tomatoes on the plate. Let the water drain from the courgettes for 1 hour.

2. Rinse the salt from the courgettes and repeat the weighting and draining to remove the water.

3. While the courgettes are draining, pour the oil into a wide sauté pan and add the onion and red pepper. Cook over a high heat until the vegetables start to sizzle, then reduce the heat and sauté gently until they are tender.

4. Increase the heat again and add the courgettes. Cook, tossing or stirring, until the courgettes are very tender, reducing the heat to prevent burning if necessary.

5. Taste for seasoning and adjust with salt. Stir in the chilli flakes and the marjoram.

6. Set a rack at the lowest level in the oven and preheat to 200°C/gas mark 6.

7. Whisk the eggs in a bowl and add the cheese and black pepper. Stir in the cooked courgette mixture and pour the filling into the tart crust. Use a fork to make sure the vegetables are evenly distributed throughout the filing.

8. Place the tart in the oven and reduce the temperature to 190°C/gas mark 5. Bake for 35-40 minutes until the crust is baked through and the filling has set.

9. Cool the tart on a rack and unmould it to a serving plate. Serve it warm or at room temperature.

Makes one 25cm tart, about 8 servings

One 25cm tart crust made from Flaky Buttery Dough (page 14)

450g young, tender courgettes, rinsed, trimmed, halved lengthways and cut into 0.5cm semicircles

Fine sea salt

3 tablespoons olive oil

115g sliced white onion

1 large red pepper or fresh pimento, about 225g, cut into 1.25cm dice

1 teaspoon urfa chilli flakes or another crushed dried chilli of your choice

1 tablespoon chopped fresh marjoram or oregano leaves

5 medium eggs

40g finely grated Pecorino Romano cheese

Freshly ground black pepper

SUMMERY TOMATO TARTS

Makes eight 11.5cm tartlets

Eight 11.5cm tartlet crusts made from Flaky Buttery Dough or Olive Oil Dough (page 14)

225g fresh goat's cheese such as Montrachet or a domestic brand, at room temperature

1 tablespoon finely cut fresh chives

1 tablespoon chopped fresh flat-leaf parsley

Freshly ground black pepper

1 teaspoon plus 2 tablespoons best-quality olive oil

570g cherry tomatoes, rinsed, dried and quartered

Fine sea salt to taste (see Note)

A handful of tiny top leaves of basil, or 6 large leaves, stacked and cut into thin ribbons

NOTE
Don't salt the tomatoes before baking, as it draws moisture from them and might make the tarts soggy.

Perfectly ripe tomatoes, cheese and herbs are a great combination, so much so that I think I've done at least three recipes featuring them before. This time around, though, I decided that the combo needed revamping, because I wanted to be able to serve the tart completely cooled as well as fresh from the oven and during seasons when the sweetest field-ripened tomatoes might not be available. That ruled out cheeses I've used in the past, like Gruyère, Cantal or Mozzarella, all of which get rubbery on cooling. Fresh cow's or goat's milk cheese is perfect – but because I don't like how goat's cheese dries out when exposed to the oven's heat, I hid it under the tomatoes.

1. Set a rack at the lowest level in the oven and preheat to 200°C/gas mark 6.

2. Use a rubber spatula to mash the cheese in a bowl, then stir in the herbs and a few grinds of pepper. Spread the cheese mixture in the bottom of the tart crusts. Drizzle the cheese in each crust with about ½ teaspoon of the olive oil.

3. Divide the tomatoes equally among the tart crusts. Drizzle on a tablespoon of the oil, dividing it equally among the tarts. Grind some pepper over each.

4. Bake for 30-40 minutes until the crusts are deep golden and the tomatoes have softened.

5. If you're serving the tarts hot, unmould to a serving plate, sprinkle with salt and scatter the basil on each. To serve them cooled, wait to add the salt and basil until you're ready to serve the tarts.

Savoury Pies

These are meatier and more substantial than the tarts in this chapter and are served as a main course or on a buffet of savoury dishes. The double-crusted ones are also perfect picnic food, because they can easily be eaten out of hand. Just unmould the pie to a cardboard cake board and wrap for transport. All you'll need is a knife to cut and some napkins for serving.

MEXICAN CHICKEN PIE (TARTA DE POLLO Y CHILTOMATE)

My friend Roberto Santibañez, chef/owner of Fonda restaurants in New York City, suggested this combination when I asked him about a chicken pie with Mexican flair. Chicken and vegetables are cooked in a chilli salsa from the Yucatan called *chiltomate*, then topped with polenta dough before baking. Though the *habanero* is classic for this, *serrano* or *jalapeño* could be substituted. Sour cream harmonises well served alongside.

1. For the *chiltomate*, preheat the grill and set a rack about 20cm from the heat. Cover a pie tin or other small pan with foil. Place the chillies and tomatoes stem-sides up on the pan and grill for about 20 minutes until the tops begin to blacken and the tomatoes start to soften. Turn the chillies once or twice – it should take less than 10 minutes for them to soften and for the skin to blacken in spots. By the time the chillies are cooked, the tomatoes should be starting to collapse; let cool for a few minutes. If necessary, remove the chillies and let the tomatoes finish cooking.

2. Once the tomatoes and chillies have cooled, slip the skins from the tomatoes and pull the stems from the chillies. Pour the tomato pulp, chillies, garlic, onion and salt into a blender and blend to a fine purée.

3. Sprinkle the chicken pieces all over with salt. Heat the oil in a casserole and brown the chicken on both sides in batches, making sure not to overcrowd it. Once all the chicken has been seared and set aside, pour the excess fat from the pan and add the *chiltomate*. Bring the salsa to the boil, scraping up any brown bits clinging to the bottom of the pan. Add the chicken, potatoes and carrots and return to the boil. Lower to a simmer, partly cover the pan and cook for about 30 minutes until the chicken and vegetables are tender.

4. Set a rack at the middle level in the oven and preheat to 190°C/gas mark 5. Lightly oil a 2-litre baking dish.

5. Stir the peas, coriander, mint, sugar and vinegar into the chicken and vegetables. Taste and adjust with salt if necessary. Tip into the prepared dish.

6. Roll the polenta dough out on a floured surface until roughly the size of the baking dish. Lift the dough onto the filling using a flexible baking tray, and cut several vent holes in the top. Or cut the dough into 6.5–7.5cm disks and overlap on the filling to cover.

7. Bake for 25–30 minutes until the crust is deep golden and the filling is bubbling. Cool the pie for a few minutes before serving.

8. To serve, spoon a portion of the crust into a shallow bowl and pour the filling alongside.

Makes one large pie, 6-8 servings

1 batch Polenta Dough with or without cheese (page 18)

CHILTOMATE

2 green *habanero* chillies

5 large tomatoes, about 900g, stem ends removed and a cross cut into the blossom end

2-3 small garlic cloves, crushed and peeled

55g white onion, coarsely chopped

½ teaspoon fine sea salt

900g skinless and boneless chicken thighs, trimmed of fat and cartilage and cut into bite-sized pieces

Fine sea salt

2 tablespoons olive or sunflower oil

225g Maris Piper or other all-rounder or waxy potatoes, peeled and cut into 1.25cm dice

2 medium carrots, about 170g, peeled and cut into 0.5cm thick rounds

125g frozen petit pois

15g coarsely chopped fresh coriander

2 tablespoons coarsely chopped fresh mint

½ teaspoon caster sugar

1 teaspoon sherry vinegar

PIZZA RUSTICA ALLA PARMIGIANA

Makes one 23cm pie, about 12 starter servings

One 23cm cake tin, 5cm deep, lined with 1 batch Olive Oil Dough (page 14), using two-thirds for the bottom crust and the remainder for the top crust

340g ricotta cheese

Fine sea salt and freshly ground black pepper

4 tablespoons finely chopped fresh flat-leaf parsley

45g finely grated Parmigiano-Reggiano cheese

2 medium eggs, well-beaten

170g boiled ham, thinly sliced

170g fresh Mozzarella cheese, thinly sliced

4 medium Hard Boiled Eggs (recipe follows), sliced

I call this Italianate savoury pie by this name because I use Parmigiano-Reggiano cheese as opposed to the more typical Pecorino Romano cheese in the filling. Cooked ham, thinly sliced Mozzarella cheese, parsley-flecked ricotta cheese filling and hard-boiled eggs make for a lighter *Pizza Rustica* than the traditional prosciutto, dried sausage and *soppressata*. Serve this as part of a selection of *antipasti* or as the main course of a light meal.

1. Set a rack at the lowest level in the oven and preheat to 190°C/gas mark 5.

2. Use a rubber spatula to mash the ricotta cheese smooth in a mixing bowl and beat in the pepper, parsley and Parmesan cheese. Taste for seasoning and add a pinch or two of salt if necessary. Stir in the beaten eggs.

3. Spread a third of the filling in the pastry crust and top it with a layer of half the ham, half the Mozzarella cheese, and half the sliced eggs.

4. Spread another third of the filling on the eggs and repeat the layering with the remaining ham, Mozzarella and eggs. Spread on the last third of the filling.

5. Put the top crust in place and seal the edges (page 32).

6. Bake the pie for 15 minutes, then reduce the temperature to 180°C/gas mark 4 and continue baking for a further 20-30 minutes until the filling puffs slightly and the crust is baked through. Avoid overbaking as this will cause the whey to drain from the ricotta and make the crust soggy.

7. Cool the pie on a rack, unmould it to a serving plate and serve it at room temperature. Wrap and refrigerate leftovers.

Hard-Boiled Eggs

1. Put as many medium eggs as you need in a saucepan to fit in a single layer and generously cover with cold water. Place the pan over a medium heat and bring to a full rolling boil. Set a timer and cook the eggs for exactly 6 minutes; the yolks will be set but not overcooked.

2. Put a large bowl in the sink and use a slotted spoon to transfer the eggs to the bowl. Let cold water run over the eggs as you use the back of the spoon to gently smash the shell of each one in several places, then add a few handfuls of ice cubes and enough water to cover the eggs.

3. Peel, then rinse each egg under running water and return to the bowl of ice. Once fully cold, place the eggs in a bowl, cover it with clingfilm and refrigerate until needed.

BIANCO FAMILY PIZZA CHIENA

While *Pizza Rustica* and *Pizza Chiena* are similar, the latter started out with a yeast dough crust and was made like a Neapolitan *calzone*. Today in southern Italy and among many Italian American families, either sweet or unsweetened pastry dough is used and the pie is baked in a tin. I always use sweet dough for the simple reason that that's the way my family did it. The fresh basket cheese used in the filling of this pie is all but impossible to obtain, even in New York City, except at Easter – you will probably need to substitute ricotta cheese. Try to get the freshly made type; it's much firmer than the supermarket variety.

Thanks to my longtime friend and colleague Andrea Tutunjian for sharing the recipe she learned from her mother, Barbara Bianco Tutunjian.

Makes one 23cm pie, about 12 appetiser servings

One 23cm cake tin, 5cm deep, lined with 1 batch Olive Oil Dough (page 14), using two-thirds of the dough for the bottom crust and the remainder for the top crust

4 medium eggs

115g Genoa salami, sliced 3mm thick and cut into 1.25cm squares

115g sweet dried Italian sausage, peeled, sliced 3mm thick and cut into 1.25cm squares

85g *soppressata*, peeled, sliced 3mm thick and cut into 1.25cm squares

140g fresh Mozzarella cheese, cut into 1.25cm dice

55g Provolone cheese, cut into 1.25cm dice

170g fresh basket cheese, cut into 1.25cm dice, or firm ricotta cheese

5 medium Hard-Boiled Eggs (page 114), coarsely chopped

1. Set a rack at the lowest level in the oven and preheat to 190°C/gas mark 5.

2. Whisk the eggs in a large bowl, then add the meats, cheeses and hard-boiled eggs and thoroughly fold everything together.

3. Scrape the filling into the pastry crust and smooth the top.

4. Put the top crust in place and seal the edges (page 32).

5. Bake the pie for 15 minutes, then reduce the temperature to 180°C/gas mark 4 and continue baking for a further 20–30 minutes until the filling puffs slightly and the crust is baked through. Avoid overbaking as this will cause whey to drain from the cheese and make the crust soggy.

6. Cool the pie on a rack, unmould to a serving plate and serve at room temperature.

ITALIAN KALE PIE (TORTA DI CAVOLO NERO)

In Italy, where they make savoury pies from almost every vegetable imaginable, kale is a popular choice, especially in Tuscany, where it's known as *cavolo nero* or black cabbage. Teamed up with pancetta, onion, garlic, ricotta cheese, eggs and grated Pecorino cheese, its slightly bitter flavour is complemented rather than hidden. This is another great solo dish or delicious accompaniment to plain grilled meat or fish.

1. Bring a large pan of salted water to the boil. Add the kale and return to the boil. Cook for about 5 minutes until tender. Drain well, pressing the kale against the colander, cool and coarsely chop.

2. Combine the pancetta and oil in a large pan and cook over a medium heat, stirring often, for 2 or 3 minutes until the pancetta has coloured but is still soft. Using a slotted spoon, transfer the pancetta to a plate covered with kitchen towels to drain.

3. Add the onion to the pan and cook over a medium-low heat for about 10 minutes until softened, then stir in the garlic, cook for a few seconds and stir in the kale. Heat through and taste for seasoning, adding salt and pepper if necessary. Let cool.

4. Set a rack at the lowest level in the oven and preheat to 200°C/gas mark 6.

5. To finish the filling, whisk the ricotta cheese and eggs in a large bowl and whisk in the parsley and Pecorino cheese. Fold in the kale mixture and the pancetta.

6. Scrape the filling into the prepared crust and spread evenly. Roll the remaining dough for the top crust and use a template to cut it to a 23cm disk. Fold the dough at the side of the tin down over the filling and place the disk of dough on the filling and folded dough. Cut several vent holes in the top of the pie and brush with oil.

7. Set the pie in the oven and reduce the temperature to 190°C/gas mark 5. Bake for 35–40 minutes until the crust is deep golden and the filling is set.

8. Cool the pie on a rack and serve at room temperature.

Makes one 23cm pie, about 8 servings

One 23cm cake tin, 5cm deep, lined with Olive Oil Dough (page 14), using two-thirds of the dough for the bottom crust and the remaining dough for the top crust

Fine sea salt

680g kale, leaves separated from the lower and interior stems, washed and drained, (see Note)

55g pancetta, cut into 0.5cm dice

1 tablespoon olive oil, plus more for brushing

115g finely chopped white or yellow onion

1 garlic clove, finely grated

Freshly ground black pepper

680g ricotta cheese

4 medium eggs

2 tablespoons finely chopped flat-leaf parsley

45g finely grated Pecorino Romano cheese

NOTE

If you find kale that has long, thick stems, start with 900g.

SUMMER VEGETABLE PIE

Makes one 23cm pie, about 8 servings

One 23cm pie crust made from Flaky Buttery Dough (page 14), plus dough for an open-lattice top crust

45g unsalted butter

1 medium white onion, cut into 0.5cm dice, about 85g

450g young, tender courgettes, cut into 1.25cm dice

450g young, tender crookneck yellow squash, cut into 1.25cm dice (see Note)

Fine sea salt and freshly ground black pepper

Kernels cut from 2 large ears sweetcorn

240g single cream

20g finely grated Parmigiano-Reggiano cheese

4 tablespoons finely cut fresh chives

½ teaspoon fresh marjoram leaves, finely chopped, or ¼ teaspoon dried

3 medium eggs

NOTE
If you can't source crookneck squash, you may substitute any other tender summer squash.

This pie came about when my friend Nancy Nicholas shared some of the produce of her Long Island garden with me. I had a couple of several kinds of vegetables, and not having enough to make a full dish from just one type, I combined them. You can add and subtract at will as long as you keep to the same weight of vegetables so you'll have the right amount of filling for the pie. This pie is excellent on its own, but it's also a handy side dish for simple grilled meats or fish.

1. Melt the butter in a casserole that has a lid and stir in the onion. Cook over a medium heat until the onion starts to sizzle. Stirring often, cook for 3–4 minutes until the onion starts to colour a little. Stir in the courgettes and crookneck squash, let them start to sizzle, then reduce the heat, season the mixture lightly with salt and pepper and stir in the sweetcorn kernels. Cover and cook, stirring occasionally, for 10–15 minutes until the vegetables are tender.

2. Remove the lid, increase the heat and let any accumulated water evaporate. Stir in the cream and cheese. Cook, stirring often, until the mixture comes to the boil.

3. Taste for seasoning (the filling should be slightly overseasoned before the final step of adding the eggs) and stir in the herbs. Cool the filling to room temperature.

4. Set a rack at the lowest level in the oven and preheat to 200°C/gas mark 6.

5. Whisk the eggs in a medium bowl and gently fold them into the cooled filling. Pour the filling into the pie crust and set the lattice top on the pie (page 33).

6. Bake the pie for 15 minutes, then reduce the temperature to 180°C/gas mark 4. Continue baking for about 30 minutes longer until the crust is deep golden and the filling is set.

7. Cool the pie on a rack and serve at room temperature.

PROVENÇAL SPINACH PIE (TOURTE D'ÉPINARDS)

Makes one 25cm pie, about 10 servings

One 25cm tart crust made from Olive Oil Dough (page 14), using two-thirds of the dough for the bottom crust and the remaining dough for the top crust

900g baby spinach, rinsed and drained

2 tablespoons olive oil, plus more for brushing

1 large white onion, finely chopped

1 large garlic clove, finely grated

Fine sea salt and freshly ground black pepper

2 medium eggs

65g finely grated Parmigiano-Reggiano cheese

65g pine nuts, lightly toasted

VARIATIONS

Sometimes a pie like this has a little soft cheese added to the filling. The closest we can come to that type of cheese is ricotta; if you want to try it, use 115g whole milk ricotta, pressed through a fine sieve.

While the official leafy green vegetable of Provence is Swiss chard, I've substituted spinach here for a variety of reasons. First, chard is not a vegetable you can get everywhere, and in the United States we never get the young, tender leaves with entirely undeveloped stems that are required for this pie. On the other hand, baby spinach is only as far away as the nearest supermarket. All sorts of elaborate versions of this pie exist; I gave one of those in a previous book. This time, I've made it simple, straightforward and easy to prepare. Great alone, it's also an excellent vegetable accompaniment to plain grilled meat or fish. Unlike the other savoury pies here, this one is made in a 2.5cm-deep French tart tin.

1. Place the spinach, with the rinse water still clinging to it, in a large casserole with a cover and place over a high heat. Cover, lower the heat to medium and steam the spinach for 1–2 minutes, stirring once or twice, until wilted and reduced. Drain, let cool, then coarsely chop.

2. Set a rack at the lowest level in the oven and preheat to 200°C/gas mark 6.

3. Rinse the pan and cook the oil and onion slowly for about 10 minutes until the onion is soft. Stir in the garlic, cook for a few seconds, then stir in the spinach. Generously salt the spinach and taste to make sure you've added enough. Add pepper, then remove the pan from the heat.

4. Whisk the eggs in a medium bowl, then whisk in the cheese. Fold in the cooled spinach mixture along with the pine nuts.

5. Scrape the filling into the prepared crust and spread evenly. Roll the remaining dough for the top crust and use a template to cut it to a 25cm disk. Fold the dough at the side of the pan down over the filling and place the disk of dough on the filling and folded dough. Cut several vent holes in the top of the pie and brush with oil.

6. Set the pie in the oven and reduce the temperature to 190°C/gas mark 5. Bake for 35–40 minutes until the crust is deep golden.

7. Cool the pie on a rack and serve at room temperature.

FRENCH CANADIAN MEAT PIE (TOURTIÈRE)

Rich, hearty and perfect for a winter lunch, a *tourtière* is one of the most beloved and argued over French Canadian dishes. What with slight regional variations, familial preferences and other influences that have crept in over the years, no one agrees about exactly what's in the filling besides minced meat. This version is adapted from my friend Rhonda Caplan, the recipe developer at Robin Hood Flour, Canada's largest miller.

1. Heat the oil in a large sauté pan and add the celery, onion and mushrooms and cook on a medium heat until the mixture starts to sizzle. Cook, stirring occasionally, for about 10 minutes until the water from the mushrooms has evaporated and the celery and onion are softened.

2. Stir in the garlic and cook for a few seconds, then add the minced meat. Use a wooden spoon to mash the meat and vegetables together so that the meat doesn't cook into large clumps. Continue cooking and mashing until the meat is separated into fine crumbs and starting to colour.

3. Stir in the grated potato, salt, pepper, thyme and spices. Cook, stirring, for about 5 minutes until the filling is well-mixed and very aromatic.

4. Scrape the filling into a bowl and cover loosely; refrigerate until completely cooled.

5. Set a rack at the lowest level in the oven and preheat to 200°C/gas mark 6.

6. Stir up the filling and taste for seasoning, adding more salt and pepper if necessary. Scrape it into the pie crust and set the top crust in place (page 33). Cut vent holes in the top of the pie and brush with the egg wash.

7. Place the pie in the oven and reduce the temperature to 190°C/gas mark 5. Bake for 45–50 minutes until the crust has turned deep golden.

8. Cool the *tourtière* slightly on a rack and serve warm.

Makes one 23cm pie, about 8 servings

One 23cm pie crust made from Flaky Buttery Dough or Flaky Dough Using Lard (page 14 or 15), plus dough for the top crust

2 tablespoons sunflower oil or lard

1 outer stalk celery, finely chopped

1 medium yellow onion, finely chopped

85g mushrooms, rinsed, trimmed and thinly sliced

2 garlic cloves, finely grated

680g minced pork, beef, veal or a combination

1 small baking potato (170–225g), peeled and coarsely grated

2 teaspoons fine sea salt

½ teaspoon freshly ground black pepper

2 teaspoons fresh thyme leaves, finely chopped, or 1 teaspoon dried

Pinch of ground cinnamon

Pinch of ground cloves

Pinch of freshly grated nutmeg

Egg wash: 1 egg whisked with a pinch of salt

Empanadas & Pasties

While the word *empanada* merely means 'in bread', empanadas are a popular casual snack in all Spanish-speaking parts of the world. The term refers to the familiar turnover-shaped pastry in the following recipes but may also be used for a large round or rectangular pie.

Doughs for empanadas can vary: in Mexico and Argentina they often use dough that's similar to puff pastry. I've substituted extra-flaky Sour Cream Dough (page 16) for that one. For non-flaky empanadas, I like to use the yeasted dough on page 17 – it always bakes to a tender and moist texture.

From Cornwall come the famous pasties; turnovers of flaky pastry with a meat and vegetable filling. They're easy to make and have a simple, homely flavour. Though the vegetables may be blanched first, the meat, usually beef, is entirely cooked inside the pasty while it's baking. Today's pasties have all sorts of fillings – even eggs and cheese for breakfast.

ARGENTINE CHICKEN EMPANADAS (EMPANADAS DE FAMAILLÁ)

Makes twelve 18cm empanadas

450g skinless, boneless chicken thighs, trimmed of fat and cartilage

½ teaspoon fine sea salt

Bouquet garni: 2 small stalks celery, 2 sprigs flat-leaf parsley, 1 large bay leaf, 2 sprigs fresh thyme, tied together

2 tablespoons olive oil

40g finely chopped onion

1 Maris Piper or other all-rounder or waxy potato, boiled until tender and cooled

½ teaspoon ground cumin

½ teaspoon hot Spanish paprika (pimentón)

2 teaspoons chopped fresh oregano leaves or 1 teaspoon crumbled dried leaves

60g coarsely chopped green Spanish olives

70g raisins

2 medium Hard-Boiled Eggs (page 114), coarsely chopped

1 batch Yeast-Risen Dough for Empanadas (page 17)

Egg wash: 1 egg whisked with a pinch of salt

A city in northern Argentina, Famaillá is also referred to as that country's empanada capital; a well-deserved title since an annual empanada festival is held there. Don't be put off by the long ingredient list for the filling; it's an easy recipe.

1. Put the chicken in a medium saucepan and cover with water. Add the salt and bouquet garni and bring to a simmer. Cook at an active simmer for 20 minutes, skimming the foam as it rises to the surface, then let the chicken cool in the stock. If you like, cook the chicken in advance, then refrigerate it in the strained stock, covered, for a couple of days.

2. Drain and cut the chicken into 1.25cm dice. Reserve 120ml of the stock.

3. Put the oil and onion in a sauté pan and cook over a medium heat until the onion starts to sizzle. Stir once, reduce the heat and cook for about 10 minutes until the onion is soft.

4. Off the heat, stir in the chicken, potato and reserved stock, then transfer the mixture into a bowl. Sprinkle on the cumin, paprika, oregano, olives, raisins and eggs.

5. While the filling is cooling, divide the dough into 80g pieces and shape each into a flat disk. Roll each piece of dough into an 20cm disk and chill if you're not going to assemble the empanadas immediately.

6. Arrange the disks of dough on the work surface and brush the edges with water. Divide the filling equally among the dough rounds, mounding it in the centre of each one. Fold the dough over to make a fat crescent-shaped pastry. >>

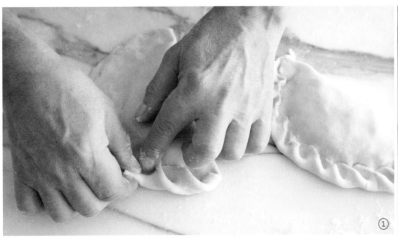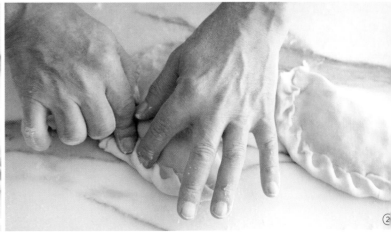

EMPANADAS WITH SAUSAGE FILLING
(EMPANADAS DE SALCICA): Omit the chicken
and begin with step 3. Remove the casings
from 450g Italian sausage without fennel and
crumble the meat. Add the meat after the onion
has begun to soften and cook, breaking the
meat up so that it doesn't set in clumps, until
any juices have evaporated and the meat is
starting to colour. Resume with step 4, adding
stock if you have it; if not, skip it.

Makes eight 18cm empanadas

**900g baby spinach, rinsed and drained, or 570g
frozen chopped spinach, thawed, squeezed dry
and chopped**

3 tablespoons olive oil

**70g finely sliced spring onions (the white part
and half the green)**

2 garlic cloves, finely grated

**30g anchovy fillets packed in olive oil, finely
chopped**

Fine sea salt and freshly ground black pepper

2 tablespoons chopped fresh flat-leaf parsley

1½ teaspoons hot Spanish paprika (pimentón)

1 batch Sour Cream Dough (page 16), chilled

Egg wash: 1 egg whisked with a pinch of salt

7. Press the edges of the pastry together with a fingertip ①, then fold and overlap the edge of
the dough ② to seal the empanadas, as in the photographs above.

8. Chill the empanadas, loosely covered with clingfilm, until you're ready to bake them, up to 24
hours. When you're ready to bake, set a rack in the lower third of the oven and preheat to 200°C/gas
mark 6.

9. Arrange the empanadas on a baking tray lined with parchment paper and brush them with
the egg wash, making sure not to let puddles accumulate on or under the empanadas. Place the
tin in the oven, reduce the temperature to 190°C/gas mark 5 and bake for 20–25 minutes until
deep golden.

10. Cool the empanadas briefly on the tray on a rack and serve warm.

ARGENTINE CHRISTMAS EVE EMPANADAS
(EMPANADAS DE VIGILIA)

These spinach empanadas make a delicious alternative to the typical meat-laden ones
and are traditionally eaten on Christmas Eve, a day of abstinence from meat in Catholic
countries. These are usually deep-fried, but I decided to bake them – it's easier, and they
turn out much less rich.

1. Put the fresh spinach with the rinse water still clinging to it in a large casserole with a lid. Place
over a medium heat, cover and steam for a few minutes until it reduces in volume. Uncover and
stirring occasionally, cook for 1–2 minutes longer. Drain, cool and chop the spinach.

2. Put the oil and spring onions into a large saucepan over a medium heat. Once the spring
onions start to sizzle, reduce the heat and cook slowly, stirring often, for about 5 minutes until
tender. Stir in the garlic and cook for a few seconds. Stir in the chopped spinach and anchovies;
cook for a minute or two. If using frozen spinach, cook for a couple of minutes longer at this point.

3. Taste the spinach and season with salt and pepper, then stir in the parsley and paprika. Cool
the filling.

4. Roll the dough, finish and bake the empanadas according to steps 5 through 10 on page 122.

CORNISH-STYLE PASTIES

The recipe below is for the steak-filled classic, with a few Variations for taking off on your own. Many thanks to my London friends Rachel Fletcher and her husband, Stephen Fagg, for devoting part of a Cornwall vacation to tasting and photographing pasties for me.

1. Put the potatoes and swede in a saucepan and fill with enough water to cover. Bring to the boil over a medium heat and cook for 2 minutes. Drain and cool.

2. Combine the potatoes, swede and onion in a bowl and sprinkle with the salt and pepper. Use a rubber spatula to fold the vegetables together and then fold in the meat.

3. To form the pasties, divide the dough into 6 equal pieces and form each into a fat disk. Flatten one of the disks and roll to form a 25cm round or 18cm round for 12 smaller pasties. Use a template such as a cake board to trim the pastry evenly all around. Repeat with the remaining pieces of dough and line them up on your work surface.

4. Divide the filling among the disks of dough, arranging it in a pile in the centre. Top each with a piece of butter.

5. Slide your hands, palms up, under opposite sides of a disk; fold your hands to bring the sides of the pasty together. Holding the pasty in one hand, pinch the edges of the dough together to seal them. Place the pasty on the work surface with the fold facing you and pleat and seal the open edge of the dough. As you finish each pasty, set it on a baking tray lined with parchment paper.

6. Let the pasties rest at room temperature for an hour or so before baking. When you're ready to bake, set a rack at the middle level in the oven and preheat to 200°C/gas mark 6.

7. Carefully brush the pasties with the egg wash. For darker colour and sheen, let the pasties dry for 10 minutes and then egg wash again. Bake for 20 minutes, then reduce the temperature to 180°C/gas mark 4. Continue baking for at least 20 minutes longer until the dough turns a deep golden colour.

8. Cool the pasties on a rack and serve warm. Or let cool completely and reheat at 190°C/gas mark 5 for 10 minutes before serving.

Makes six large pasties or twelve smaller ones

450g Maris Piper or other all-rounder or waxy potatoes, peeled and cut into 1.25cm dice

225g swede, peeled and cut into 1.25cm dice

200g white onion, cut into 1.25cm dice

1 teaspoon fine sea salt

½ teaspoon freshly ground black pepper

680g beef skirt steak, trimmed of excess fat and cut into 1.25cm chunks

1 batch Pasty Dough (page 16)

45g unsalted butter, chilled and cut into 6 or 12 pieces

Egg wash: 1 egg whisked with a pinch of salt

VARIATIONS

Substitute an equal amount of diced skinless, boneless chicken thigh meat for the steak. A tender cut of lamb from the top end of the leg also works well. Or mix the vegetables and seasonings with a pound of lean minced beef and evenly divide the mixture among the pieces of dough.

If you want a little more seasoning, try a sprinkling of finely chopped fresh thyme leaves or flat-leaf parsley, curry powder or some hot Spanish paprika (pimentón).

CHAPTER 6

STRUDEL & OTHER THIN DOUGHS & PASTRIES

If you've never tried making strudel from scratch, you'll be amazed at how easy it is. All you need to do is knead the dough well (or let a stand mixer do the work for you), and you've already taken the necessary steps to make sure that the dough will stretch to the required transparent thinness.

Before completing this book, I had an opportunity to visit Turkey and find out about traditional Turkish pastry doughs first-hand. In both Istanbul and Gaziantep, I visited bakeries and gained some experience in preparing doughs for both savoury and sweet specialities.

While I understand that it's faster and easier to purchase a package of filo dough at the supermarket, I urge you to try the Turkish *yufka* dough (it's rolled, not stretched). Both homemade and packaged versions are far superior to any packaged filo dough in flavour and performance. Hand-rolled and partially baked *yufka* leaves are available from Turkish and Middle Eastern shops.

For some sweet Turkish *baklava* specialities, I've given a dough recipe for those who wish to try it. It's neither difficult to prepare nor tricky to roll, but it is a slow, exacting process that not everyone will have time to attempt. If you decide to resort to using packaged dough, try to find the absolute thinnest dough available, and your results will be as similar as possible to homemade.

STRUDEL DOUGH

Strudel has been made in Austria and Hungary for hundreds of years. My own history with this pastry is a long one. I first tried a strudel recipe in one of my mother's cookbooks as a teenager and was amazed that the dough was so easy to stretch paper thin, especially since I had absolutely no pastry skills at the time. This recipe is straightforward and easy to follow, and outlines the basic method for pulling the dough to the required transparent thinness. When you make a strudel, it is best to prepare the dough up to the point described here, then prepare the filling while the dough is resting. Once the filling has cooled, you can go ahead and stretch the dough, as instructed opposite. Don't try to get away with putting a warm filling in the dough – the strudel will disintegrate when you try to move it to the baking tin. Using an egg in the dough makes it easier to stretch, but a little less fragile after it's baked.

Makes about 340g dough, enough for one 38–45cm strudel

200g unbleached bread flour

¼ teaspoon fine sea salt

1 tablespoon vegetable oil or melted butter

1 medium egg, optional

Warm water

STRETCHING THE STRUDEL DOUGH

A square or rectangular table 60 x 90cm or larger

A cloth to cover the table; either an old tablecloth or a clean bedsheet

Flour for dusting

Vegetable oil and a brush

1. Stir the flour and salt together in the bowl of an electric mixer.

2. If you're using the egg, beat the oil and egg together with a fork in a 250ml measuring cup; if not, just add the oil. Add enough warm water to make 150ml.

3. Use a rubber spatula to mix the liquid into the flour; make sure no flour remains on the side of the bowl and clean off the spatula.

4. Attach the dough hook and mix the dough on the lowest speed for about 1 minute until it begins to hold together. Increase the speed a couple of notches to just below medium and mix for another 2 minutes until the dough is smooth and elastic.

5. Scrape the dough onto a lightly floured work surface and knead for 1 minute. Coat a small bowl with a very thin layer of oil and invert the dough into it; turn the dough over so that the top is oiled, and cover with clingfilm. Let rest for 1 hour.

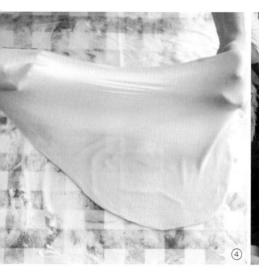

Stretching the Strudel Dough

1. Before beginning to stretch the strudel dough, be sure that your filling is ready to go. If a cooked filling needs to cool, the dough can wait in the bowl where it's resting. Once the dough is fully stretched, you have only 10 minutes before you need to fill and bake the strudel.

2. Cover the table with the cloth and dust flour all over it, especially in the centre.

3. Take the rested strudel dough out of the bowl without folding it over on itself and set it in the centre of the table. Use the palms of your hands to flatten the dough ①.

4. Dust a little flour on the dough and roll it in all directions, going over the edges of the dough too. Make it as thin as you can ②.

5. Brush the top of the dough with oil ③, then begin to stretch it: Place both hands under the centre of the dough, make fists, and stretch from the centre outward over the backs of your hands ④. Don't worry about the rest of the dough at this point, but keep stretching from the centre outward. The dough will lighten in colour as it becomes thinner.

6. Again place your fists under the dough; this time, work them hand over hand to stretch the outer thicker part of the dough, going all around the piece of dough.

7. Eventually, the dough will become thin and large enough that you can secure one of the corners over a corner of the table ⑤. Continue stretching from all directions, pulling on the thick ends of the dough until you cover the table ⑥ or until the dough is at least 60 x 75cm. Be careful not to pull too hard or too fast – this is what tears the dough.

8. Once the dough has been stretched, let it dry for 10 minutes. While the dough is drying, use scissors to trim away the thick edges and discard them. The following strudel recipes pick up the process from this point.

POPPY SEED STRUDEL

Makes one 38-45cm strudel, 10-12 servings

1 batch Strudel Dough (page 128), stretched and ready to be filled

POPPY SEED FILLING

120ml whole milk

60g unsalted butter

1 tablespoon honey

Large pinch of ground cinnamon

1 teaspoon finely grated lemon zest

180g ground poppy seeds

35g raisins or dried currants

60g fine dry breadcrumbs

1 medium egg yolk

60ml orange juice, strained before measuring

60ml dark rum

2 medium egg whites

60g sugar

60g unsalted butter, melted

Icing sugar for finishing

Crème Anglaise (page 180) for serving

NOTE

The correct size *Rehrücken* tin is available online. It's called a 'half-round loaf cake tin, 31.5cm'. In a pinch, you can substitute a 30cm-long loaf tin.

This is adapted from the recipe used at Demel, Vienna's most famous pastry shop, which I visited for an article that appeared in *Saveur* magazine in 2009. I remember testing this recipe at the time, but it never appeared in the article. I like it because it's baked in a *Rehrücken* pan (see Note), and if the strudel bursts while it's in the oven, once it's unmoulded, the unsightly part is safely concealed underneath. Viennese deception at its most sophisticated . . .

1. For the filling, bring the milk, butter and honey to the boil in a small pan and remove from the heat. Stir in the cinnamon, lemon zest, ground poppy seeds, raisins and breadcrumbs; scrape into a bowl and let cool.

2. Once the mixture has cooled, stir in the egg yolk, orange juice and rum, one at a time.

3. Whisk the egg whites in a stand mixer on a medium-high speed using the whisk attachment. Once white, opaque and beginning to hold their shape, increase the speed to high and add the sugar in a slow stream; continue whisking until the egg whites hold a soft peak – don't overwhisk.

4. Use a rubber spatula to fold the egg whites into the filling.

5. Set a rack at the middle of the oven and preheat to 190°C/gas mark 5. Butter a 3cm Rehrücken tin.

6. Trim your piece of dough to a 60 x 75cm rectangle. Spread the filling on a 25 x 30cm rectangle with the 25cm side centred about 7.5cm in from the edge of the 60cm side.

7. Use a brush to drizzle the melted butter over the unfilled portions of the dough, leaving a little to brush onto the outside of the strudel.

8. Begin rolling the strudel: Fold the 7.5cm of dough over the filling, then fold the unfilled dough in from each side. Lift the cloth and roll the strudel ①, stopping and folding the edges inward as you go ②. End with the edge of the dough on the bottom of the strudel ③.

9. Fold back the excess cloth so that the strudel is right-side up at the cloth's edge, then invert it into the tin seam side up ④. Brush the top with butter and snip vent holes with scissors.

10. Place the strudel in the oven and reduce the heat to 180°C/gas mark 4. Bake for about 30 minutes until golden, then lower the temperature to 160°C/gas mark 3 and bake for about 20 minutes longer until the internal temperature reaches 82°C.

11. Unmould the strudel to a rack to cool. Dust lightly with icing sugar and slide onto a serving plate; serve it with Crème Anglaise.

OLD VIENNA APPLE STRUDEL

Makes one 38–45cm strudel, 10–12 servings

1 batch Strudel Dough (page 128), stretched and ready to be filled

APPLE FILLING

900g Golden Delicious apples, peeled, halved, cored and thinly sliced

100g caster sugar

½ teaspoon ground cinnamon

70g raisins

60ml water

120g unsalted butter

60g dry breadcrumbs

90g coarsely chopped walnut pieces

240ml sour cream

Icing sugar for finishing

Lightly sweetened whipped cream for serving

VARIATION

For a simpler filling, omit the sour cream and walnuts.

This is justifiably the most popular strudel in Vienna, whether homemade, enjoyed at a coffee house, or bought from a pastry shop. In Vienna it's common to use very tart raw apples in the filling; all the steam and juices generated by the apples result in a strudel where the dough is soft and moist rather than crisp. I like cooking the apples for the filling so that the strudel bakes crisp. Spooning some sour cream in with the apples is a classic old-fashioned Viennese way with strudel. See the Variations for a plain apple strudel.

1. For the filling, combine the apples, sugar, cinnamon and raisins in a non-reactive pan with a cover. Add the water and bring to the boil over a medium heat, stirring occasionally. Cover and steam for 5 minutes. Uncover the pan, increase the heat to high, and let the juices concentrate for a couple of minutes. Pour the filling into a shallow serving dish and let cool to room temperature.

2. Melt 75g of the butter in a small sauté pan and add the breadcrumbs. Cook over a medium-low heat, stirring often, for about 5 minutes until toasted and golden. Set aside to cool. Wipe the pan and melt the remaining 45g butter.

3. Set a rack at the middle level in the oven and preheat to 200°C/gas mark 6. Cover a large Swiss roll tin with heavy-duty tin foil or a double thickness of parchment paper.

4. Trim your piece of dough to a 75 x 60cm rectangle and arrange it with the long edge facing you. Scatter the breadcrumbs on a 30 x 40cm rectangle of dough centred about 7.5cm in from the 60cm edge so that the 40cm side of filling is parallel to the 60cm side of dough. Scatter the cooled filling over the breadcrumbs, followed by the walnuts. Use a teaspoon to drop the sour cream all over.

5. Use a brush to drizzle the remaining butter all over the unfilled portions of the dough, leaving a little to brush on the outside of the rolled strudel.

6. Roll the strudel and transfer to the tin (see the photos on page 131). If your tin is too short, position the strudel diagonally.

7. Brush the outside of the strudel with the remaining butter and use sharp scissors to snip some vent holes in the top.

8. Place the strudel in the oven and reduce the heat to 190°C/gas mark 5. Bake for 30–40 minutes until deep golden and crisp. Cool on a rack. If you are going to serve the strudel soon after it's baked, cut into portions and transfer one at a time to a serving plate, reassembling the strudel. (In Vienna, strudel is almost always cut in the tin.) Dust lightly with icing sugar and serve with lightly sweetened whipped cream.

APRICOT & CHEESE STRUDEL

Both this and the plainer cheese strudel with raisins described in the Variations are Viennese classics. This cheese filling is equally good with sour cherries, prune plums or blueberries, though in Vienna soft fruits and berries are usually used with a nut-based filling that bakes somewhat dry to accommodate the juices from the fruit.

1. For the filling, bring the milk to a simmer in a small saucepan and stir in the cubed bread off the heat. Leave the mixture to soak for 1 minute, then force the bread through a sieve into a bowl, followed by the cheese.

2. In another bowl, use a rubber spatula to beat the butter and sugar together, then beat in the egg yolks, lemon zest and vanilla extract. Beat in the bread and cheese, then stir in the cream.

3. Set a rack at the middle level in the oven and preheat to 200°C/gas mark 6. Butter a large Swiss roll tin.

4. Trim your piece of dough to a 75 x 60cm rectangle and arrange it with the long edge facing you. Spread the cheese filling on a 30 x 40cm rectangle of dough centred about 7.5cm in from the 60cm edge so that the 40cm side of filling is parallel to the 60cm side of dough. Scatter the sliced apricots all over the filling.

5. Use a brush to drizzle the melted butter over the unfilled portions of the dough, leaving a little to brush onto the outside of the rolled strudel.

6. Roll the strudel and transfer to the tin (see the photos on page 131). If your tin is too short, position the strudel diagonally.

7. Brush the outside of the strudel with the remaining butter and use sharp scissors to snip some vent holes in the top.

8. Place the strudel in the oven and reduce the heat to 190°C/gas mark 5. Bake the strudel for 30–40 minutes until it is deep golden and crisp. Cool it on a rack. If you are going to serve the strudel soon after it's baked, cut it into portions and transfer them one at a time to a serving plate, reassembling the strudel. (In Vienna, strudel is almost always cut in the tin.) Dust lightly with icing sugar.

Makes one 38–45cm strudel, 10-12 servings

1 batch Strudel Dough (page 128), stretched and ready to be filled

APRICOT AND CHEESE FILLING

75ml whole milk

85g good-quality white bread, trimmed of crusts before measuring, diced

680g salted farmer's cheese or ricotta cheese

45g unsalted butter, softened

100g caster sugar

3 medium egg yolks

2 teaspoons finely grated lemon zest

1½ teaspoons vanilla extract

120ml double cream

450g fresh apricots, rinsed, stemmed, halved, stoned and sliced

60g unsalted butter, melted

Icing sugar for finishing

VARIATION

Omit the apricots and use 140g sultanas, soaked in a tablespoon of rum for 1 hour.

TYROLEAN STRUDEL See page 134

See page 134

Makes one 38–45cm strudel, 10–12 servings

**1 batch Strudel Dough (page 128), stretched
and ready to be filled**

DRIED FRUIT AND NUT FILLING

360ml whole milk

65g caster sugar

2 tablespoons unbleached plain flour

4 medium eggs, separated

Finely grated zest of 1 small lemon

¼ teaspoon ground cinnamon

130g dried currants

135g stoned dates, diced

150g stemmed dried figs, diced

120g coarsely chopped walnut pieces

60g unsalted butter, melted

Icing sugar for finishing

VARIATION

The classic Viennese recipe for this also calls
for dried pears. If you wish to add them, reduce
the other dried fruits to 100g each and add
125g diced dried pears.

This rich strudel, studded with dried fruit and nuts, is a perfect dessert for winter when fresh fruit is not as plentiful. This strudel is particularly beloved in Austria; anything referred to as coming from the Tyrol makes the Austrians recall the pleasure of vacationing in the mountains and donning *Lederhosen* or *Dirndln*. This is adapted from *Wiener Susspeisen/Viennese Sweet Foods* by Eduard Mayer, the bible of Viennese baking.

1. For the filling, bring the milk to the boil with one-third of the sugar over a low heat. Meanwhile, mix another third of the sugar with the flour and whisk in the egg yolks smoothly. Once the milk boils, whisk half into the egg yolk mixture. Return the remaining milk to the boil and pour in the egg yolk mixture, whisking constantly, until the milk thickens and comes to a full boil. Whisk in the lemon zest and cinnamon. Scrape the milk mixture into a bowl, press clingfilm against the surface and chill until cold.

2. Stir in the dried fruits and walnuts.

3. Whisk the egg whites in a stand mixer on a medium-high speed using the whisk attachment. Once the egg whites are opaque and beginning to hold their shape, increase the speed to high and add the remaining third of the sugar in a slow stream; continue whisking until the egg whites hold a soft peak – don't overwhisk.

4. Use a rubber spatula to fold the egg whites into the filling.

5. Set a rack at the middle level in the oven and preheat to 200°C/gas mark 6. Butter a large Swiss roll tin.

6. Trim your piece of dough to a 75 x 60cm rectangle arranged with a long edge facing you. Spread the filling on a 30 x 60cm rectangle of dough centred about 7.5cm in from the 75cm edge closest to you. Use a brush to drizzle the melted butter all over the unfilled portions of the dough, leaving a little to brush onto the outside of the strudel.

7. Roll the strudel and transfer to the tin (see the photos on page 131). If your pan is too short, position the strudel diagonally.

8. Brush the outside of the strudel with the remaining butter and use sharp scissors to snip some vent holes in the top.

9. Place the strudel in the oven and reduce the heat to 190°C/gas mark 5. Bake for 30–40 minutes until deep golden and crisp. Cool the strudel on a rack. If you are going to serve the strudel soon after it's baked, cut into portions and transfer to a serving plate one at a time, reassembling the strudel. (In Vienna, strudel is almost always cut in the tin.) Dust lightly with icing sugar.

STRUDEL OF GREENS, BACON & GOAT'S CHEESE See page 135

Savoury strudels are home-style fare in Vienna, and cabbage strudel is the most popular by far. I like cabbage, but for a strudel, I prefer the idea of using darker greens. When buying the greens, make sure the leafy, tender parts will add up to 450g after you've removed any tough stems. Feel free to substitute another cheese like Feta, Gruyère or a blue-veined cheese like Roquefort.

1. For the filling, bring a large pan of salted water to the boil. Add the greens and bring back to the boil. For spinach and other tender greens, drain immediately. For tougher ones like kale, let the greens cook until tender, then drain. Cool, coarsely chop and place the greens in a large bowl.

2. Cook the bacon until nicely coloured but not too crisp; transfer to the bowl of greens.

3. Bring the milk and butter to the boil over a low heat; remove the pan from the heat, stir in the flour until the mixture is smooth and cool slightly. Stir in the eggs one at a time; fold the mixture into the greens and bacon. Season well with salt and pepper.

4. Set a rack at the middle level in the oven and preheat to 200°C/gas mark 6. Butter a large Swiss roll tin.

5. Trim your piece of dough to a 75 x 60cm rectangle and arrange it with a long edge facing you. Spread the filling on a 30 x 60 rectangle of dough centred about 7.5cm in from the long edge closest to you. Scatter the cheese, walnuts and chives on the filling.

6. Use a brush to drizzle the melted butter over the unfilled portions of the dough, leaving a little to brush onto the outside of the rolled strudel.

7. Roll the strudel and transfer to the tin (see the photos on page 131). If your pan is too short, position the strudel diagonally.

8. Brush the outside of the strudel with the remaining butter and use sharp scissors to snip some vent holes in the top.

9. Place the strudel in the oven and reduce the heat to 190°C/gas mark 5. Bake for 30-40 minutes until deep golden and crisp. Cool on a rack. If you are going to serve it soon after it's baked, cut into portions and transfer to a serving plate one at a time, reassembling the strudel. (In Vienna, strudel is almost always cut in the tin.) If you are making the strudel ahead of time and would like to serve it warm, leave it whole; when you are ready to serve, reheat it at 180°C/gas mark 4 for 10 minutes, then cut and place on plates or a serving plate.

Makes one 38–45cm strudel, 10-12 servings

1 batch Strudel Dough (page 128), stretched and ready to be filled

GREENS, BACON AND GOAT'S CHEESE FILLING

Fine sea salt

570g assorted greens, such as baby spinach, Swiss chard, kale, watercress or a combination, tough stems removed, rinsed and drained

115g slab skinless bacon or thick-cut bacon, cut into 0.5cm dice

120ml whole milk

45g unsalted butter

65g unbleached plain flour

2 medium eggs

Freshly ground black pepper

225g crumbled fresh goat's cheese, such as Montrachet

120g coarsely chopped walnut pieces, lightly toasted

20g finely snipped fresh chives

60g unsalted butter, melted

TURKISH PISTACHIO PASTRY (KATMER)

Makes two 23cm square *katmer*, about 6 servings

KATMER DOUGH

200g unbleached plain flour

¼ teaspoon fine sea salt

1 medium egg

1 tablespoon vegetable or light olive oil, plus more for rolling the dough

Warm water

55g *kaymak* (Turkish clotted cream; see Note)

170g unsalted very green pistachio nuts, finely chopped

50g caster sugar

NOTE

Kaymak, made from the cream that solidifies on the surface when milk is boiled to make yogurt, is available both fresh and frozen in Middle Eastern grocery shops.

My friend Cenk Sönmeszoy first told me about *katmer* – a square pastry containing several layers of dough as well as Turkish clotted cream, sugar and finely chopped pistachios – and sent me links to videos of some very skilled bakers who throw the dough around like a bed sheet to make it larger and thinner. I even had a chance to try my hand at it when I visited Mustafa Özgüler's Orkide pastry shop in Gaziantep and had a lesson from *katmer* master Murat Güney. The method here is simplified but gives excellent results. Try it first on your own – it's really easy. Then invite some friends over and make *katmer* for dessert after a simple meal – they'll think you're a baking genius.

1. For the dough, stir the flour and salt together in the bowl of an electric mixer.

2. Use a fork to beat the egg and oil in a 250g liquid measuring cup, then add enough warm water to make 150ml. (Or place a bowl on the digital scales, set it to zero, and add the eggs, oil and enough water to make 150g.) Use a rubber spatula to stir the liquid and the flour together. Scrape the bowl and spatula, then beat the dough on the lowest speed using the dough hook for about 3 minutes until it begins to turn smooth. Stop the mixer and let the dough rest for 15 minutes.

3. Beat the dough on a medium speed for about 1 minute until smooth and elastic. Then scrape the dough onto an oiled surface, and repeatedly smack it against the table ①, folding and kneading it between smacks. After smacking the dough against the work surface 100 times, knead it together and divide into 2 pieces, each about 225g.

4. Round, then oil the pieces of dough. Place them close together on a plate and cover them with clingfilm. Let the dough rest for at least 1 hour and up to 8 hours; longer is better.

5. Set a rack at the middle level in the oven and preheat to 230°C/gas mark 8. Lightly oil two Swiss roll tins.

6. Oil a smooth work surface and the dough and roll it as thinly as possible ②. Once the dough is rolled, oil the top of it again. Starting at the edge of the dough closest to you, lift the edge of the dough and pull it thinner towards you ③. Continue around each side of the dough, lifting and pulling thinner as you do, until the dough is approximately a 45cm square ④.

7. Tear or cut the thick edges from the dough, then fold it inward on 4 sides to make a 30cm square ⑤. Dot the surface of the dough with half of the kaymak, followed with half each of pistachios and sugar ⑥.

8. Fold the corners of the square in towards the centre, overlapping them slightly - you'll have an approximate 23cm square ⑦. Slide the *katmer* onto one of the prepared tins, then repeat the process with the remaining piece of dough. Bake for 10–15 minutes until deep golden and crisp.

9. Slide each *katmer* to a cutting board and cut into 5cm squares. Slide the squares onto a serving plate and serve immediately.

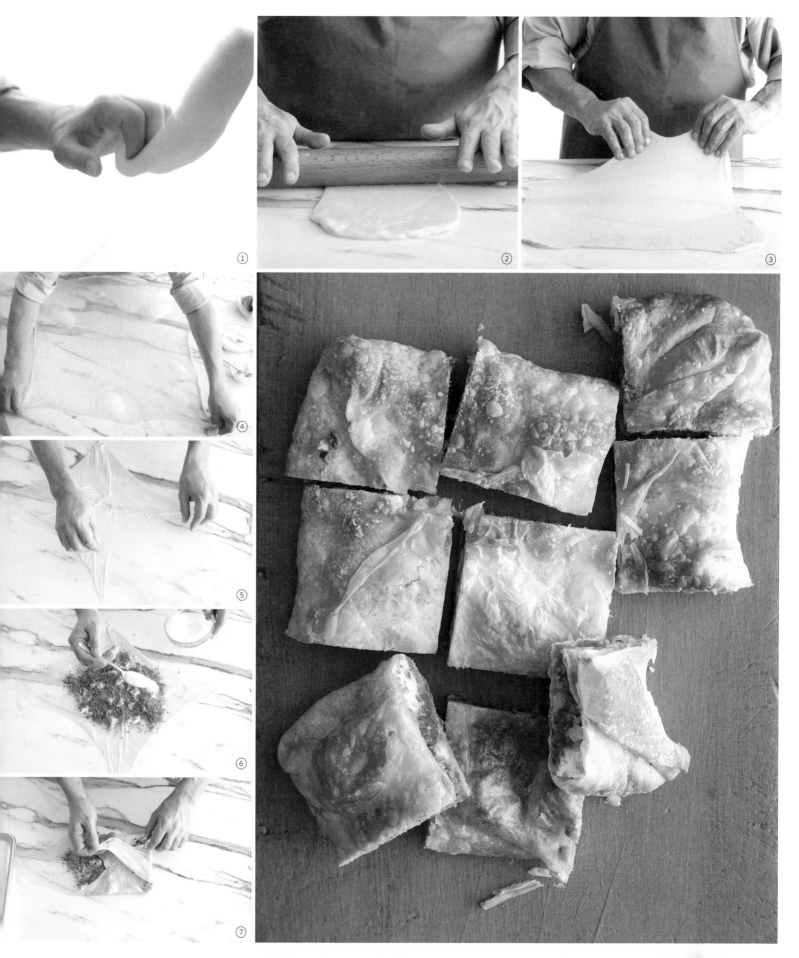

① ② ③ ④ ⑤ ⑥ ⑦

Thin Doughs

Though once a dough is pulled, stretched or rolled to paper thinness, it might look exactly like other doughs in this category, there are subtle differences in ingredients, thickness and even storage. Here are some of the principal types, with a short explanation of how each one is made:

Packaged filo dough: made from a combination of bread or other strong flour, water, a little oil or vegetable shortening and salt, most Greek-style filo is sold refrigerated and often loaded with preservatives and/or solid vegetable fat; unfortunately, it remains the best choice available for making *baklava* if you don't prepare the dough yourself.

Yufka: a thin Turkish dough made from flour, water and a little salt, it is stretched over a thin dowel. *Yufka* is mostly used for savoury Turkish pastries.

Baklava: a generic term for sweet pastries made from thin dough in Turkey. The dough is made from high-gluten flour, eggs, water and salt. While most of us think of *baklava* as many layers of pastry stacked with a nut filling between, in Turkey, *baklava* takes on many different shapes. Nuts, most often pistachios, are always used for the filling and may be accompanied by an unsweetened 'cream' made from reduced milk thickened with semolina.

TURKISH BAKLAVA DOUGH

Unlike dough for strudel, *baklava* dough is entirely rolled, and the end result is much thinner. Professional baklava makers roll a stack of eight layers of dough simultaneously, a feat you don't need to duplicate. Using a pasta machine at the beginning of the process is helpful, letting you start with pieces of dough that are evenly squared off. Try rolling four pieces of dough at a time; if that's too difficult, then try with two, and it will go much more quickly. You will need a 2cm diameter dowel, 60cm long, preferably hardwood, for rolling the dough. Also, have everything ready to assemble your *baklava* before you start rolling. The dough has to be used immediately after it's rolled or it will dry out and shatter.

Makes 16 30 x 45cm sheets of dough

2 medium eggs

Warm water

1 teaspoon lemon juice, strained before measuring

½ teaspoon fine sea salt

500g bread or other high-gluten flour

Wheat starch for rolling the dough (can be sourced online)

MIXING THE DOUGH

1. Place the bowl of an electric mixer on your digital scales and set it to zero. Crack the eggs into the bowl and break them up with a fork. Add enough warm water to bring the total weight to 300g and whisk the eggs and water together. Whisk in the lemon juice and salt.

2. Use a rubber spatula to stir in the flour, making sure that none sticks to the side of the bowl.

3. Place the bowl on the mixer with the dough hook and mix on the lowest speed until it pulls cleanly away from the side of the bowl, about 5 minutes. Let rest for 15 minutes.

4. Start the mixer again on a low-medium speed and mix for a further 3–5 minutes until smooth and elastic ①. Cover the bowl and let the dough rest for 1 hour.

INITIAL ROLLING

1. Scrape the dough onto a floured surface and divide it into 4 pieces, each 200g.

2. Dust the surface and one piece of dough with wheat starch and roll to an even 10cm square. Set aside covered with a towel and repeat with the remaining pieces.

3. Start running the pieces of dough, one at a time, through the widest setting on the pasta machine ②. If a piece of dough comes through with a narrow strip on either end, fold the narrower area back onto the dough so that the ends of the piece are straight and even. Remember to dust the dough often with starch while rolling it through the machine.

4. Once the sheets of dough are smooth and even, start running them through every other setting, stopping when the dough is a little less than 3mm thick, 10cm wide and about 60cm long ③ (this is usually the third setting before the thinnest, depending on the machine).

5. Cut each of the strips of dough crossways into 4 pieces, so that you have 16 that are approximately 10 x 15cm. Stack the sheets of dough on a starch-dusted work surface, sprinkling starch between each one. Cover with clingfilm and a towel. >>

ROLLING THE DOUGH

1. Dust the work surface with starch and place a sheet of dough on it. Dust the top with more starch and place another sheet of dough on it; repeat until you have stacked 4 layers of dough. Turn the stack of dough so that the narrower end is facing you and dust the top with starch. It's also possible to roll only 2 pieces of dough at a time according to all the instructions below, or even a single piece – see step 10.

2. Roll over the stack of dough from the end closest to you toward the far end and back 2 or 3 times ①. Roll over the width of the dough, without rolling over the ends, to make the sheets of dough wider ②.

3. Place the rolling pin about 4cm onto the dough and begin wrapping the whole stack of dough around the rolling pin, rolling it away from you.

4. Place both hands on the dough while it's wrapped on the pin and roll it back and forth, also stretching horizontally with your hands to widen it. Roll and stretch the stack 4 or 5 times, then unfurl from the rolling pin.

5. Dust the top piece of dough with starch and roll it up onto the rolling pin. Repeat with the remaining pieces of dough so that you add another piece right up against the end of the previous one ③; the four sheets of dough are now rolled consecutively around the rolling pin.

6. Wrap both hands around the dough on the rolling pin and hold the rolling pin out in front of you. Gently pull on the dough to widen it ④.

7. Repeat step 4.

8. Unfurl the outside sheet of dough onto the work surface and dust with starch. One by one, unfurl the remaining dough pieces and stack them on top, dusting the surface of each with starch.

9. Repeat steps 2 through 7.

10. Alternatively, follow steps 2, 3, 4, 6 and 7 with a single piece of dough ⑤ and ⑥. Cover the dough stack with clingfilm and a towel.

11. Repeat steps 1 through 11 with the remaining 12 pieces of dough, rolling them 4 or 1 at a time.

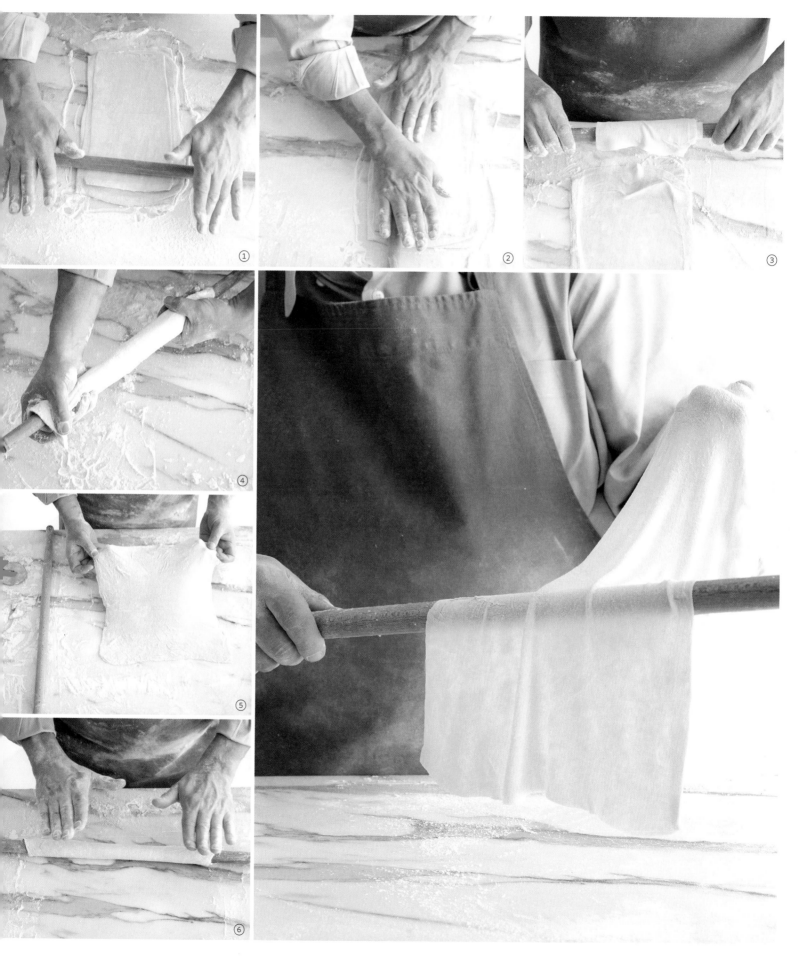

TURKISH 'CARROT SLICE' BAKLAVA (HAVUÇ DİLİMİ BAKLAVA)

Makes one 25cm diameter baklava, about
16 servings

1 batch Turkish Baklava Dough (page 140)

CREAM FILLING

240ml whole milk

120ml single or double cream

3 tablespoons fine semolina

SYRUP

360ml water

300g caster sugar

**2 teaspoons lemon juice, strained before
measuring**

450g unsalted butter, clarified (see Note)

**450g very green pistachio nuts, finely ground,
plus more for serving, optional**

Kaymak **(Turkish clotted cream); see Note,
page 138, optional**

NOTE

To clarify butter, melt slowly over a low heat in
a medium saucepan. Let stand for 10 minutes,
then use a spoon to skim off the foamy solids
on top. Pour off the clarified butter, leaving
the watery residue in the pan. Cool, then put
the butter into a plastic container, cover and
refrigerate for up to a month.

VARIATION

To substitute packaged filo pastry, use about
680g of filo.

This traditional Turkish *baklava* derives its name from the shape of its cut wedges – it's baked in a round tin and filled with a generous amount of chopped pistachios and a creamy, unsweetened mixture of milk and cream thickened with fine semolina. All the sweetening arrives when hot sugar syrup is poured over the freshly baked pastry.

1. Prepare the cream right before assembling the *baklava*: Bring the milk and cream to a simmer in a non-stick saucepan. Skim any skin from the surface and sift the semolina in, whisking constantly to avoid lumps. Place on a medium-low heat and cook, stirring constantly, until the cream thickens and comes to the boil; it will do so very quickly. Scrape the cream into a bowl, press clingfilm directly against the surface and set aside at room temperature.

2. For the syrup, bring the water and sugar to the boil, stirring occasionally over a medium heat. Once it boils, reduce the heat and simmer for 10 minutes. Remove from the heat and set aside.

3. Set a rack at the middle level in the oven and preheat to 200°C/gas mark 6.

4. Line a buttered round 25cm x 5cm deep tin with one of the dough sheets, letting it cover the sides of the tin and hang over the edges. Sprinkle with butter. Lay another sheet of dough into the tin, placing it perpendicular to the first and sprinkle with butter.

5. Stack the remaining sheets of dough on a work surface and, using the tin as a template, use a sharp knife to cut the stack into 14 round layers. Save the dough scraps.

6. Place 6 of the round layers in the tin, one at a time, sprinkling butter between them. Set the remaining round layers and half of the scraps aside, covered.

7. Use the other half of the dough scraps to build more layers in the tin, assembling them next to each other without overlapping too much. It's not necessary to sprinkle butter between these layers of dough.

8. Use an offset spatula to spread the cream filling on the dough. Sprinkle the pistachios on top.

9. Make more unbuttered layers of dough using the remaining scraps as in step 7. Fold the overhanging dough inward to cover the scraps, and sprinkle butter on top.

10. Cover with the remaining 8 round layers, sprinkling butter between them but not on top of the last layer.

11. Use a 7.5cm cutter to mark a circle in the centre and then use a small, sharp knife to cut along the circle, slicing almost through to the bottom. Cut the outer ring of the *baklava* into 16 even wedges, again slicing almost to the bottom.

12. Reheat the remaining clarified butter slightly if it has started to solidify and pour half of it onto the *baklava*, tilting the pan in all directions to evenly distribute. Let the pastry stand for a minute or two, then pour on the remaining butter.

13. Bake the *baklava* for about 30 minutes until the top layers are deep golden and crisp. Use a small knife to lift the layers of dough from the bottom upward to check that they are baked through. If they are still white and soft, bake for 10-15 minutes and check again.

14. About 10 minutes before the *baklava* is ready, reheat the syrup to boiling, remove from the heat and stir in the lemon juice.

15. Place the tin of baked *baklava* in your kitchen sink. Evenly pour the hot syrup over the *baklava*, averting your face, as the syrup will bubble up and steam. Let the *baklava* stand in the sink for a minute, then set it on a rack to cool completely.

16. Finish cutting through the *baklava*, this time slicing down to the bottom of the tin. Sprinkle the very centre with the reserved chopped pistachios. Serve at room temperature with some *kaymak* and more chopped pistachios if you wish.

1 batch Turkish Baklava Dough (page 140)

240ml water

200g caster sugar

225g very green fragrant pistachios, finely ground

225g unsalted butter, clarified (see Note, page 144)

2 teaspoons lemon juice, strained before measuring

VARIATION

To substitute packaged filo pastry, use a little more than half (16 sheets) of a 450g packet of filo.

TURKISH PISTACHIO ROLLS (FISTIKLI SARI BURMA)

You will need a 1cm wooden dowel, about 60cm long, to make this simple and beautiful *baklava* variation, in which dough and chopped pistachios are rolled around the dowel and the outside layer of dough wrinkles as the roll is removed. A hint of lemon that emphasises the pistachio flavour is added to the syrup used to moisten these after baking.

1. For the syrup, bring the water and sugar to the boil, stirring occasionally over a medium heat. Once the syrup boils, remove the pan from the heat and set it aside.

2. Set a rack at the middle level in the oven and preheat to 230°C/gas mark 8. Fill a clean spray bottle with cool water. Butter a 23 x 33 x 5cm metal tin.

3. To form the pastries, place a sheet of dough on the work surface. If using packaged filo dough, spray it lightly with water.

4. Fold over 5cm of the 30cm side of the dough; place the dowel at the narrow end of the dough closest to you and roll the dough around it once. Sprinkle about 2 tablespoons of the pistachios directly in front of the rolled area, then begin rolling so that the pistachios roll into the dough. Some will fall out the side; just scrape them back onto the dough as you go.

5. When you reach the end of the dough, push the roll to the end of the dowel and ease it off, leaving the dough wrinkled and about 15cm long. Set the roll lengthways into the prepared tin, placing it to one side of the tin. Repeat the rolling process with the remaining pieces of dough, placing them side by side in the tin as you go.

6. Once the tin is filled with the pastries, use a small sharp knife to cut down the centre of each row to make 32 pastries in all.

7. Pour on the clarified butter, then place the tin in the oven. Reduce the heat to 200°C/gas mark 6 and bake for 20–25 minutes until the tops of the rolls are very light golden.

8. Ten minutes before the rolls are ready, reheat the syrup to boiling. Stir in the lemon juice.

9. Place the tin in your kitchen sink and pour the hot syrup over the rolls, averting your face, as the syrup will bubble up and steam. Let the pastry stand in the sink for a minute, then set it on a rack to finish cooling. Use a narrow spatula to remove the rolls from the tin and slice each one into 16 pieces. Serve the pastries at room temperature.

YUFKA

Originally used as a griddle-baked flatbread by Turkic nomads, in today's Turkey, *yufka* leaves are the principal dough for preparing savoury pastries. Most Turkish cooks buy *yufka* from a shop called a *yufkası* (yoof-ka-suh) that specialises in the preparation. Like the dough for *baklava*, *yufka* is rolled substantially by hand, and you'll need a 50–60cm long dowel, 2.5cm in diameter, preferably made of hardwood.

1. Whisk the water and salt together in the bowl of a stand mixer; use a rubber spatula to stir in the flour, being careful that none sticks to the side of the bowl.

2. Place the bowl on the mixer with the dough hook and mix on a low speed for about 5 minutes until the dough pulls cleanly away from the side of the bowl. Let the dough rest for 15 minutes.

3. Mix on a medium-low speed for a further 3–5 minutes until the dough is smooth and elastic.

4. Scrape the dough onto a floured work surface and divide it into 9 pieces, each 75g. Round each piece of dough and place it, rounded side downwards, on a floured work surface. Cover with clingfilm and a towel and let rest for 1 hour.

5. Place a piece of parchment paper on a large tray or board near the rolling surface.

6. Flour the work surface and place a piece of dough on it, rounded side upward. Press it to a flat disk using the palm of your hand. Flour underneath and on top of the dough again and roll it as for a tart crust, rolling away and back toward yourself, from 6 o'clock to 12 o'clock and back, never rolling over the edges closest and furthest from you, then turning the disk of dough 60° to the right (to 2 o'clock) and repeating until the dough is 25–30cm in diameter.

7. Flour the work surface and the dough and place the rolling pin 2.5cm or so away from the edge closest to you; roll the dough around the rolling pin. Place your hands in the middle of the pin and begin rolling, and at the same time, pressing and moving your hands away from each other to widen the sheet of dough. Unfurl it from the rolling pin and rotate it 120°.

8. Repeat step 7 twice. If the dough isn't yet fully 40–45cm in diameter at that point, repeat the process one more time.

9. Slide the rolling pin under the dough across the diameter of the round, lift the dough from the work surface, and unfurl it onto the parchment. Place another piece of parchment paper on top. Continue rolling and stacking the remaining pieces of dough.

10. Cover the last piece of dough with parchment and fold the entire stack into quarters. Slide into a large plastic bag and refrigerate until you're ready to use. Homemade *yufka* of this type stays fresh for a week. It can't be frozen or it will become brittle.

Makes nine 40–45cm diameter leaves of dough

300ml water

2½ teaspoons fine sea salt

500g high-gluten or bread flour

NOTE

When *yufka* leaves are prepared at a *yufkasi*, they're baked on one side on a round griddle, then cooled, dampened to prevent cracking, and blotted between cloths to absorb excess moisture. The partially baked leaves are wrapped airtight and will keep refrigerated for a couple of weeks. Turkish import shops sell hand-rolled *yufka* made in Turkey in packets of 3 round sheets for pan-baked *börek* or 24 or more triangular wedges to make fried 'cigarette' *börek* (see the recipes that follow).

Rolling *yufka* is good practise for attempting the hand-rolled dough for *baklava*. In one *yufkasi* I visited in Istanbul, the 22-year-old son of the owner told me he'd mastered the rolling in two months – not quite the 7 years it takes for *baklava* dough (see page 140).

FETA AND MINT BÖREK (PEYNIRLI BÖREK)

This savoury pie made from thin *yufka* dough was shared by my friend Cenk Sönmeszoy, an accomplished cookbook author, food stylist and blogger in Istanbul. This is a typical Turkish savoury pie with crisp, flaky layers on the outside and moist, creamy ones within. In Turkey, *yufka* is used to make many types of savoury pies, up to 40cm in diameter, some of which are eaten for breakfast. To make this for family or guests, I would suggest using a slope-sided pie dish or a porcelain quiche dish.

1. Set a rack in the lower third of the oven and preheat to 190°C/gas mark 5. Butter a 23cm pie dish.

2. Melt 60g of the butter; cube the remaining butter and set aside.

3. Whisk the milk and eggs together and whisk in the melted butter.

4. Centre one of the *yufka* leaves on the prepared dish and ease it in so that it's wrinkled rather than stretched. Pour in 75ml of the egg and milk mixture.

5. Take the second *yufka* leaf, tear it into large pieces, and stack them in the dish; pour in another 75ml of the milk mixture.

6. Mix the Feta and mint together and evenly distribute half in the lined dish. Sprinkle on a third of the butter cubes.

7. Top with another torn layer of *yufka*, as in step 5 above. Pour in another 75ml of the milk mixture, followed by the remaining Feta and mint and another third of the butter cubes.

8. Top with another whole layer of *yufka*, centring it on the filling. Fold in any overhanging *yufka* over the top of the pie and use a sharp knife to cut the pastry into 8 wedges, cutting almost but not quite through the dough on the bottom of the dish, then pour the remaining milk mixture over all. Scatter on the remaining butter cubes and sprinkle with sesame seeds.

9. Bake the *börek* for 30–40 minutes until the top layer is crisp and the filling is hot.

10. Cool slightly on a rack and serve warm.

VARIATIONS

MINCED MEAT FILLING: Coat a sauté pan with 2 tablespoons olive oil and add 55g finely chopped white onion. Cook slowly over a low heat for 15–20 minutes until soft and translucent, stirring occasionally. Increase the heat to medium and add 450g minced beef or lamb; use a wooden spoon to stir and break up the meat for a few minutes, until it starts to colour and separate into fine granules. Season with salt, pepper and a large pinch of ground allspice. Pour into a sieve set over a bowl to allow excess fat to drain; let cool. Right before assembling the *börek*, stir in 15g each chopped mint and flat-leaf parsley. Fill the pastry as above, using the meat filling in place of the mint and Feta mixture and omitting the cubed butter in steps 6 and 7. Top the pie with 2 tablespoons butter cubes and the sesame seeds as in step 8 and bake.

Makes one 23–25cm *börek*, 8–10 servings

4 leaves homemade *Yufka* (page 147). To use packaged *yufka*, see Note

115g unsalted butter

240ml whole milk

3 medium eggs

250g crumbled Feta cheese

40g chopped fresh mint leaves

1–2 tablespoons sesame seeds for finishing

NOTE

To use packaged *yufka*, which has much larger leaves, in steps 5 and 7 use half of one of the large leaves, torn apart.

TURKISH FRIED 'CIGARETTE' PASTRIES (SİGARA BÖREĞİ)

Makes 24 small hors d'oeuvre pastries

3 sheets homemade *Yufka* (page 147) or 1 packet triangular *yufka* leaves (to use packaged filo dough, see Note)

125g finely crumbled Feta cheese

4 tablespoons chopped fresh mint leaves

4 tablespoons chopped flat-leaf parsley or dill

700ml sunflower oil for frying

NOTE

To use packaged filo dough, you'll need 12 sheets of dough, 2 tablespoons olive oil and a brush. Place 1 filo sheet on the work surface. Drizzle very lightly with oil and place another sheet on top. Cut across widthways into 2 smaller rectangles, then cut each rectangle diagonally into 2 triangles. Repeat with the remaining sheets and proceed as above.

These are so-called because of their shape. Since cigarettes have fallen into such disgrace, though, there is even a movement afoot to change the name of this pastry to 'pen' *böreği*. The G in *böreği* is silent.

1. Let the dough come to room temperature.

2. Stir the cheese and herbs together.

3. If you're using homemade *yufka*, stack the 3 leaves and use a small, sharp paring knife to cut 8 equal-size wedges for a total of 24 pieces.

4. To form each roll, place 1 teaspoon of filling in a line 1.25cm in from the base of a triangle then fold the sides in. Roll up Swiss roll-style. Use a brush to moisten the tip of the triangle with water to seal the pastry. Arrange the roll with the point underneath.

5. Heat the oil in a deep casserole or wok to 180°C/gas mark 4.

6. Fry several pastries at a time, taking care not to crowd them, then use a slotted spoon to transfer them to a Swiss roll tin lined with kitchen towels to drain. Serve while still warm and crisp.

CHAPTER 7

PUFF PASTRY, CROISSANTS & OTHER LAMINATED DOUGHS

Doughs like puff pastry that consist of alternating layers of dough and butter formed by repeated rolling and folding are known as 'laminated'. You start with a slightly elastic, lean dough that has only a small amount of butter in it and use that to enclose a large, flat piece of butter that has been mixed with a little flour to make for easier handling. The dough is rolled to press the layers of dough and butter thinner, then folded to increase the number of layers. On paper, the process is pretty easy to explain; it's not difficult to execute either, but it requires close attention to detail.

The following rules are important to follow for all laminated doughs:

• Give the base dough plenty of time to rest and chill before wrapping it around the butter.

• Always start with cold butter and soften it to a malleable consistency quickly – leaving the butter at room temperature too long will soften it too much. >>

• For maximum success in rolling the dough and butter together, both should be at approximately the same temperature and have a similar consistency. Butter that's too soft will make the layers of dough slide apart from each other, and butter that's too hard will pierce through the dough and resist forming even layers.

• Always make the dough very thin on the initial rolling. If the butter layer is too thick after the first couple of rollings, it will fragment into flakes when the chilled, rested dough is rolled again; fragments of butter melt and leak out of the dough instead of forming even layers.

• Take your time with the rolling and keep the dough even; you'll be rewarded with a beautiful result.

• Traditional puff pastry may be made in dozens of ways. The version here is one I've used for years and have taught thousands of students to prepare successfully. It's a slight twist on the classic formula that also helps to guarantee a good, even rise; the proof that the pastry is well-made.

• Quick puff pastry is just that, a faster and easier way to get almost the same results as the traditional method. Perfect for thin pieces of dough, like a baked sheet to make Napoleons or a *mille-feuille*, quick puff pastry is also excellent for small puff pastries.

• Croissant dough is made in a manner similar to traditional puff pastry, but the base dough contains yeast, so that the croissants rise both from the puffing of the layers and from the action of the yeast.

• *Plunderteig*, or Viennese layered dough, is a sweeter version of croissant dough. It contains yeast, but also more sugar, as well as eggs. It's richer than the typical Danish pastry made in the United States, yet not as rich and flaky as that made in Scandinavia.

PUFF PASTRY

All the laminated doughs in this chapter are made the same way – with a square of butter at one end of a rectangle of dough so that a single fold of the dough over the butter encloses it. This method requires starting with a thin layer of butter, which makes it easier to get even layers of butter in your dough and consequently a better rise and a more delicate texture after baking. This recipe makes more than enough dough for any pastry in this chapter.

Makes about 900g dough

DOUGH

315g unbleached plain flour

85g unsalted butter, softened

150ml cold water, plus about
1 tablespoon more if necessary

1 teaspoon fine sea salt

BUTTER BLOCK

30g unbleached plain flour

310g unsalted butter, cold

1. For the dough, combine the flour and butter in a bowl and rub in the butter so that no visible pieces remain. Don't mix so much that it starts to become pasty. Stir the water and salt together and sprinkle all over the flour. Use a rubber spatula to dig to the bottom of the bowl and bring up the unmoistened flour, turning the bowl as you go. Don't exert pressure on the dough, just bring the spatula up from the bottom of the bowl. After 10 or 12 strokes, if there are any dry bits of flour remaining, sprinkle a few drops of water until they adhere to the main mass of dough.

2. Scrape the dough from the bowl to a lightly floured surface and dust the top with flour. Use your hands, the straight side of a dough scraper, and a ruler to shape the dough into a 20cm square. Wrap the dough in clingfilm and chill for 1 hour.

3. Shortly before the hour is up, prepare the butter block: scatter half the flour on the work surface and cut the butter into 5 or 6 pieces. Turn the pieces in the flour to coat them and use a rolling pin to gently pound each piece of butter to soften it. Once all the butter has been pounded, scatter on some of the remaining flour, dusting the work surface again if necessary; stack one piece of butter on another and use the rolling pin to hammer them together. Repeat, adding the remaining pieces of butter to the stack. Scatter on the last of the flour, then quickly knead the butter into a solid mass and use your hands, the straight side of a dough scraper and a ruler to shape the butter into a 20cm square ①.

4. Set the butter aside for a moment, scrape the surface free of any sticky bits of butter, and flour it. Unwrap the dough and place it on the work surface; flour the dough and roll it evenly to an 20 x 40cm rectangle, with a short edge near you ②. Brush away any excess flour on the dough's surface and place the butter on the end closest to you. Fold the dough down to enclose the butter ③ and pinch the edges of the dough together ④. >>

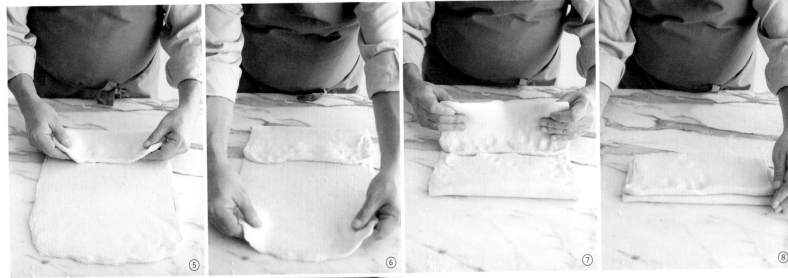

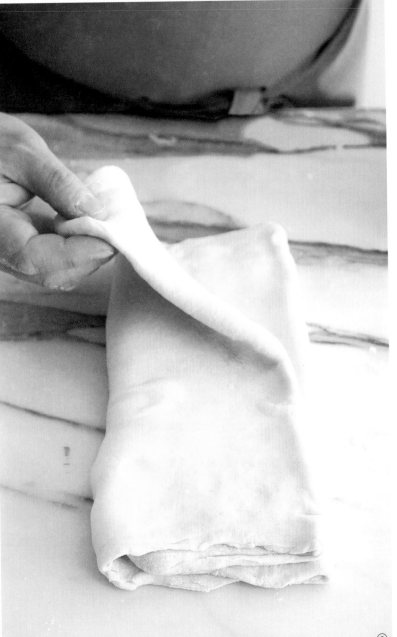

5. Flour under and on top of the dough and use the rolling pin to start pressing the package of dough and butter in a succession of gentle and even strokes, moving from the closest edge to the furthest edge. Gently roll the dough in one direction, starting at the end nearest to you and without going over the opposite edge. Repeat, rolling from the far end back toward yourself. Repeat the rolling once more and make the dough a 20 x 40cm rectangle.

6. Brush excess flour from the dough, then fold both narrow ends towards the middle, leaving about a 1.25cm space between them ⑤⑥. Fold the dough in half along that centre line to make 4 layers ⑦⑧.

7. Position the folded package of dough so that the closed fold, resembling the spine of a book, is on your left ⑨. Repeat step 5, this time rolling across as well as lengthways, until the dough is as close to 20 x 40cm as possible. Repeat step 6.

8. Wrap and chill the dough for an hour or so. If you wait longer, you will need to let the dough soften slightly at room temperature before completing the rolling and folding process.

9. When ready to resume rolling, repeat step 7 twice more.

10. You've now rolled and folded the dough 4 times, giving it 4 'turns'. Wrap and chill the dough for at least half a day. After this, it's ready to be used in any recipe that calls for it.

MAKE AHEAD
Keep the dough refrigerated for up to 2 days. For longer storage, double wrap and freeze. Thaw in the refrigerator overnight before using.

QUICK PUFF PASTRY

Variously called rough, half, express and even Scottish puff pastry, this quick method works especially well for thin or small pastries when you don't need the dough to rise to great heights. It's much faster to prepare because all the ingredients are mixed together from the outset with no separate rolling and layering of dough and butter. The ingredients are the same as the traditional dough; the assembly is completely different and the dough gets only three instead of four turns.

1. Combine the flour and 85g of the butter in a bowl and rub in the butter so that no visible pieces remain. Don't mix so much that it starts to become pasty.

2. Add the remaining butter to the bowl and toss it through the flour. Use your fingertips to slightly soften and flatten the pieces of butter, making sure they stay covered in flour.

3. Stir the water and salt together and sprinkle it all over the flour and butter mixture. Use a rubber spatula to dig to the bottom of the bowl and bring up the unmoistened flour, turning the bowl as you do. Don't exert pressure on the dough, just bring the spatula up from the bottom of the bowl. After 10 or 12 strokes, if there are any dry bits of flour remaining, sprinkle a few drops of water until they adhere to the main mass of dough.

4. Scrape the dough from the bowl onto a lightly floured surface and dust the top with flour. Squeeze the dough together, shaping it into a fat sausage shape. Flour under and on top of the dough again and press it into a rough rectangle. If the dough feels soft, wrap and chill it for half an hour to firm up the butter.

5. Flour under and on top of the dough and use the rolling pin to start pressing in a succession of gentle and even strokes, moving from the closest edge outward. Gently roll the dough in one direction, starting at the end nearest to you and without going over the opposite edge. Repeat, rolling from the far end back towards yourself. Repeat the rolling once more and make the dough a 20 x 40cm rectangle.

6. Brush excess flour from the dough, then fold both narrow ends toward the middle, leaving about a 1.25cm space between. Fold the dough in half along that centre line to make 4 layers.

7. Position the folded parcel of dough so that the closed fold, resembling the spine of a book, is on your left. Repeat step 5, this time rolling across as well as lengthways, until the dough is as close to 20 x 40cm as possible.

8. If feasible, give the dough a third turn by repeating steps 5 and 6. If the dough is too soft to handle, chill it for 1 hour and then perform the third turn.

9. After the third turn, wrap and chill the dough; it's ready for use once it has chilled and rested for a couple of hours.

Makes about 900g dough

315g unbleached plain flour

400g unsalted butter, chilled and cut into 1.25cm pieces

170ml cold water, plus about 1 tablespoon more if necessary

1 teaspoon fine sea salt

MAKE AHEAD
Keep the dough refrigerated for up to 2 days. For longer storage, double-wrap and freeze the dough. Thaw it in the refrigerator overnight before using.

VARIATION
You can use a food processor for steps 1 and 2 by adding in the first, smaller quantity of butter into the flour and pulsing it repeatedly at 1-second intervals until it has been completely absorbed. Add the second, larger quantity of butter and give two 1-second pulses, then use a long metal spatula to scrape the side of the bowl. Repeat the two pulses and invert the food processor bowl into a large mixing bowl, carefully remove the blade, and resume the recipe at step 3.

PROFESSOR CALVEL'S CROISSANT DOUGH

Makes 1.12kg, enough for 30–40 pastries

DOUGH

120ml room-temperature tap water, about 24°C

3½ teaspoons fine granulated active dried yeast or instant yeast

180ml whole milk, scalded and cooled to room temperature

50g caster sugar

1 teaspoon organic malt syrup or honey

500g unbleached bread flour

2 teaspoons fine sea salt

15g unsalted butter, softened

BUTTER BLOCK

35g unbleached bread flour

225g unsalted butter, cold

The late Raymond Calvel, the father of modern French breadmaking, wrote about croissants in his second book, *Le Goût du Pain (The Flavour of Bread)*. This recipe is modified from his in that I've used whole milk instead of dried milk because whole milk contributes a fresher taste to the croissants and I have not added ascorbic acid (vitamin C).

1. Whisk the water and yeast together in the bowl of a stand mixer, then whisk in the milk, sugar and malt syrup. Use a large rubber spatula to stir in the flour; make sure there is no flour stuck to the sides or bottom of the bowl. Place the bowl on the mixer fitted with the dough hook and mix on the lowest speed for 2 minutes. Let the dough rest for 15 minutes.

2. Mix the dough on a medium speed, adding the salt and butter, for a further 2–3 minutes until smooth and elastic. Cover the bowl with clingfilm and let the dough ferment at room temperature for 30–60 minutes until it starts to puff. Without deflating the dough, place the bowl in the refrigerator for 2 hours.

3. Once the second hour is almost up, prepare the butter block: scatter half the flour on the work surface and cut the butter into 5 or 6 pieces. Turn the pieces in the flour to coat them and use a rolling pin to gently pound each piece of butter to soften it. Once all the butter has been pounded, scatter on some of the remaining flour, dusting the work surface again if necessary; stack one piece of butter on another and use the rolling pin to hammer them together. Repeat, adding the remaining pieces of butter. Scatter on the last of the flour, then quickly knead the butter into a solid mass and shape into a 20cm square. Set aside.

4. Scrape the work surface free of any sticky bits of butter and flour it. Unwrap the dough onto the surface, flour it and roll evenly to an 20 x 40cm rectangle, with a short edge near you. Brush away any excess flour on the dough's surface and place the butter on the end closest to you. Fold the dough down to enclose the butter and pinch the edges together around it.

5. Flour under and on top of the dough and use the rolling pin to start pressing in a succession of gentle and even strokes, moving from the closest edge to the furthest edge. Gently roll the dough in one direction, starting at the end nearest to you and without going over the opposite edge. Repeat, rolling from the far end back towards yourself. Repeat the rolling once more and make the dough a 20 x 40cm rectangle.

6. Brush excess flour from the dough, then fold both narrow ends toward the middle, leaving about a 1.25cm space between. Fold the dough in half along that centre line to make 4 layers.

7. Position the folded parcel of dough so that the closed fold, resembling the spine of a book, is on your left. Repeat step 5, this time rolling across as well as lengthways, until the dough is as close to 20 x 40cm as possible. Repeat step 6.

8. Wrap and chill the dough and be ready to form and bake the croissants within 2–4 hours.

VIENNESE DANISH DOUGH (PLUNDERTEIG)

The German word *Plunder* can refer to stacked planks or beams of wood, which is how the term came to be applied to a laminated pastry dough. Recently, I visited with my old friend Hans Diglas, proprietor of *Café Diglas* and *Konditorei Diglas* in Vienna. Herr Diglas gave me some pastries made with *plunderteig*, and I was an immediate convert. Over the following several days, I spent some time at his production facility and this recipe is the result.

1. Whisk the milk and yeast together in the bowl of a stand mixer, then whisk in the egg yolks, vanilla extract and sugar. Use a large rubber spatula to stir in the flour, making sure there is none stuck to the sides or bottom of the bowl. Place the bowl on the mixer fitted with the dough hook and mix on the lowest speed for 2 minutes.

2. Increase the speed to medium, adding the salt and butter and mix for a further 2–3 minutes until smooth and elastic. Cover the bowl with clingfilm and chill in the refrigerator for 2 hours.

3. Once the second hour is almost up, prepare the butter block: scatter half the flour on the work surface and cut the butter into 5 or 6 pieces. Turn the pieces in the flour to coat them and use a rolling pin to gently pound each piece to soften it. Once all the butter has been pounded, scatter on some of the remaining flour, dusting the work surface again if necessary; stack one piece of butter on another and use the rolling pin to hammer them together. Repeat, adding the remaining pieces of butter. Scatter on the last of the flour, then quickly knead the butter into a solid mass and shape into a 20cm square. Set aside.

4. Scrape the work surface free of any sticky bits of butter, and flour it. Unwrap the dough and place it on the surface, flour it and roll evenly to an 20 x 40cm rectangle, with a short edge near you. Brush away any excess flour on the dough's surface and place the butter on the end closest to you. Fold the dough down to enclose the butter and pinch the edges together around it.

5. Flour under and on top of the dough and use the rolling pin to start pressing in a succession of gentle and even strokes, moving from the closest edge to the furthest edge. Gently roll the dough in one direction, starting at the end nearest to you and without going over the opposite edge. Repeat, rolling from the far end back towards yourself. Repeat the rolling once more and make the dough a 20 x 40cm rectangle.

6. Brush any excess flour from the dough, then fold both narrow ends toward the middle, leaving about a 1.25cm space between. Fold the dough in half along that centre line to make 4 layers.

7. Position the folded parcel of dough so that the closed fold, resembling the spine of a book, is on your left. Repeat step 5, this time rolling across as well as lengthways, until the dough is as close to 20 x 40cm as possible. Repeat step 6.

8. Wrap and chill the dough; use it the same day or chill overnight and form and bake the pastries the next morning.

Makes 850g dough, enough for 18–24 finished pastries

DOUGH

180ml whole milk, scalded and cooled to 38°C

4½ teaspoons fine granulated active dried yeast or instant yeast

2 medium egg yolks, at room temperature

1 teaspoon vanilla extract

3 tablespoons caster sugar

300g unbleached bread flour

½ teaspoon fine sea salt

30g unsalted butter, softened

BUTTER BLOCK

35g unbleached bread flour

225g unsalted butter, cold

CARAMELISED PUFF PASTRY LAYERS

Makes one 25 x 38cm layer

300g Puff Pastry or Quick Puff Pastry (page 155 or 157)

2 tablespoons caster sugar

2 tablespoons icing sugar

VARIATION

If you don't need the layer to be caramelised, omit both sugars. Bake the pastry at 190°C/gas mark 5, and at the end of step 4, invert the stack of tins and dough and continue baking until the layer is crisp and golden, 10–15 minutes longer. Cut and store as in step 7.

Thin, fragile baked layers of puff pastry are a must for any kind of *mille-feuille*, large or individual, or classic Napoleons. Start with these instructions to prepare the pastry; further instructions for finished desserts using these layers are in the recipes that follow. This is loosely adapted from a recipe by Pierre Hermé that appears in his first book, *Secrets Gourmands*. See the Variation for a plain puff pastry layer.

1. Lightly flour the work surface and the dough and roll it to a 25 x 38cm rectangle. (It's helpful to roll the dough part of the way, then transfer one of the pieces of parchment paper for lining a tin to your work surface, flour it and finish rolling the dough directly on the paper.)

2. Slide the paper and dough into one of the tins and use a fork to pierce it all over at 1.25cm intervals. Cover the dough loosely with clingfilm and let it rest for several hours.

3. When you're ready to bake the layer, set a rack in the upper third of the oven and preheat to 200°C/gas mark 6. Line two 25 x 38cm Swiss roll tins with parchment paper.

4. Sprinkle the dough with the caster sugar and place the second piece of parchment paper on top; stack the second tin on top of the parchment. Place in the oven and reduce the temperature to 190°C/gas mark 5. Bake for about 15 minutes until the layer is almost cooked through.

5. Remove the stack of tins and dough from the oven and invert them, grasping both sides to avoid having the dough slide out. Increase the oven temperature to 230°C/gas mark 8.

6. The dough will now be resting on a piece of parchment on the back of a Swiss roll tin. Lift off the top tin, peel away the top paper, and slide the layer of dough, still on the second piece of paper, back into the original tin. Evenly sprinkle with the icing sugar and bake, watching carefully, for 7–10 minutes until the sugar melts and glazes. Don't walk away or it will definitely burn.

7. Slide the baked layer, still on its paper, to a cutting board and slice it into the desired pieces while it is still warm. To prevent the pastry from warping once it has cooled, slide it or the pieces back between the papers and tins until you are ready to proceed.

TRADITIONAL VANILLA MILLE-FEUILLE

It's a mystery why this is referred to as a 'Napoleon' in the United States and UK, though the best explanation is that it has nothing to do with the French emperor but is a corruption of the word *Neapolitan*. In any case, this version of a *mille-feuille* combines the simple elements of crisp, buttery caramelised puff pastry layers and pastry cream perfumed with vanilla pod and lightened with whipped cream. It's definitely a case where the whole is much greater than the sum of the separate parts.

1. For the pastry cream, whisk together the milk, 2 tablespoons of the sugar and the vanilla pod in a small saucepan; if you're using vanilla bean paste, add it in step 3 when you take the pastry cream off the heat. Bring the mixture to the full boil over a low heat. Meanwhile, in a bowl, whisk the yolks and then whisk in 2 tablespoons of the remaining sugar. Sift over and whisk in the flour.

2. When the milk mixture boils, whisk it into the egg yolk mixture. Strain the mixture back into the pan (leaving the vanilla pod in the sieve) and place over a medium heat. Using a small, pointed-end whisk, whisk constantly, being sure to reach into the corners of the pan, until the cream comes to a full boil and thickens. Cook, whisking constantly, for 30 seconds more.

3. Scrape the cream into a glass bowl, stir in the vanilla paste, if using, and press clingfilm directly against the surface. Chill until cold.

4. When you're ready to assemble the *mille-feuille*, no more than 3–4 hours before you intend to serve it, prepare the whipped cream: Whip the cream and remaining 2 tablespoons sugar to a firm peak, but not until dry or grainy. Fold into the chilled pastry cream.

5. Place one of the baked layers, glaze-side up, on a serving plate or serving board, and spread it with half the pastry cream. Add a second layer and the remaining cream.

6. Use a sharp serrated knife to cut the last layer into 8 separate pieces, each 4 x 7.5cm. Dust half with icing sugar. Alternate the dusted and plain glazed pieces of pastry on top of the pastry cream.

7. Use a sharp serrated knife to cut the *mille-feuille* all the way through; having the top layer already cut eliminates most of the squish factor during this process.

Makes 8 individual servings

1 batch Caramelised Puff Pastry Layers (opposite), cut into three 7.5 x 30cm layers

VANILLA POD PASTRY CREAM

240ml whole milk

6 tablespoons caster sugar

1 Madagascar Bourbon vanilla pod (see Note below) split, or 1 teaspoon vanilla pod paste

3 medium egg yolks

2 tablespoons unbleached plain flour

240ml double cream

Icing sugar

NOTE

After using the vanilla pod, rinse and let it dry for a day at room temperature. Embed it in your sugar canister to lightly scent the sugar.

VARIATION

Fold a couple of tablespoons of Lemon Curd (page 48), into the pastry cream along with the whipped cream for a subtle lemon flavour.

STRAWBERRY RASPBERRY MILLE-FEUILLES

Makes 8 individual servings

1 batch Caramelised Puff Pastry Layers (page 160), cut into two 19cm square layers

VANILLA ORANGE PASTRY CREAM

180ml whole milk

60ml double cream

50ml caster sugar

Zest of 1 small orange, removed in large strips with a vegetable peeler

3 medium egg yolks

2 tablespoons unbleached plain flour

1 teaspoon vanilla extract or vanilla bean paste

FINISHING

240ml double cream

2 tablespoons caster sugar

350g berries, a mixture of small strawberries, rinsed and hulled and raspberries, picked over, but not washed

VARIATIONS

Any ripe fruit that's sweet and not excessively juicy can be substituted for the berries. Try really ripe apricot halves, sliced stoned plums or prune plums, or even well-drained sliced poached pears.

In France it's popular during the summer to make tarts and other pastries like *mille-feuille aux fruits rouges* or 'with red fruits', meaning basically whatever berries are available. We can't obtain the tiny, intensely flavoured wild strawberries or *fraises des bois* as easily as they do in France, but small, perfectly sweet, height-of-the-season berries work very well in this dessert. It's fun and tasty to combine several types of berries, and if you have access to redcurrants, sprinkle in a few – not too many, or the fruit mix might be too tart.

1. For the pastry cream, combine the milk, cream, half the sugar and the orange zest in a small saucepan and whisk to combine. Bring to the full boil over a low heat. Meanwhile, in a bowl, whisk the egg yolks and then whisk in the remaining sugar. Sift over and whisk in the flour.

2. When the milk mixture boils, whisk it into the egg yolk mixture. Strain the mixture back into the pan (leaving the orange zest in the strainer) and place over a medium heat. Use a small, pointed-end whisk to stir constantly, being sure to reach into the corners of the pan, until the cream comes to the full boil and thickens. Cook, whisking constantly for another 30 seconds. Off the heat, whisk in the vanilla extract or paste. Scrape the cream into a glass bowl and press clingfilm directly against the surface. Chill until cold.

3. A few hours before serving the *mille-feuilles*, use a sharp serrated knife to cut each of the layers into 8 rectangles, each about 4.5 x 9.5cm.

4. Just before assembling, whip the cream with the sugar to a soft peak.

5. Arrange 8 of the cut layers, caramelised side up, on dessert plates. Top each with a heaped tablespoon of pastry cream. Arrange some of the strawberries and raspberries on the pastry cream, then top with a spoonful of whipped cream. Cover each with another puff pastry layer, caramelised side up, and gently press to adhere the layer to the whipped cream.

6. Serve immediately; these can wait an hour at a cool room temperature but not much longer.

PUFF PASTRY TART CRUST

Makes one 25cm round crust (see Variation for the square shape)

300g Puff Pastry or Quick Puff Pastry (page 155 or 157)

Water for brushing the dough

VARIATION

For a square crust, place the dough on a floured surface and lightly flour it. Press with a rolling pin to soften and thin the dough, then roll to a 20 x 40cm rectangle. Use a sharp pastry wheel to trim the long edges straight, then cut the dough lengthways into two 2.5cm strips, and one 15cm strip. Fold the 15cm strip in thirds and transfer to the prepared tin. Unfold and use a fork to pierce the dough all over at 1.25cm intervals. Moisten the long edges of the 15cm strip, then place one of the 2.5cm strips on each moistened edge to form a lip (the narrow ends of the crust will be left open). Flour a fingertip and press the side strips down to adhere. Use the back of a paring knife to make indentations on the side strips to help them stay in place. Finally, pierce the top of the side strips down through the bottom with the point of a paring knife at 1.25cm intervals. Then rest and bake, as described in steps 7 through 9.

These are versatile, easy to prepare, and a lifesaver when you want a simple tart with a layer of pastry cream and some fresh fruit but you don't have a special tin to bake it in. You can use any dimensions you like and make the tart crust round, square or rectangular. When planning the size and shape of your tart if it's different from the ones below, remember to consider the size and shape of your serving plate.

1. Roll the dough into a 28cm square, then cut three 2.5cm-wide strips from one side ①②.

2. Roll the remaining large piece of dough back into a 28cm square and place on a Swiss roll tin lined with parchment paper ③.

3. Place a 25cm round template, such as a cake board on the dough and use a sharp pastry wheel to cut around it ④. Remove the scraps of dough.

4. Pierce the large disk of dough with a fork at 1.25cm intervals ⑤.

5. To make the sides of the crust, moisten the edge of the disk ⑥ and then apply one of the strips at the edge, letting 2.5cm or so at each end of the strip stray off the edge onto the work surface. Moisten the ends of the strip and apply another one the same way. Repeat for the third strip. You'll now have 6 strip ends that need to be trimmed away. Use a fingertip to press the strips so they will adhere to the disk of dough beneath ⑦.

6. Use a sharp pastry wheel to cut away the dangling ends and make the edge of the disk even ⑧. Indent and pierce the strips using a paring knife, as in photo 5 on page 166.

7. Loosely cover the crust with clingfilm, and refrigerate for at least 2 hours or overnight.

8. When you're ready to bake, set a rack at the middle level in the oven and preheat to 200°C/gas mark 6.

9. Place the tin in the oven, reduce the temperature to 190°C/gas mark 5 and bake for 20–25 minutes until golden and dry. Cool the crust on a rack and fill and serve that same day.

INDIVIDUAL HAZELNUT PITHIVIERS

A large *Gâteau Pithiviers* is one of France's most famous pastries. Named for a town outside Paris, the puff pastry cake usually has an almond filling. Here, I've recast it as an individual dessert with a hazelnut filling and a creamy caramel sauce to offset the richness of the buttery dough. Using traditional puff pastry is preferable, since you want plenty of rise from even layering.

1. For the filling, pulse the hazelnuts and sugar in a food processor until finely ground. Add the butter, rum, vanilla, cinnamon and egg yolks and pulse again to mix. You might need to use a metal spatula to scrape down the bowl. Add the flour, pulse again, then invert the filling into a bowl; carefully remove the blade and use a rubber spatula to scrape any remaining filling into the bowl. Cover loosely and set aside.

2. Roll the dough on a floured surface to an 20 x 30cm rectangle; cut in half. Roll one half to 20 x 30cm and the other half to 25 x 38cm. If the dough begins to get soft, slide the pieces onto a baking tray and chill for a few minutes.

3. Place the smaller sheet of dough on the work surface and use a ruler and dough scraper to mark it into 10cm squares. Use a sharp pastry wheel or knife to cut them apart. Line the squares up on a Swiss roll tin lined with parchment paper and divide the filling equally among them, making a 5cm diameter mound in the centre ①.

4. Mark, then cut the remaining, large piece of dough into 12.5cm squares. Carefully brush egg wash around each pastry's filling and place a 12.5cm square of dough on top ②. Cup your hand over the centre and press the dough around the filling, leaving no air pockets, then line up the sides of the dough. As long as the top square covers the bottom one, it's okay.

5. Invert a 5cm round biscuit cutter over the filling and press just enough to seal the layers of dough together ③. Then use a 10cm round cutter to cut each of the pastries, saving the scraps for another use ④.

6. Indent the side of the pastries at 1.25cm intervals using the back of a paring knife ⑤. Make several arc-shaped slashes in the top of the pastry over the filling, only cutting about halfway through the dough. Cover and chill the pastries for at least 4 hours or overnight.

Makes 6 individual (10cm) cakes

600g (⅔ batch) Puff Pastry or Quick Puff Pastry (page 155 or 157)

HAZELNUT FILLING

115g whole hazelnuts

100g caster sugar

85g unsalted butter, softened

1 tablespoon dark rum

1 teaspoon vanilla extract

Large pinch of ground cinnamon

3 medium egg yolks

45g unbleached plain flour

Egg wash: 1 egg whisked with a pinch of salt

CARAMEL SAUCE

200g caster sugar

2 tablespoons light corn syrup or golden syrup

60ml water

150ml double cream

Pinch of fine sea salt or *fleur de sel*

7. Set a rack in the lower third of the oven and preheat to 200°C/gas mark 6.

8. Brush the pastries with egg wash using a fairly dry brush to avoid puddles. Bake for 45–55 minutes until well-risen and deeply golden. Cool on a rack.

9. Meanwhile, for the caramel sauce, stir the sugar, corn syrup and water together in a medium saucepan and melt over a low heat undisturbed. Meanwhile, heat the cream in another small pan until scalded; turn off the heat. Stir the sugar occasionally, but only until completely liquefied. Then cook, still over a low heat, until the syrup is a deep caramel colour. Holding the pan at arm's length and averting your face, pour the cream into the caramel in 3 additions, letting it boil up and recede before adding more. Once all the cream has been added, give the caramel sauce a good stir and bring to the full boil. Season with salt.

10. To serve, reheat the sauce to lukewarm and the pastries briefly at 180°C/gas mark 4. Place the pastries on dessert plates and pass the caramel sauce separately.

VARIATIONS
Substitute almonds for the hazelnuts and omit the cinnamon in the filling. You could press a small apricot or plum half onto the filling before placing the top layer of dough, but avoid overfilling the pastries, or they will burst open while baking.

MAKE AHEAD
Make the filling ahead of time, cover and chill it. It will keep for several days.

PEAR & ALMOND DUMPLINGS

Most fruit dumplings are constructed by wrapping a piece of fruit in a square of dough. This one is a little different – the fruit and a dab of almond filling are sandwiched between two layers of puff pastry, and the dough never shrinks, falls away or does anything but rise to flaky perfection around the fruit.

1. For the poached pears, half-fill a 4–5-litre casserole with a cover with ice water and the lemon juice. Peel, halve and core the pears, dropping them in one piece at a time. Skim out the ice, add the sugar, vanilla pod and cinnamon and bring to the boil over a medium heat. Boil for 1 minute, cover the pan, remove from the heat and let the pears cool in the syrup. Remove the vanilla pod and cinnamon stick and refrigerate for up to several days.

2. For the almond filling, beat the almond paste and sugar together at medium speed in a stand mixer using the paddle attachment. Beat in 1 egg yolk and continue beating until smooth and free of lumps. Beat in the remaining egg yolk and the butter, followed by the flour. Set aside.

3. Drain the pears and trim the stem ends off, to make them round. Line a Swiss roll tin with parchment paper.

4. Roll the dough on a floured surface to a 20 x 40cm rectangle. Cut it half and roll each half to 20 x 40cm. If the dough begins to get soft, slide the pieces onto a baking tray and chill for a few minutes.

5. Place one sheet of dough on the work surface and use a ruler and dough scraper to mark it into 10cm squares. Cut them apart, line them up on the prepared tin and spoon a dab of almond filling into the centre of each ①. Cover the filling with a pear half ②.

6. Mark and cut the second piece of dough as above, then use a sharp pastry wheel to cut a 5cm cross in the centre of each piece, ends pointing towards the corners of the square. Lightly brush egg wash around each pastry's pear, then lay one of the dough squares over it, lining up the edges of the pastry so that the top of the dumpling opens at the cut cross ③. Press with a fingertip all around the perimeter of the square ④. Repeat with the remaining pastry squares, then cover the dumplings loosely with clingfilm and chill for at least 4 hours.

7. Set a rack in the lower third of the oven and preheat to 200°C/gas mark 6. Use a dry brush to dab egg wash on the pastries, then bake for 45–55 minutes until well-risen and baked through.

8. Cool the dumplings on a rack and serve warm. Dust lightly with icing sugar right before serving.

Makes 8 pastries

600g Puff Pastry or Quick Puff Pastry (page 155 or 157)

POACHED PEARS

Ice water

2 tablespoons lemon juice, strained before measuring

4 firm-ripe Williams pears, about 900g

200g caster sugar

1 vanilla pod, left whole

7.5cm piece of cinnamon stick

ALMOND FILLING

75g almond paste (see Note)

2 tablespoons caster sugar

2 medium egg yolks

30g unsalted butter, softened

2 tablespoons unbleached plain flour

Egg wash: 1 egg whisked with a pinch of salt

Icing sugar for finishing

VARIATIONS
Substitute firm-ripe peaches, apricots or prune plums for the pears. The apricots and plums don't need to be poached. For the peaches, just halve and stone them before poaching them – the skins will easily slip off.

NOTE
In the UK, almond paste can be a little hard to find. You can substitute marzipan instead but as it has a higher sugar content, I recommend you reduce the sugar quantity in the almond filling by half.

CROISSANTS

Once your dough is made and well-chilled, you can use it for croissants or for a variant such as the two recipes that follow, *pains au chocolat* or chocolate twists. Here, I'm giving the dimensions and instructions for using half the dough for croissants. See the Note for dimensions and instructions for using a third in case you'd like to make all three pastries at once.

Makes 16 large croissants

½ batch/560g Professor Calvel's Croissant Dough (page 158), chilled

Egg wash: 1 egg whisked with a pinch of salt

2 large Swiss roll tins covered with parchment paper

1. Place the dough on a floured surface and roll to a 40cm square, then cut into 2 strips, each 40 x 20cm. Patch the strips together by overlapping them by 0.5cm ① so you have a 80 x 20cm rectangle.

2. Mark one long side every 10cm. On the other long side, start marking at 5cm in from the left, then mark every 10cm – you'll have one 5cm section at the end. Use your dough scraper to mark triangles ②, then use a sharp pastry wheel to cut them ③. You'll have 15 triangles and a half triangle at each end. Patch the halves together.

3. Form the croissants by positioning the base of the triangle so it faces you. Pull the corners of the base to widen it. With one hand, start rolling upward ④ from the base while gently pulling on the apex of the triangle to lengthen it ⑤. Roll toward the point and leave the point on top. Curve the pastries slightly as you put them on the prepared tins ⑥.

4. Cover the croissants with a lightweight tea towel and let prove until almost doubled in size, about 1 hour, depending on the temperature of the room.

5. Once the croissants have started to puff, set racks in the upper and lower thirds of the oven and preheat to 230°C/gas mark 8.

6. Gently brush the croissants with the egg wash. Place in the oven and reduce the temperature to 200°C/gas mark 6. Bake for about 10 minutes until well-risen and starting to colour.

7. Switch the positions of the tins, swapping from one oven rack to the other and turning from front to back. Bake for about 10 minutes more, until baked through.

8. Cool on a rack and serve the day they are baked, or bag and freeze. Reheat frozen croissants at 180°C/gas mark 4 for 10 minutes, then cool slightly before serving.

NOTE

To use a third of the dough, roll a 30 x 40cm rectangle, then cut it into two 30 x 20cm rectangles, patching them together as above and cutting them the same way. This will yield 11 full croissants and 2 patched ones.

④ ⑤ ⑥

PUFF PASTRY BOW TIES

This beautiful variation on caramelised puff pastry can be a little challenging to prepare. If the dough gets sticky, just refrigerate it for 10 minutes or so and continue.

Makes about 24 cookie-sized pastries

200g caster sugar

⅓ batch/300g Puff Pastry or Quick Puff Pastry (page 155 or 157)

1. Scatter about a third of the sugar on the work surface and place the dough on it. Turn the dough over to coat the other side with sugar and begin to press and roll into a 30cm square. Move the dough frequently while rolling and add sugar under and on top.

2. Slide the dough onto a baking tray lined with parchment paper and refrigerate for 10–15 minutes until firm.

3. Trim the side edges even and cut the dough into 6 approximately 5cm strips. Stack 3 strips together, making 2 separate stacks.

4. Use the handle of a wooden spoon to press a narrow trough lengthways into the centre of each stack, turn the stacks over, and repeat on the other side.

5. Carefully cut each stack of dough lengthways into long slices 0.85cm thick. One at a time, take the slices and twist them at the indentation, making a bow-tie shape.

6. Put a pile of the remaining sugar on the work surface and dip one side of each pastry into it. Arrange the bow ties, sugared sides down, on the parchment-lined baking tray (you may need two), leaving a couple of centimetres around each one.

7. Let rest at room temperature while you set a rack at the middle level in the oven and preheat to 190°C/gas mark 5.

8. Bake one baking tray at a time until the bow ties expand and the sugar on the bottom caramelises, about 20 minutes.

9. Cool the bow ties on a rack and turn the caramelised side upward to serve. They're great on their own or to accompany any plain fruit, custard or frozen dessert. They can be stored for a couple of days between sheets of greaseproof paper in a tin or plastic container with a tight-fitting cover, but they're best on the day they're baked.

MAKE AHEAD
Cut and bake one of the stacks of sugared dough, then double-wrap and freeze the other. Thaw in the refrigerator for several hours or overnight, then proceed from step 6. Much of the sugar will melt, but they'll bake very well.

PAINS AU CHOCOLAT

Makes 16 large pastries

½ batch/560g Professor Calvel's Croissant Dough (page 158), chilled

32 chocolate sticks, or two 100g bars plain dark chocolate cut into 16 pieces measuring 2 x 10cm

Egg wash: 1 egg whisked with a pinch of salt

VARIATION
To use a third of the croissant dough, roll it to a 30 x 40cm rectangle, then cut it into twelve 10cm squares. Resume at step 2, above.

These 'chocolate loaves' are usually filled with tiny specially made bars of plain chocolate called *batons boulangers* (bakers' sticks). You can order those online, or you can buy two 100g bars of premium plain dark chocolate, let it soften at room temperature, and cut it into 2cm strips using a thin sharp knife run under hot water and wiped between cuts.

1. Place the dough on a floured surface and roll to a 40cm square. Mark, then cut the dough into sixteen 10cm squares. Line 2 large Swiss roll tins with parchment paper.

2. Place 2 small chocolate sticks or 1 larger piece of chocolate about 4cm in from one side of the dough square, then fold the dough over to enclose it. Fold the dough over once more and place the pastry, seam side down, on one of the prepared tins. Repeat until all the dough squares have been filled with chocolate, leaving as much space as possible between them on the tins.

3. Cover with a lightweight tea towel and let prove until almost doubled in size, about 1 hour or a little longer, depending on the temperature of the room.

4. Once the pastries have started to puff, set racks in the upper and lower thirds of the oven and preheat to 230°C/gas mark 8.

5. Gently brush the *pains au chocolat* with the egg wash. Place in the oven and reduce the temperature to 200°C/gas mark 6. Bake for about 10 minutes until well-risen and starting to colour.

6. Switch the positions of the tins, swapping from one oven rack to the other and turning from front to back. Bake about 10 minutes more, until the pastries are baked through.

7. Cool on a rack and serve the day they are baked, or bag and freeze them. Reheat frozen *pains au chocolat* at 180°C for 10 minutes, then cool slightly before serving.

VIENNESE CHEESE-FILLED SQUARES (TOPFENTASCHERL)

Viennese pot cheese, or *Topfen*, isn't unlike our part-skim milk ricotta, but it's a little firmer. In this recipe, I've combined the ricotta with some cream cheese, and it works perfectly. This is another wonderful recipe shared by Hans Diglas in Vienna.

Makes 12 pastries

½ batch/425g Viennese Danish Dough (page 159)

70g dried currants or sultanas

1 teaspoon dark rum

115g cream cheese, at room temperature

50g caster sugar

2 medium egg yolks

1 teaspoon vanilla extract

225g ricotta cheese

Icing sugar for finishing

1. Toss the currants with the rum and set aside. Line a baking tray with parchment paper.

2. Use a rubber spatula to beat together the cream cheese, sugar, egg yolks and vanilla extract. Gently fold in the ricotta cheese.

3. Roll the dough on a floured surface to a 30 x 40cm rectangle. Mark, then cut the dough into twelve 10cm squares.

4. Carefully fold the currants and rum into the cheese filling and distribute evenly among the squares of dough, spooning into the centre of each.

5. Pick up opposite corners of the dough ①, stretching slightly ②. Overlap the corners, then pinch together ③; repeat with the two other corners ④. Repeat with the rest of the dough.

6. Arrange the pastries on the prepared baking tray, leaving a couple of centimetres all around each one.

7. Cover with a lightweight tea towel and prove until almost doubled in size, about 1 hour, depending on the temperature of the room.

8. Once they have started to puff, set racks in middle level in the oven and preheat to 200°C/gas mark 6.

9. Place the pastries in the oven and reduce the temperature to 190°C/gas mark 5. Bake for about 15 minutes until well-risen and starting to colour.

10. Turn the baking tray from back to front and continue baking for about 10 minutes longer until the pastries are baked through.

11. Cool on a rack and serve the day they are baked; dust with icing sugar right before serving. Because the filling is delicate, these don't freeze well.

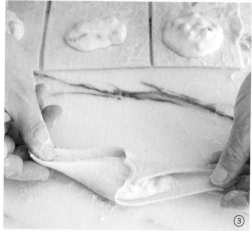

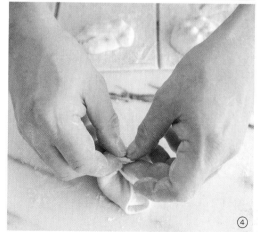

CHOCOLATE CINNAMON TWISTS (TORSADES AU CHOCOLAT)

Makes 16 pastries

½ batch/560g Professor Calvel's Croissant Dough (page 158), chilled

ALMOND FILLING

75g almond paste (see Note)

2 tablespoons sugar

2 medium egg yolks

30g unsalted butter, softened

2 tablespoons unbleached plain flour

170g plain chocolate mini chips, or plain chocolate cut into small pieces

1 teaspoon ground cinnamon

Egg wash: 1 egg whisked with a pinch of salt

NOTE

To use a third of the dough, roll it to a 40cm square, then cut it into two 20cm strips. Fill and finish the pastry as described, but cut only ten 4cm pieces in step 4.

In the UK, almond paste can be a little hard to find. You can substitute marzipan instead but as it has a higher sugar content, I recommend you reduce the sugar quantity in the almond filling by half.

These aren't a classic croissant variation but a French way of having croissant dough stand in for Danish pastry. The dough is spread with almond filling, then sprinkled with chocolate and cinnamon. You could easily substitute or add raisins or currants.

1. For the almond filling, beat the almond paste and sugar together at a medium speed in a stand mixer using the paddle attachment. Beat in 1 egg yolk and continue beating until smooth and free of lumps. Beat in the remaining egg yolk and the butter, followed by the flour.

2. Place the dough on a floured surface and roll it to a 40 x 60cm rectangle. Mark, then cut the dough into 2 strips, each 20 x 60cm. Line 2 large Swiss roll tins with parchment paper.

3. Spread the almond filling on one of the strips, then evenly sprinkle the chocolate and cinnamon over it. Cover with the second piece of dough, gently pressing them together.

4. Use a sharp pastry wheel to cut the dough crossways into 16 strips, each 4cm wide.

5. Give each strip a couple of twists as you put it on one of the prepared tins, arranging the pastries about 5cm apart in all directions.

6. Cover with a lightweight tea towel and let prove until almost doubled in size, about 1 hour or a little longer, depending on the temperature of the room.

7. Once they have started to puff, set racks in the upper and lower thirds of the oven and preheat to 230°C/gas mark 8.

8. Gently brush the torsades with the egg wash. Place in the oven and reduce the temperature to 200°C/gas mark 6. Bake for about 10 minutes until well-risen and starting to colour.

9. Switch the positions of the tins, swapping from one oven rack to the other and turning from front to back. Continue baking until the torsades are baked through, about 10 minutes longer.

10. Cool on a rack and serve the day they are baked, or bag and freeze. Reheat frozen torsades at 180°C/gas mark 4 for 10 minutes, then cool them slightly before serving.

VIENNESE WALNUT CINNAMON CRESCENTS

(ISCHLER KIPFERL)

Bad Ischl, not far from Salzburg, was a favourite watering place among nineteenth-century Viennese aristocracy, including Emperor Franz Josef. These sweet and indulgent crescents are a speciality of a pastry shop in Bad Ischl, but they've been widely copied all over Austria. This version comes from Café Diglas in Vienna.

1. Roll the dough on a floured surface to a 30cm square. Cut it into 2 strips, each 15 x 30cm, then join them together into a long strip that's 15 x 60cm. Following the instructions for cutting croissant dough in step 2 on page 170, mark, then cut the strip into triangles with a 10cm base. You will get 11 full triangles, along with 2 half-triangles on the ends, which you can patch together to make a twelfth pastry. Line 2 large Swiss roll tins with parchment paper.

2. Stir the caster sugar and cinnamon together in a small bowl. Generously brush the dough with the butter, then evenly sprinkle with the cinnamon sugar and walnuts. Use the palm of your hand to press the sugar and nuts against the dough to adhere.

3. Invert one pastry so that the sugar and nuts are underneath. Roll from the base of the triangle toward the point, pulling gently on the point to lengthen it. If some of the sugar and nuts fall off, just sprinkle them back on as you roll. Finish with the point at the top of the roll, then curve the pastry slightly and arrange it on one of the prepared tins. Repeat with the remaining pastries.

4. Cover with a lightweight tea towel and prove until almost doubled in size, about 1 hour, depending on the temperature of the room.

5. Once they have started to puff, set racks in the upper and lower thirds of the oven and preheat to 200°C/gas mark 6.

6. Place the tins in the oven and reduce the temperature to 190°C/gas mark 5. Bake for about 10 minutes until well-risen and starting to colour.

7. Switch the positions of the tins, swapping from one oven rack to the other and turning from front to back. Continue baking for about 10 minutes longer until the pastries are baked through.

8. Cool on a rack and serve the day they are baked; dust with icing sugar right before serving. Because the topping is delicate, these don't freeze well.

Makes 12 pastries

½ batch/425g Viennese Danish Dough (page 159)

TOPPINGS

65g caster sugar

½ teaspoon ground cinnamon

60g unsalted butter, melted and cooled

120g walnut pieces, finely chopped

Icing sugar for finishing

DANISH DOUGH COFFEE CAKE (PLUNDERKRANZKUCHEN)

Baking this filled, split, and twisted cake in a ring or tube tin is a perfect way to get a symmetrical and moist result. The original recipe calls for candied orange peel, but I've substituted dried apricots to offset the sweetness of the currants and the almond filling.

1. Butter a 25cm ring or tube tin. For the filling, combine the milk and almond paste in a medium saucepan and set over a low heat. Whisk often to avoid lumps.

2. Thoroughly mix the sugar and flour in a small bowl, then whisk in the egg yolks all at once. When the milk mixture comes to the boil, whisk one-third of it into the egg yolk mixture, then return the milk to a medium heat. Once the milk boils again, begin to whisk in the yolk mixture, continuing to whisk until the filling thickens and comes to the boil. Cook, whisking constantly, for 30 seconds more.

3. Off the heat, whisk in the lemon zest and vanilla extract; scrape the filling into a bowl, press clingfilm directly against the surface and chill thoroughly.

4. Place the dough on a floured work surface and lightly dust the top with flour. Roll to a 30 x 40cm rectangle. Use an offset metal spatula to spread the chilled filling on the dough – it will be a thin layer. Set aside 2 tablespoons each of the currants and apricots for finishing the cake, then sprinkle the rest on top of the filling.

5. Tightly roll up the dough, starting from one of the long sides, then use a sharp knife to split the roll lengthways. Leave the halves, cut sides up, next to each other.

6. Without stretching the filled and split pieces of dough, gently twist the halves together and arrange in the prepared tin so that some of the split areas are facing upwards.

7. Cover the tin with a lightweight tea towel and prove the cake for several hours, until it puffs to double its original volume.

8. Set a rack in the lower third of the oven and preheat to 190°C/gas mark 5.

9. Set the tin in the oven and reduce the temperature to 180°C/gas mark 4. Bake for about 1 hour until well-risen and golden with an internal temperature of 93°C.

10. Cool the cake on a rack and unmould onto the rack or a cake board. Replace the tin with another rack or cake board and turn the cake right side up.

11. For the icing, stir the icing sugar, milk and vanilla extract together in a small saucepan and heat, stirring constantly, until just lukewarm. Use a spoon to generously drizzle the icing on the cake. Quickly sprinkle with the reserved currants and apricots, then the sliced almonds.

12. Slide the cake to a serving plate and serve on the day it is baked. Store loosely covered at room temperature.

Makes one 25cm ring, about 12 servings

½ batch/425g Viennese Danish Dough (page 159)

ALMOND CREAM FILLING

360ml whole milk

150g almond paste, cut into 0.5cm pieces (see Note)

65g caster sugar

35g unbleached plain flour

5 medium egg yolks

Finely grated zest of 1 small lemon

2 teaspoons vanilla extract

140g dried currants

150g snipped dried apricots

VANILLA ICING

210g icing sugar, sifted

3 tablespoons whole milk

1 teaspoon vanilla extract

75g lightly toasted flaked almonds

VARIATIONS

To substitute almonds or other nuts for the marzipan, combine 80g shelled nuts and 50g caster sugar and grind until fine and beginning to become pasty. When using almonds, add ¼ teaspoon almond extract.

NOTE

In the UK, almond paste can be a little hard to find. You can substitute marzipan instead but as it has a higher sugar content, I recommend you reduce the sugar quantity in the almond filling by half.

VIENNESE APRICOT POCKETS (MARILLENTASCHERL)

Makes about 16 small pastries, or 8 servings

½ batch/425g Viennese Danish Dough (page 159)

16 very small whole apricots (see Note)

100g almond paste, cut into 16 pieces (see Note)

Egg wash: 1 egg whisked with a pinch or salt

1 tablespoon dark rum

55g flaked almonds

Icing sugar for finishing

Crème Anglaise **(recipe follows)**

NOTE

Out of season, tinned apricot halves in light syrup, well drained, work well for this recipe.

In the UK, almond paste can be a little hard to find. You can substitute marzipan instead bust as it has a higher sugar content, I recommend you reduce the sugar quantity in the recipe by half.

CRÈME ANGLAISE

360ml whole milk

180ml double cream

65g caster sugar

1 vanilla pod, split

4 medium egg yolks

Ice water for cooling

Plunderteig is a perfect sweet and tender covering for small individual fruits like apricots, prune plums and tiny apples or pears. Here, the dough is wrapped *around* the fruit, unlike the puff pastry version on page 169, where the fruit is sandwiched between two layers of dough. This is excellent served with the Crème Anglaise that follows the recipe.

1. Rinse, stem and stone the apricots without fully cutting them in half. Stuff each with a small piece of almond paste and set aside.

2. Set a rack at the middle level in the oven and preheat to 200°C/gas mark 6. Line a large baking tray with parchment paper.

3. Roll the dough to a 30 x 35cm rectangle. Cut away a 5cm strip to make the dough a 30cm square. Slide the extra strip of dough onto a baking tray and chill.

4. Mark, then cut the dough square into sixteen 7.5cm squares. Lightly brush the egg wash onto the edges of the squares, then position an apricot in the centre of each. Sprinkle each apricot with a drop or two of the rum.

5. Bring 2 opposite corners of the dough together over the apricot, pinching them together; repeat with the other corners. Repeat with the remaining pastries and arrange on the prepared baking tray, seam side up.

6. Use a small fluted biscuit cutter or a serrated pastry wheel to cut the reserved strip of dough into 2.5cm disks or squares. Egg wash the pastries and press a piece of dough onto each one, placing it over the juncture of the corners of dough. Brush the added pieces of dough with egg wash and sprinkle with the flaked almonds.

7. Without proving them beforehand, place the pastries in the oven and reduce the temperature to 190°C/gas mark 5. Bake for about 15 minutes until well-risen and starting to colour.

8. Turn the baking tray from back to front and bake until the pastries are fully baked through, about 10 minutes more.

9. Cool the pastries on a rack and plan on serving warm. Dust with icing sugar right before serving with the *Crème Anglaise*.

Crème Anglaise

In a saucepan, bring the milk, cream and sugar to the boil with the vanilla pod. Whisk the egg yolks in a bowl, then whisk them into the boiling liquid; remove the vanilla pod. Strain the mixture back into the pan and cook it over a low heat, stirring constantly, until it is slightly thickened. Be careful not to let the sauce boil, or it will scramble. Pour the thickened sauce into a bowl set over ice water. Use it the same day or on the following day; if necessary, store it in the refrigerator.

VIENNESE ALMOND CRESCENTS (KLOSTERKIPFERL)

These aren't anything like croissants or the *Viennese Ischler Kipferl* on page 177, but they are a traditional pastry nonetheless. Here the Viennese Danish Dough is spread with an almond filling, folded, creased into a vague crescent shape, then strewn with flaked almonds. It's creamy, crunchy and sweet all at the same time – and thoroughly delicious.

1. Roll the dough on a floured surface to a 30 x 45cm rectangle. Mark, then cut the dough into four 7.5 x 45cm rectangles and line them up in a row.

2. Spread the almond filling in a 4cm strip at the closer end of each rectangle, then fold the tops of the rectangles over the filling so that the long edges meet. Cut each rectangle into 4 x 15cm strips.

3. Ease each strip into a crescent shape and transfer to a baking tray lined with parchment.

4. Cover the pastries with a lightweight tea towel and prove until almost doubled in size, about 1 hour, depending on the temperature of the room.

5. Set a rack at the middle level in the oven and preheat to 200°C/gas mark 6.

6. Carefully brush the pastries with the egg wash and sprinkle with the almonds.

7. Place in the oven and reduce the temperature to 190°C/gas mark 5. Bake for about 15 minutes until well-risen and starting to colour.

8. Turn the baking tray from back to front and continue baking the crescents for about 10 minutes longer until baked through.

9. Cool on a rack and serve them the day they are baked; dust with icing sugar just before serving.

Makes 12 pastries

½ batch/425g Viennese Danish Dough (page 159)

1 batch Almond Filling as in Chocolate Cinnamon Twists (page 176)

Egg wash: 1 egg whisked with a pinch of salt

55g flaked almonds, lightly crushed

Icing sugar for finishing

CHAPTER 8

BRIOCHE & OTHER YEAST-RISEN PASTRIES

Most of the recipes in this chapter are best as breakfast, brunch or tea pastries, though there are a couple like the brioche tart and shortcake that can be varied with different fruit and served as a dessert. The advantage to using brioche dough as a tart crust, aside from its tender sweetness, is its ability to absorb any juices the fruit generates while baking. Unlike a thinner pastry dough, which would become soggy, the thicker and slightly drier brioche dough welcomes the additional flavour and moisture. Both the tart and the shortcake are light and elegant enough to serve in the evening, also.

Of course, there are a few Viennese pastries here too. It's not for no reason that brioches, croissants, Danish pastries and the whole assortment of breakfast baking is referred to as *Viennoiserie* in French. I've included some personal favourites, like *Beugelteig*, which is a sweet but not especially rich yeast dough that can be used to make poppy seed or walnut-filled bows or strudels.

BRIOCHE MOUSSELINE DOUGH

Makes 900g, enough for 15-18 individual brioches depending on the size of the moulds used or one large or two smaller loaves baked in loaf or round tins

25g caster sugar

7g sachet fine granulated active dried yeast or instant yeast

75ml whole milk, scalded and cooled to 38°C

4 medium eggs, at room temperature

400g unbleached strong bread flour

1 teaspoon fine sea salt

225g unsalted butter, softened

This is a richer, softer and in some ways lighter dough than the brioche recipes in *BAKE!* and *BREAD*. Use it for a standard or round loaf baked in a tin or for any of the brioche roll variations on page 186. Softer and stickier than a leaner brioche dough, it's a little difficult to handle but don't let that stop you from trying it. Flour the palms of your hands rather than the work surface or the dough and you'll have no problems forming the dough. No matter what size or shape tin you choose, it will look appealing and taste even better.

1. Stir the sugar and yeast together in the bowl of a stand mixer, then whisk in the cooled milk. Let sit for 1 minute, then whisk again. Whisk in the eggs.

2. Use a large rubber spatula to stir in the flour, making sure not to leave any in the bottom of the bowl or stuck to its sides.

3. Using the dough hook, beat the dough on the lowest speed for 2-3 minutes until it comes together but isn't completely smooth. Let the dough rest for 15 minutes.

4. Mix again on a medium-low speed and sprinkle in the salt. Add the butter in 8 or 10 separate pieces, then let the dough mix for about 5 minutes until it completely absorbs the butter and becomes smooth, shiny and elastic. If the dough doesn't absorb the butter easily, stop and scrape down the bowl and dough hook every couple of minutes. Once you see that the butter is on its way to being completely absorbed, increase the speed to medium for about 1 minute.

5. Scrape the dough into a buttered bowl, turn it over so that the top is buttered and cover with clingfilm. Let ferment for 1-2 hours (depending on the temperature of the room) until it doubles in bulk.

6. Once the dough has fermented, scrape onto a floured surface and give it a turn: press the dough into a fat disk and fold one side over the centre, then fold the other side over both. Roll the dough down from the top to form an uneven sphere. Place the dough back in the bowl (butter the top again if necessary) seam-side down and cover again.

7. Refrigerate the dough for a couple of hours or until it rises again and then chills down. It's now ready to use. You can leave the dough in the refrigerator overnight, but you should bake it within 18 hours of beginning to mix it.

VIENNESE SWEET YEAST-RISEN DOUGH (BEUGELTEIG)

This versatile dough is tender and buttery, but is always meant to surround a filling, whether as individual pastries like the Walnut Bows and Poppy Seed Crescents or a large Walnut Strudel, all of which appear later in this chapter. *Beugel* is the German word for bow, as in bow and arrow. The Poppy Seed Crescents resemble the wood handle of the bow, while the Walnut Bows are made to somewhat resemble the bowstring after it's pulled to shooting position.

1. Stir the sugar and yeast together in the bowl of a stand mixer, then whisk in the cooled milk. Let sit for 1 minute, then whisk again. Whisk in the egg.

2. Use a large rubber spatula to stir in the flour, making sure not to leave any in the bottom of the bowl or stuck to its sides.

3. Sprinkle on the salt and distribute the butter in 8 or 10 pieces on the dough. Using the dough hook, beat on a medium-low speed for about 5 minutes until the butter is absorbed. Stop and scrape down the sides of the bowl and the dough hook several times, more often if the butter is staying stuck to the sides of the bowl instead of being incorporated.

4. Once the butter is incorporated, increase the speed to medium and beat the dough for 2–3 minutes until it is no longer stuck to the sides of the bowl and is more elastic.

5. Scrape the dough into a buttered bowl, turn it over so that the top is buttered and cover with clingfilm. Let ferment for 1–2 hours (depending on the temperature of the room) until it doubles in bulk.

6. Once the dough has fermented, scrape to a floured surface and deflate it. Use immediately or place the dough back in the bowl, cover and refrigerate. Chill for an hour or two or overnight, but be sure to use within 18 hours of beginning to mix it.

Makes about 450g, enough for any recipe in this chapter that calls for it

30g icing sugar, sifted

3 teaspoons (10g) fine granulated active dried yeast or instant yeast

75ml whole milk, scalded and cooled to 38°C

1 medium egg, at room temperature

225g unbleached strong bread flour

1 teaspoon fine sea salt

100g unsalted butter, softened

INDIVIDUAL BRIOCHES

Individual brioches are a typical breakfast bread in France. Here I include descriptions and instructions for the principal ones, plus a few suggestions for inventing your own.

Brioche Rolls

Divide the dough into 60g pieces. Round them into perfect little spheres and place them, about 7.5cm apart, on the prepared tin. Cover and let the rolls prove. Once almost doubled in size, brush the rolls with egg wash, using a very dry brush to avoid puddles, and leave plain or sprinkle with pearl sugar, coarse demerara sugar or coarsely chopped flaked almonds.

Raisin Brioches

When preparing the dough, add 140g dried currants, raisins or sultanas at the end of step 4, mixing them in for a minute or two on the lowest speed. Don't worry if they're not very evenly distributed; when the dough is turned in a later step, they will get mixed in. Proceed as for Brioche Rolls, above, but don't sprinkle with sugar or nuts before baking. If, when you're rounding the rolls, some raisins break through the top of the roll, poke them back in and pinch the dough over them; they'll burn if they stay on the surface.

Brioche Croissants

Press the finished dough out to a thick square on a floured baking tray and cover with clingfilm. Chill until firm, about 1 hour. Roll the dough to a 30cm square, then cut into 2 rectangles, each 30x 15cm. Join them together, overlapping the 15cm sides by 0.5cm to make a 15 x 60cm rectangle. Cut the dough into triangles with a 10cm base, roll the crescents and place in the prepared pans, following the instructions for shaping croissant dough on page 170. Cover the crescents with a lightweight tea towel and prove for about 1 hour (depending on the temperature of the room) until almost doubled in size. Brush with egg wash and sprinkle sparingly with pearl sugar; bake as above.

For all the following rolls you'll need to:

1. **Use one batch of Brioche Mousseline dough (page 184).**

2. **Line a large baking tray or Swiss roll tin with parchment paper.**

3. **Have a thin tea towel, or oiled or sprayed clingfilm to cover the formed rolls.**

4. **Make egg wash out of 1 egg whisked with a pinch of salt.**

5. **Set a rack at the middle level in the oven and preheat to 190°C/gas mark 5.**

6. **Bake the rolls until they are well-risen, deep golden, and firm, about 20 minutes.**

7. **Cool on a rack and serve them the same day. Alternatively, you can bag and freeze them, then reheat at 180°C/gas mark 4 before serving.**

NOTE
Brioche pans come in dozens of different sizes. Weigh a piece of dough that fills one of your pans by two thirds, then divide the dough accordingly. Any leftover dough may be used to make one of the variations that doesn't need a special pan.

Brioches à Tête

These are a little tricky at first, but once you get the hang of forming them, they are quite easy. (And if this all seems too complicated, you can just use plain rounded pieces of dough . . .) Divide the dough into 40–60g pieces. Have ready 12 buttered fluted brioche tins that have about an 80ml volume. Set the rounded piece of dough ① on its side with the smooth top facing to the right ②. Use the side of your hand, karate chop style, to indent the dough a third of the way in from the smooth side ③. Then roll back and forth at the indentation to make a little 'neck' under the head ④. Turn the brioche so that the head is upward and use the fingers of one hand to make a trough in the body ⑤ so that the head is surrounded with an even doughnut-shaped piece of dough ⑥. Drop the brioches into the prepared tins as they're formed ⑦⑧. Cover, proof, and brush with egg wash. (*Brioches à tête* are not sprinkled with sugar or nuts.) Bake and cool.

BRIOCHE LOAVES

Makes two medium loaves

1 batch Brioche Mousseline Dough (page 184)

Egg wash: 1 egg whisked with a pinch of salt, optional

2 x 450-680g loaf tins, buttered

VARIATION
ROUND BRIOCHE LOAVES: Butter two 5cm deep, 20cm round tins and line each with a disk of parchment paper. In step 1, above, divide each half of the dough into 10 pieces. Round and place them so that 6 pieces of dough line the perimeter of the tin and 4 are in the centre. Continue with the recipe at step 3.

The lighter and richer Brioche Mousseline dough is perfect for these. They can be baked in a standard loaf tin or in the same type of round tin used for cake layers. You can also make a single loaf and use the rest of the dough for one of the individual roll variations.

1. Divide the fully risen dough in half, making two 450g pieces. Divide each half into 5 pieces and round them all.

2. Stretching the dough balls slightly, place 5 pieces of dough in a line in each pan. Don't worry if the pans aren't full - they will be once the loaves have proved.

3. Cover with a lightweight tea towel and let rise until doubled and filling the pan.

4. Set a rack in the lower third of the oven and preheat to 190°C/gas mark 5.

5. Once the dough has fully proved, brush with egg wash if you like, being careful not to let any run between the loaf and the tin, which would make it stick.

6. Bake the loaves for 30-40 minutes until well-risen and deep golden, with an internal temperature of 94°C.

7. Unmould the loaves onto a rack and cool them on their sides to prevent them from falling.

8. Wrap and keep the loaves at room temperature. For longer storage, freeze them; defrost and reheat briefly at 180°C/gas mark 4 and cool before serving.

SWISS BRIOCHE CREAM CAKE (NIDELKUCHEN)

This is a specialty of the Konditorei Aebersold in Murten, a charming walled medieval town in Switzerland's Canton Fribourg. After tasting and speaking with Hans Aebersold about the topping in 2005, I came home and worked out this version. While the original recipe remains a secret, my efforts got me pretty close. One difference is that the bakery uses a dough similar to a rich white bread, though this brioche dough version certainly makes for a delicate result. This is a great coffee cake to serve for breakfast or brunch.

1. Round the dough to a sphere. Cover with a tea towel or clingfilm and let rest for 10 minutes. Butter and spray a 23cm springform tin, buttering the sides thickly as the topping may run over while baking.

2. Using the floured palm of your hand, press the dough into the prepared pan. If it resists, cover for 10 minutes, then press again. Cover and let the dough prove for 30–40 minutes until about 50% thicker.

3. After about 20 minutes, set a rack at the middle level in the oven and preheat to 190°C/gas mark 5. Slide a sheet of foil onto the bottom of the oven to catch any drips of butter.

4. For the topping, whisk the crème fraîche and egg yolks together. Use the palm of your hand to gently press a 20cm round area in the centre of the dough to deflate it, leaving a 1.25cm thicker rim at the side of the tin all around. Use a small offset spatula to spread the topping to within 1.25cm of the side of the pan. Sprinkle with half the sugar.

5. Place the tin in the oven, reduce the temperature to 180°C/gas mark 4 and bake for 15 minutes. Open the oven and pull out the rack; quickly sprinkle on the remaining sugar.

6. Bake the cake for about 20 minutes longer until well-risen and the topping is set and golden.

7. Cool the cake on a rack, then remove the side of the tin and slide the cake from the base onto a serving plate. Serve on the day it's baked.

Makes one 23cm cake, 8–10 servings

½ batch Brioche Mousseline Dough (page 184)

60ml crème fraîche or other thick cream

2 medium egg yolks

3 tablespoons caster sugar

PRUNE PLUM TART IN A BRIOCHE CRUST

Makes one 28 or 30cm tart, about 12 servings

½ batch Brioche Mousseline Dough (page 184)

ALMOND FILLING

200g almond paste (see Note)

3 tablespoons sugar

1 medium egg

85g unsalted butter, softened

2 teaspoons finely grated orange zest

1 medium egg yolk

1 teaspoon vanilla extract

35g unbleached plain flour

¼ teaspoon baking powder

1.14kg prune plums, rinsed, halved and stoned

2 tablespoons sugar for the plums

VARIATIONS
Substitute halves or quarters of small apricots (pictured at right) or peaches (to cut the peaches, see page 85). To use pears, peel, halve and slice them from stem to blossom end, cutting each half into quarters or sixths. If pear slices are too thick, they'll generate too much water for the filling to absorb.

NOTE
In the UK, almond paste can be a little hard to find. You can substitute marzipan instead but as it has a higher sugar content, I recommend you reduce the sugar quantity in the recipe by half.

Brioche dough makes a perfect crust for a tart of juicy fruit like these plums – or apricots, peaches or even small pears. A thin coating of almond filling helps to keep the crust drier, but the brioche can also absorb most of the fruit juices without becoming soggy. This is an excellent tart for brunch or teatime, served with thick unwhipped cream like crème fraîche, or with some lightly sweetened whipped cream. The almond filling here is twice as much as you need; freeze the rest in a plastic container, covered tightly, and use within a few weeks.

1. Set a rack at the lowest level in the oven; preheat to 200°C/gas mark 6. Butter a 28cm or 30cm round tart tin.

2. Set the dough on a floured surface and lightly dust with flour. Roll to a disk a little larger than the pan. Fold the dough in half and transfer to the prepared pan, lining up the fold with the diameter of the pan. Unfold the dough and press into the pan. Cover and let rest at room temperature while preparing the filling.

3. For the almond filling, beat the almond paste and sugar on a low speed in the bowl of a stand mixer fitted with the paddle attachment until reduced to fine crumbs. Add the whole egg and beat for 1–2 minutes until completely smooth. Beat in the butter until smooth, then stop and scrape the bowl and beater. Beat in the orange zest, egg yolk and vanilla extract. Quickly mix the flour and baking powder together and fold into the filling using a rubber spatula.

4. Uncover the dough and press a 20cm round area in the centre of the dough to deflate it, leaving a 1.25cm thicker rim at the side of the pan all around. Spread the almond filling on the dough – it will be a thin layer. Starting at the outside edge of the crust, arrange the plums, cut-side upwards, close to each other. Continue making concentric rows of plum halves until you reach the centre of the crust. Sprinkle the plums with sugar.

5. Place the tart in the oven and reduce the heat to 190°C/gas mark 5. Bake for about 45 minutes until the crust is well-coloured and dry and the plums are softened and juicy.

6. Cool the tart on a rack and serve warm or at room temperature.

BOSTOCK

Makes about eight bostocks

Eight 3cm-thick slices of day-old brioche loaf

ALMOND SYRUP

150ml water

65g caster sugar

2 strips orange zest, each 5cm wide and 5cm long, removed with a vegetable peeler

2 tablespoons *orgeat* (French almond syrup; see Note)

1 teaspoon vanilla extract

1 teaspoon orange flower water, optional

Almond Filling (page 192)

55g flaked almonds

Icing sugar

NOTE

If you have no orgeat syrup, substitute ½–1 teaspoon almond extract (taste the syrup after adding ½ teaspoon and use more only if necessary).

Originally crafted from leftover brioche, Bostock has taken its rightful place at the breakfast (or tea) table. A thick slice is moistened with an almond-flavoured syrup, then spread with almond cream and sprinkled with sliced almonds. Moist, sweet, perfumed and slightly crunchy around the edges, Bostock always pleases. Traditionally, these were round because the slices were cut from a cylindrical loaf; you can use rectangular slices of brioche or trim them into rounds using a cutter.

1. Set a rack at the middle level in the oven and preheat to 190°C/gas mark 5. Line a Swiss roll tin with buttered aluminium foil.

2. For the syrup, bring the water and sugar to a simmer, stirring to dissolve the sugar. Off the heat, add the orange zest; let the syrup cool. Remove the zest and stir in the *orgeat*, vanilla and orange flower water, if using.

3. Arrange the brioche slices on the prepared tin and use a brush to moisten with the syrup.

4. Spread each slice with a tablespoon or two of the almond filling, then sprinkle the sliced almonds on top.

5. Place the tin in the oven and reduce the temperature to 180°C/gas mark 4. Bake until the filling is set and the Bostocks are well-toasted and crisp around the edges.

6. Dust with icing sugar. Serve warm or cool on a rack and serve at room temperature.

VIENNESE BRIOCHE DUMPLINGS (BUCHTELN)

While *Buchteln* are originally from Bohemia, one of the countries that lost its national identity after being swallowed up by the Austrian Empire, today they're thought of as thoroughly Viennese. Small balls of rich dough (here I'm using brioche dough) usually filled with jam, *Buchteln* are baked in a heavily buttered pan so that the bases become quite crisp. They are served with just a sprinkling of icing sugar or with a vanilla custard sauce. I love pastries like this that are made in coffeehouses as well as in the home.

1. Place the dough on a floured surface and press or pat it to a 30cm square. Mark, then cut the dough into 5cm squares.

2. Place a small dab of jam or filling in the centre of each square. Pull the corners upward, pinch together, and invert the little filled bun as it's formed. Work quickly so that the dough doesn't soften too much.

3. Once you've formed the dumplings, spread half the butter in the bottom of a 5cm-deep 23cm square tin, then brush the rest of the butter on the formed pastries. Place them in the tin in 6 rows of 6 pastries in each. Cover and let the dumplings prove while the oven is preheating.

4. Set a rack at the middle level in the oven and preheat to 200°C/gas mark 6.

5. Once the oven is ready, uncover and place the dumplings inside. Reduce the temperature to 190°C/gas mark 5 and bake for about 20 minutes until well-risen and deep golden.

6. Serve the dumplings directly from the baking tin, placing a portion on a plate and dusting with icing sugar. Serve the sauce on the side.

Makes about 36 small pastries, 3 or 4 to a portion

½ batch Brioche Mousseline Dough (page 184)

140g apricot jam or any fruit jam you like, fruit butter, Poppy Seed Filling (page 200), or Walnut Filling (page 199), any large pieces chopped

120g unsalted butter, melted

Icing sugar for finishing

Crème Anglaise (page 180) for serving, optional

RASPBERRY BRIOCHE SHORTCAKE

Back in the 1990s, we used to have a demonstration class every afternoon at Peter Kump's New York Cooking School. Occasionally the chef *garde-manger* or the pastry chef from the celebrated restaurant Le Cirque would do one of them. José, the young French pastry chef, once made this lovely take on a shortcake. I made it for a class soon after I tasted it and have always wanted to share the recipe as a memorial to his talent, because José passed away very young.

1. Round the brioche dough to a sphere and let it rest, covered, on the work surface for 10 minutes. Butter a 5cm deep, 23cm round tin and line with parchment paper.

2. Use the floured palm of your hand to evenly press the dough into the prepared tin. Cover and let prove until almost doubled in bulk, about 45 minutes.

3. Set a rack at the middle level in the oven and preheat to 180°C/gas mark 4.

4. Bake the cake for 30–40 minutes until well-risen and deep golden, with an internal temperature of 94°C. Unmould and cool on a rack.

5. Meanwhile, make the filling by whisking the caster sugar, flour and salt together in a non-reactive saucepan. Whisk in the milk and the egg yolks. Place the pan over a low heat and whisk until the mixture thickens and comes to the full boil. Cook, whisking constantly, for 1 minute. Off the heat, whisk in 3 tablespoons of the orange liqueur and scrape the pastry cream into a bowl. Press clingfilm directly against the surface and refrigerate until cold.

6. Use a sharp serrated knife to split the brioche cake horizontally into 2 layers. Place the bottom layer on a serving plate, cut-side up and sprinkle with half of the remaining orange liqueur.

7. Whip the cream and fold into the cooled pastry cream. Spread half the cream on the bottom layer. Top the cream with the raspberries, then spread the remaining cream over the berries.

8. Sprinkle the cut surface of the top layer with the remaining orange liqueur, then invert the cut side onto the filling.

9. Dust the cake with icing sugar right before serving.

Makes one 23cm cake, 8-10 servings

½ batch Brioche Mousseline Dough (page 184)

100g caster sugar

45g unbleached plain flour

Pinch of salt

360ml whole milk

4 medium egg yolks

6 tablespoons orange liqueur

180ml double cream

340g fresh raspberries, picked over but not washed

Icing sugar for finishing

VARIATIONS

Tiny hulled strawberries or a mixture of different berries can replace the raspberries.

YEAST-RISEN WALNUT STRUDEL (NUSSBEUGELSTRUDEL)

Strudel made with a slightly sweet, buttery yeast dough is one of my favourite treats; in this recipe I'm using the Beugelteig on page 185 that's also used for the Poppy Seed and Walnut Bows that follow. One thing is important in preparing this: you have to be certain that the dough rolled into the centre of the strudel is baked through. Testing the temperature of the strudel with an accurate thermometer ensures perfect results.

Don't be shocked at the method of baking the strudel sealed inside a tube of parchment paper – it's the best and easiest way to make it so that it doesn't spread out and burst. Thanks to my friend Brian Pansari for sharing this method for baking a similar type of strudel at his *La Bonbonniere* bakery in Edison, New Jersey.

1. Thickly butter a 30 x 45cm sheet of parchment paper.

2. For the filling, combine the butter, milk and sugar in a medium saucepan and bring to a simmer. Stir in the walnuts and breadcrumbs and cook, stirring constantly, for 1–2 minutes; the filling will be quite thick. Off the heat, stir in the vanilla extract, lemon zest and cinnamon.

3. Scrape the filling onto a plate, press clingfilm directly against the surface, and cool to room temperature.

4. Once the filling has cooled, invert the dough onto a floured surface and lightly flour the top. Press the dough into a rough square, then press or gently roll into a 25 x 30cm rectangle. Evenly spread the cooled walnut filling all over the dough, leaving a 2.5cm margin uncovered on each of the 30cm sides.

5. Fold over the uncovered centimetres of dough at the top or bottom and roll the strudel Swiss roll style, ending seam-side up.

6. Run the palms of both hands under the strudel and move it, without stretching it, and position it centred at one of the long edges of the buttered paper, seam side up. Tightly roll the paper around the strudel; wrap 4 or 5 pieces of masking tape around the paper to keep it firmly around the strudel while baking. Leave the ends of the paper open to allow the strudel to expand.

7. Transfer the strudel to a Swiss roll tin, seam-side down, and let rest for 15–20 minutes.

8. Set a rack in the middle level of the oven and preheat to 190°C/gas mark 5.

9. Place the strudel in the oven and reduce the temperature to 180°C/gas mark 4. Bake for 45–55 minutes until it reaches an internal temperature of 94°C on an instant-read thermometer. (Pierce the strudel with the thermometer a little in from the ends, since they'll be trimmed away afterwards.)

10. Slide the strudel to a rack and remove the paper. Cool, seam-side down, on the rack. Trim the edges diagonally before serving. >>

Makes one 40cm-long strudel, about 18 servings

1 batch chilled Viennese Sweet Yeast-Risen Dough (page 185)

WALNUT FILLING

30g unsalted butter

120ml whole milk

100g caster sugar

240g walnut pieces, finely ground

45g fresh breadcrumbs

1 teaspoon vanilla extract

Finely grated zest of 1 small lemon

⅛ teaspoon ground cinnamon

VARIATIONS

POPPY SEED CRESCENTS (MOHNBEUGEL): These are given a slightly different final shaping from the Walnut Bows below, but use the same dough and a filling that's substantially the same.

In the walnut filling, page 199, substitute 170g ground poppy seeds for the walnuts and 105g raisins, coarsely chopped, for the breadcrumbs. Bring to the boil and cook, stirring, until no longer liquid, about 3 minutes. Cool, then divide the filling into 12 equal pieces, each about 40g. With lightly floured hands, roll each to a cylinder about 11.5cm long. Divide the dough into 12 pieces, each about 40g. Roll to the same size and shape as the filling.

Place the dough on a floured surface and roll to an oval about 15 x 9cm. Brush the dough with water, place the filling on it, and wrap the dough around the filling ①. Roll the pastry under the palm of your hands and shape the ends into points ②. Arrange them on the parchment-lined Swiss Roll tin and just curve 2.5cm on each end inward to form an elongated crescent shape ③.

Brush the pastries with egg wash (1 egg whisked with a pinch of salt); wait 5 minutes, then brush again.

Place the pastries in the oven and reduce the temperature to 180°C/ gas mark 4. Bake for 25–35 minutes until deep golden and baked through. Cool on a rack and serve the day they are baked.

WALNUT BOWS (NUSSBEUGEL): Use the same dough and filling as the Walnut Strudel on page 199 for this popular Viennese breakfast pastry. Shape as for the Poppy Seed Crescents above and use the side of your hand, karate-chop style, to make a crease in the middle of the pastry and bend it ③. Transfer to a parchment paper-covered Swiss roll tin. Repeat with the remaining dough and filling. Egg wash and bake.

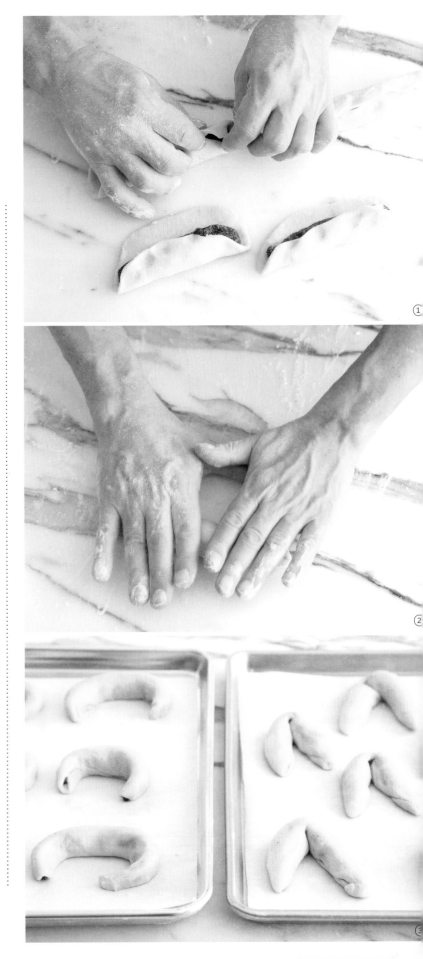

BRIOCHE FRUIT DUMPLINGS

These are a little like larger *Buchteln* and are served in a similar manner. While *Buchteln* may be left plain or filled with a jam or nut filling (see page 195), these dumplings are always filled with fresh fruit. This recipe is based on dumplings I recently tasted at Café Central in Vienna, one of the best places to enjoy traditional and contemporary Viennese pastry specialities.

1. Press or pat the dough on a floured surface to a 30cm square. Mark, then cut the dough into 7.5cm squares.

2. Place a small dab of jam and an apricot half in the centre of each square. Pull the corners upward, pinch them together and invert the little filled bun as it's formed. Work quickly so that the dough doesn't soften too much.

3. Once you've formed the dumplings, spread half the butter in the bottom of a 5cm-deep 23cm square tin, then brush the rest of the butter on the formed pastries. Place them in the tin in 4 rows of 4 dumplings in each. Cover and let prove while the oven is preheating.

4. Set a rack at the middle level in the oven and preheat to 200°C/gas mark 6.

5. Once the oven is ready, uncover and place the dumplings inside. Reduce the temperature to 190°C/gas mark 5 and bake for about 20 minutes until well-risen and deep golden.

6. Serve the dumplings directly from the baking tin, placing a portion on a plate and dusting with icing sugar. Serve the sauce on the side, if you like.

Makes about 16 small pastries, two per portion

½ batch Brioche Mousseline Dough (page 184)

70g apricot jam, any large pieces chopped

8 small apricots, rinsed, halved and stoned

60g unsalted butter, melted

Icing sugar for finishing

Crème Anglaise (page 180) for serving, optional

VARIATIONS

Substitute halves of small prune plums, a couple of plump sweet stoned cherries, or even a chunk of fresh pineapple or mango for the apricot halves.

NOTE

Traditional Viennese fruit dumplings are boiled, not baked and are served with buttered breadcrumbs and melted butter.

CHAPTER 9

PÂTE À CHOUX
OR CREAM PUFF
PASTRY

The only pastry dough that's actually cooked before it's baked, pâte à choux is not only versatile but also quite easy to prepare. Simple puffs, large or small, can be shaped by popping the dough onto a tin from a spoon, but more tailored shapes such as éclairs require piping. I've provided detailed instructions and photos on the techniques for piping, so with a little practise, the shapes should be easy to master.

Most desserts made from pâte à choux are filled with pastry cream. As you read through these recipes, you'll notice that the pastry cream fillings are similar but not exactly alike. Except for the *Crème Chiboust* filling in the *Gâteau Saint-Honoré*, you can pretty much use the fillings interchangeably, according to your taste. Further flavour variations for pastry cream are listed after the recipe for *Petits Choux au Café* on page 206.

PÂTE À CHOUX

Makes 780g

240ml whole milk

100g unsalted butter

¼ teaspoon fine sea salt

½ teaspoon caster sugar

155g unbleached plain flour

245g whole eggs

NOTE

For greatest accuracy weigh all the ingredients. For exact weight of the eggs, place a bowl on the scales and zero it. Add 4 medium eggs; if they're not enough, whisk a fifth egg and add only enough for the exact weight. This base recipe for cream puff pastry will yield enough for any of the recipes in this chapter.

Makes 24 or more small *choux*, depending on the size they're piped

1 batch *Pâte à Choux* (above)

COFFEE PASTRY CREAM

360ml whole milk

120ml double cream

65g caster sugar

1 tablespoon instant espresso powder

3 tablespoons cornflour

5 medium egg yolks

2 teaspoons vanilla extract or dark rum

60g unsalted butter, at room temperature

COFFEE GLAZE

320g icing sugar, sifted

75ml water

2 teaspoons instant espresso powder

2 tablespoons light corn syrup or golden syrup

30g unsalted butter, softened

2 teaspoons vanilla extract

For the best leavening, plan on getting the piped shapes into the oven as soon as possible after the paste is mixed and the shapes are formed. Thanks to Jeff Yoskowitz for sharing his excellent recipe.

1. Combine the milk, butter, salt and sugar in a 2-litre saucepan and place over a medium heat. Bring the mixture to the boil, stirring occasionally, to make sure the butter melts.

2. Once the liquid has come to a full rolling boil, remove the pan from the heat and add the flour all at once. Use a wooden spoon or silicon spatula to smoothly stir it in. Return the pan to the heat and beat the paste for 20–30 seconds, just until the bottom of the pan is filmed.

3. Pour the paste into the bowl of a stand mixer and fit it with the paddle attachment. Beat on the lowest speed for 30 seconds to cool slightly. Add the eggs one at a time, beating smooth after each addition. Stop and scrape the bowl and beater after the second and third eggs.

COFFEE FILLED & ICED CREAM PUFFS (PETITS CHOUX AU CAFÉ)

Small puffs like these were used to form part of the assortment of petits fours served at the Sporting Club in Monte Carlo when I worked there several summers in the 1970s. Since the recipe makes quite a few, these would be a perfect dessert to serve, along with some cookies or plainer pastries, for a large party.

1. Set racks in the upper and lower thirds of the oven and preheat to 190°C/gas mark 5. Prepare two rimmed baking trays or Swiss roll tins: use a dab of the dough in each corner ① to hold parchment paper in place for piping ②.

2. Using a pastry bag fitted with a 1cm fine French star tube (Size 4, Ateco #824), pipe the pâte à choux to make twenty-four 2cm-diameter choux on the prepared pans. Hold the bag at a 45° angle to the tin, touch the tube to the paper, squeeze quickly to make a small sphere, then stop squeezing and lift upwards ③. If you leave a point, moisten your fingertip and smooth it away.

3. Bake the choux for 20–25 minutes until golden and dry. Completely cool the tins on racks.

4. For the pastry cream, set aside 120ml of the milk in a medium bowl. Combine the remaining 240ml milk with the cream, sugar and espresso powder in a medium non-reactive saucepan and whisk to mix. Place the pan over a low heat and bring to the full boil.

5. Meanwhile, whisk the cornflour into the reserved 120ml milk and whisk in the egg yolks.

6. Once the milk boils, whisk about one-third of it into the yolk mixture. Return the remaining milk to the full boil. Beginning to whisk before pouring, add the egg yolks to the pan mixture in a quick stream, whisking constantly. >>

FLAVOURING PASTRY CREAM

In each of the following variations, omit the coffee and rum from the recipe.

VANILLA PASTRY CREAM: Flavour the pastry cream with 2 teaspoons vanilla extract instead of the rum.

LEMON OR ORANGE PASTRY CREAM: Add the grated zest of 1 large lemon or orange to the milk mixture. For lemon, add 2 tablespoons lemon juice to the egg yolk mixture; for orange, add 2 tablespoons orange juice and 1 tablespoon lemon juice. Reduce the vanilla extract to 1 teaspoon.

CHOCOLATE PASTRY CREAM: Bring an additional 120ml milk to the boil and stir in 225g plain chocolate off the heat. Whisk smooth and add to the pastry cream along with the vanilla extract and butter.

CARAMEL PASTRY CREAM: Mix 100g sugar and 2 tablespoons water in a large saucepan. Set the pan over a medium heat and cook, stirring occasionally, until the sugar melts and caramelises to a deep amber colour. Reduce the sugar in the pastry cream recipe to 50g; heat the milk, cream and sugar in a separate pan while you are cooking the caramel. Once the caramel is cooked, remove the pan from the heat and pour the hot milk mixture into the caramel, shielding the hand you use to hold the handle of the milk pan with a towel and averting your face. Afterward, bring the mixture to the boil and continue with the recipe.

LIQUEUR PASTRY CREAM: Add 1–2 tablespoons sweet liqueur, such as triple sec, or 1 tablespoon non-sugared spirits, such as rum or kirsch to the cream along with the butter and vanilla extract.

7. Cook, whisking constantly, until the pastry cream thickens, comes to the full boil and boils for 30 seconds.

8. Off the heat, whisk in the vanilla extract and butter. Pour the pastry cream into a shallow bowl so it cools quickly and press clingfilm directly against the surface. Refrigerate immediately and use it as soon as it's cold or within 24 hours.

9. Fill the choux puffs completely with the pastry cream using a pastry bag and a 0.5cm (Size 2, Ateco #802) plain tube, inserting the tube through the bottom flat side of the choux; it will feel noticeably heavier once it's fully filled ①. Set aside.

10. For the glaze, half-fill a saucepan with water and bring to the boil over a medium heat.

11. Meanwhile, use a silicon spatula to mix the icing sugar, water and espresso powder in a heatproof bowl larger than the top of the saucepan – it will be very thick. Beat in the corn or golden syrup, butter and vanilla extract.

12. Reduce the heat so that the water just simmers gently, then set the bowl over the pan. Warm the icing, whisking constantly until it is lukewarm, about 38°C. Use the glaze immediately or reheat it carefully if necessary.

13. Once the glaze is ready, quickly dip the top third of each choux puff into it, letting the excess glaze drip back into the bowl and setting the puff right-side up on a parchment paper-covered tin ②.

14. Arrange the choux on a serving plate to serve. Refrigerate them if they have to sit more than a couple of hours – but don't chill for too long, or the pastry will get soggy.

① ②

CHOCOLATE ÉCLAIRS

Makes about eighteen 10cm éclairs

1 batch *Pâte à Choux* **(page 204)**

VANILLA POD PASTRY CREAM

360ml whole milk

120ml double cream

65g caster sugar

1 vanilla pod, split lengthways

3 tablespoons cornflour

5 medium egg yolks

30g unsalted butter, at room temperature

CHOCOLATE GLAZE

75ml water

75ml light corn syrup or golden syrup

200g caster sugar

225g plain chocolate cut into 0.5cm pieces or 225g plain chocolate mini chips

VARIATION

For éclairs with a chocolate filling, use the chocolate pastry cream variation on page 206.

No one seems to agree as to whether the 'chocolate' in 'chocolate éclair' refers only to the icing or to the pastry cream filling as well. I'm partial to vanilla pastry cream with chocolate icing, but you can use chocolate or any other flavour of pastry cream you like.

1. For the pastry cream, set aside 120ml of the milk in a medium bowl. Combine the remaining 240ml milk with the cream, sugar and vanilla pod in a medium non-reactive saucepan and whisk together. Bring to the full boil over a low heat.

2. Meanwhile, whisk the cornflour into the reserved 120ml milk, then whisk in the egg yolks.

3. Once the milk boils, whisk about one third of it into the egg yolk mixture. Return the remaining milk to the full boil. While whisking constantly, add the egg yolk mixture in a quick stream. Cook, whisking constantly, until the pastry cream thickens, comes to the full boil and boils for 30 seconds more. Use tongs to discard the vanilla pod and off the heat, whisk in the butter. Pour the pastry cream into a shallow bowl to cool quickly and press clingfilm directly against the surface. Refrigerate immediately until ready to use.

4. Set a rack at the middle level in the oven and preheat to 220°C/gas mark 7. Line a baking tray with parchment paper.

5. Use a pastry bag fitted with a 13mm fine French star tube (Size 6, Ateco #826), to pipe 10cm éclairs 5cm apart on the prepared tin. Hold the bag at a 45° angle with the tube touching the paper and pull while squeezing the bag. When you reach the end, stop squeezing and lift toward the éclair to avoid leaving a point – see page 202. (If you do, moisten your fingertip and rub it smooth.)

6. Bake the éclairs for 10 minutes, then reduce the heat to 180°C/gas mark 4 and bake until dark golden and dry, about 20 minutes more. Cool the éclairs on a rack.

7. Using a pastry bag fitted with a 0.5cm (Size 2, Ateco #802) plain tube, pierce the bottom of each éclair in a couple of places and squeeze in the filling. Set the éclairs, filled-side up, on a clean parchment paper-lined tin.

8. For the glaze, stir the water, corn syrup and sugar together in a medium saucepan. Bring to the boil over a medium heat, stirring occasionally so that the sugar dissolves. When you reach a full rolling boil, boil for 30 seconds more. Off the heat, add the chocolate and shake the pan so that it submerges. Let stand for a couple of minutes, then whisk the glaze only until just smooth; too much agitation will introduce air bubbles.

9. Test the coating ability of the glaze by dipping the handle of a wooden spoon into it. If the glaze isn't covering well, let cool for a few minutes, gently stir with a spatula, and test again.

10. Pick up an éclair, filled-side up, and dip the unpierced side into the glaze. Hold for the excess to drip off, then turn glazed-side up and place back on the tin. Repeat with the remaining éclairs (if the glaze cools, reheat over simmering water without stirring too much). Let the glaze set and serve within several hours.

BIGNÈ DI RICOTTA

Makes about eighteen 6.5–7.5cm cream puffs

1 batch *Pâte à Choux* (page 204)

900g firm, dry Ricotta cheese

160g icing sugar, sifted

1 teaspoon vanilla extract

1 teaspoon finely grated orange zest

¼ teaspoon ground cinnamon

115g plain chocolate, cut into 0.5cm pieces, or 115g plain chocolate mini chips

35g candied orange peel, cut into 0.5cm dice, optional

Icing sugar for finishing

VARIATIONS

Half-fill the *choux* with any flavour of pastry cream, then top them by piping on a large rosette of sweetened whipped cream. Finish with the top and dust with icing sugar.

Or fill the puffs with a thin layer of vanilla pastry cream, add some sliced sugared strawberries or lightly sugared raspberries and top those with a rosette of whipped cream.

These cream puffs are split and filled with the same type of cream that you find inside Sicilian *cannoli*. Look for freshly-made Ricotta for the filling – the supermarket variety is too wet and loose to hold its shape. Pastry shops use a very dry Ricotta called *impastata*, and it's available nationally but only in large quantities. Maybe a friendly local grocer will order some for you.

1. Set a rack at the middle level in the oven and preheat to 220°C/gas mark 7. Line a baking tray with parchment paper.

2. Use a pastry bag fitted with a 13mm fine French star tube (Size 6, Ateco #826), to pipe the *pâte à choux* in 4cm mounds 5cm apart all around on the prepared tin. Hold the pastry bag perpendicular to the tin and about 2.5cm above it, then squeeze out a half sphere. Stop squeezing and pull away sideways to avoid leaving a point. If you do, wet a fingertip and 'erase' the point by gently smearing over it.

3. Bake the *choux* for 10 minutes, then reduce the temperature to 180°C/gas mark 4 and bake for about 20 minutes more until well-risen, deep golden and fairly dry. Slice off the top third of one of the *choux*, as in step 5, to determine doneness. Cool on a rack.

4. While the choux are baking and cooling, beat the Ricotta and sugar together on a medium-low speed in a stand mixer fitted with the paddle attachment. Remove the bowl from the mixer and use a rubber spatula to beat in the vanilla extract, orange zest and cinnamon. If you chopped the chocolate, sift away any small dusty particles in a small open-mesh sieve, then add the chocolate and if you like, the orange peel.

5. Line the pastries up on a clean tin and use a sharp serrated knife to slice off the top third of each. Pipe or spoon the filling into the choux puffs, overfilling slightly so that the Ricotta shows when the top is replaced. Dust with icing sugar before serving.

PARIS–BREST PRALINÉ

This tyre-shaped pastry was supposedly invented in honour of a bicycle race of the same name. Today, it's more common to make it as a series of separate large spheres of dough that grow together while the pastry is baking, whether in the traditional round shape or as a rectangular strip, rather than piping the dough into rings. The crunchy topping has recently become popular in fancy pastry shops in Paris.

1. For the crunch topping, beat the butter and sugar on a low speed in a stand mixer with a rubber spatula. Beat in the flour until it's absorbed, then increase the speed to medium-low and beat for about 20 seconds. Set aside at room temperature.

2. Set a rack at the middle level in the oven and preheat to 220°C/gas mark 7. Line a baking tray with parchment paper.

3. Trace a 23cm circle on the paper lining the tin and turn it over. Use a pastry bag fitted with a 2.5cm opening and no tube to pipe 5cm spheres of the *choux* paste close together just inside the circle.

4. Divide the crunch topping into as many pieces as there are spheres of *pâte à choux* and roll the topping pieces 3mm thick; cut them into even rounds using a 4cm plain or fluted cutter.

5. Paint the pastry with egg wash and top each mound of *pâte à choux* with the topping.

6. Bake the pastries for 10 minutes, then reduce the temperature to 180°C/gas mark 4 and bake until they are well-risen, deeply coloured, and crisp, about 20–30 minutes more; cool on a rack.

7. When you're ready to assemble the pastry, beat the butter and chocolate hazelnut spread on a medium speed in a stand mixer with the paddle attached until smooth. Add the chilled pastry cream all at once, then beat until the filling is soft and smooth, about 5 minutes.

8. Use a sharp serrated knife to slice off the top third of each pastry. Slide the base to a serving plate and pipe in the filling in a series of large rosettes using a pastry bag fitted with a fine French star tube (Size 4, Ateco #824).

9. Replace the top of the pastry and serve it within a couple of hours.

Makes one 23cm round pastry, about 10 servings

½ batch *Pâte à Choux* (page 204)

CRUNCH TOPPING

35g unsalted butter, cool but slightly soft

50g granulated or demerara sugar

45g unbleached plain flour

Egg wash: 1 egg whisked with a pinch of salt

FILLING

225g unsalted butter, softened

130g chocolate hazelnut spread

1 batch Vanilla Pod Pastry Cream (page 208)

VARIATIONS

For a change of shape, pipe the *pâte à choux* in 2 straight lines of spheres next to each other instead of a circle; everything else remains the same. Brush egg wash onto the pastry and sprinkle with flaked almonds or hazelnuts instead of using the crunch topping.

GÂTEAU SAINT-HONORÉ

Possibly the most elegant and impressive-looking dessert made from *pâte à choux*, Gâteau Saint-Honoré has a double pedigree: it is named in honour of a seventh-century bishop of Amiens who is venerated as the patron saint of pastry cooks and it was first made in Paris pastry shops in 1884 to celebrate the centennial of the birth of Antonin Carême, the greatest French chef of the nineteenth century. The Crème Chiboust filling, named for the nineteenth-century Parisian pastry shop in which it originated, uses a cooked meringue to lighten the pastry cream. This cake is really a combination of quite easy preparations and I've changed the round shape to a rectangular one that's even simpler to put together.

1. Set racks in the upper and lower thirds of the oven and preheat to 190°C/gas mark 5. Line 2 baking trays with parchment paper.

2. Place the Flaky Buttery Dough on a floured surface, roll to a rectangle a bit larger than 40 x 12.5cm and place on one of the prepared tins. Use a ruler and a sharp pastry wheel to trim the pastry to exactly 40 x 12.5cm. Use a fork to pierce the pastry all over at 1.25cm intervals.

3. Brush the long edges of the pastry base with water. Using a pastry bag fitted with a 1cm fine French star tube (Size 6, Ateco #826), pipe the *pâte à choux* in a straight line onto the moistened edges, holding the bag at a 45° angle to the strip of dough and squeezing out a line equal to the diameter of the tube. Don't worry about the short edges – they will be trimmed.

4. Use the remaining *pâte à choux* to make twenty-four 2.5cm puffs on the second prepared tin. Hold the bag at a 45° angle to the tin, touch the tube to the paper, and squeeze quickly to make a small sphere, then stop squeezing and lift upward. If you leave a point, moisten a fingertip and smooth it away (see photos on page 205).

5. Bake the base and *choux* for 20–25 minutes until golden and dry. Cool in the tins on racks.

6. For the filling, set aside 120ml of the milk in a medium bowl. Combine the remaining 360ml milk with 50g of the sugar and the vanilla pod in a medium non-reactive saucepan and whisk well. Place over a low heat and bring to the full boil.

7. Meanwhile, whisk the cornflour into the reserved 120ml milk and whisk in the egg yolks.

8. Once the milk boils, whisk about one-third of it into the egg yolk mixture. Return the remaining milk to the full boil. Whisk in the egg yolk mixture in a quick stream and cook, whisking constantly, until the pastry cream thickens, comes to the full boil and boils for 30 seconds. Discard the vanilla pod.

9. Off the heat, whisk in the butter. Pour the pastry cream into a shallow bowl to cool quickly and press clingfilm directly against the surface. Chill until cold and use within 24 hours.

10. Whisk the pastry cream smooth in a large bowl and set aside. Use a fork to stir the gelatine into the water in a small heatproof bowl. Half-fill a saucepan with water and bring to the boil. Whisk the egg whites and the remaining 65g sugar together in the bowl of an electric mixer>>

Makes one 40cm-long dessert, about 8 servings

½ batch/300g Flaky Buttery Dough (page 14) or ⅓ batch/300g Puff Pastry (page 155)

1 batch *Pâte à Choux* (page 204)

CRÈME CHIBOUST FILLING

480ml whole milk

50g plus 65g caster sugar

1 vanilla pod, split lengthways

3 tablespoons cornflour

5 medium egg yolks

30g unsalted butter, soft

10g (3½ scant teaspoons) unflavoured powdered gelatine

75ml water

3 medium egg whites

CARAMEL GLAZE

300g sugar

2 tablespoons water

½ teaspoon distilled white vinegar

WHIPPED CREAM

240ml double cream

2 tablespoons caster sugar

1 teaspoon vanilla extract

SPINNING THE CARAMEL

To spin the caramel in the *choux*, gently reheat the caramel and dip a spoon into it. Hold the spoon perpendicular to the pan and let the caramel begin to fall in a thin stream and then quickly run the spoon back and forth over the choux on one side of the pastry, holding the spoon about 5cm above it.

and place over the pan of boiling water. Whisk gently but constantly until the egg whites are hot, about 60°C and the sugar dissolves. Place the bowl on the mixer with the whisk attachment and whisk on medium-high speed until well-risen in volume but not dry. Once you start whisking, place the bowl of soaked gelatine over the pan of water off the heat until it becomes a clear liquid. When the egg whites are ready, quickly whisk the gelatine into the pastry cream and then fold in the meringue.

11. Fill the small *choux* puffs using a pastry bag and a 0.5cm (Size 2, Ateco #802) plain tube, inserting the tube through the bottom flat side of the *choux*. Set aside. Spread the remaining filling in the rectangular base between the two side walls of the *pâte à choux*.

12. For the caramel glaze, stir the sugar, water and vinegar together in a medium saucepan and place over a medium heat. Have a bowl of ice water ready. Make sure the bowl is wide enough for the bottom of your saucepan to be submerged in the water by a couple of inches.

13. Once the sugar starts to melt, stir occasionally with a metal spoon, but don't stir too much, or it might start to crystallise in large lumps. If a lot of sugar sticks to the side of the pan, use a clean pastry brush dipped in hot water to dissolve it. As the sugar liquefies and starts to become an even, light caramel colour, move the pan off the heat and continue cooking in the heat retained by the pan. When finished, the caramel should be clear (without any visible sugar granules) and a deep amber colour. Usually it takes a few times removing the pan from the heat and putting it back again before the caramel is the correct colour. Test by letting a few drops fall from a spoon onto a sheet of white paper – it should be a clear dark amber colour. Once the caramel has reached the right shade, immerse the base of the pan in the ice water for just a few seconds to cool the pan so that it won't keep darkening the caramel. Don't let the caramel itself cool or it will become too thick to use.

14. Immediately glaze the puffs: quickly dip the top third of each into the caramel, turning it right side up and setting it on a parchment-lined pan. Take care to prevent any crumbs or dabs of filling from dropping into the caramel – this might cause it to become lumpy and crystallised before you have glazed all your pastries. Once all the puffs are glazed, gently reheat the caramel. Carefully dip a single spot on the bottom of each choux and affix it to one of the side walls on the pastry base.

15. Whip the cream with the sugar and vanilla extract to a soft peak and spread over the pastry cream. Trim the edges of the pastry before serving. Keep the gâteau at a cool room temperature (but not in the refrigerator) until serving time.

ITALIAN CREAM PUFF FRITTERS (SFINCI)

My maternal grandmother loved to make these, and I can understand why – they're light, luscious and easy to whip up from very little in the way of ingredients. The standard coating is cinnamon sugar, but sugar mixed with grated lemon or orange zest is delicious too.

Makes about 40 small fritters

1 batch *Pâte à Choux* (page 204)

100g sugar

½ teaspoon ground cinnamon

480ml sunflower oil or light olive oil for frying

1. Combine the sugar and cinnamon in a medium bowl.

2. Heat the oil in a deep pan or wok over a medium heat to 180°C. Line a Swiss roll tin with kitchen towels.

3. Use a teaspoon to scoop up a spoonful of the dough, then use a second spoon to scrape it out into the hot oil. Work with the spoons close to the surface of the oil so it doesn't splatter.

4. Use a skimmer or slotted spoon to stir the fritters around for a few seconds until they become inflated and golden. Wait to see that they split, then that the split area colours too, as a sign of doneness.

5. Transfer the fritters to the prepared tin to drain, then one at a time, roll them in the cinnamon sugar.

6. Continue frying and sugaring the fritters; as you finish each fritter, arrange it on a serving plate.

GOUGÈRE WITH GRUYÈRE, BACON & PECANS

Hardly a French classic, this bacony and nutty version of the traditional Burgundian pastry always wins admirers. If you buy a large *gougère* in a pastry shop, it's piped as a series of spheres in a ring, but you can also make individual smaller puffs to serve as an hors d'oeuvre to nibble with drinks.

1. Scatter the diced bacon in a sauté pan and place over a low heat. Cook until the fat has melted and the pieces are beginning to crisp, about 10 minutes, stirring occasionally. Using a slotted spoon, transfer the bacon to a plate covered with kitchen towels to drain.

2. Set a rack at the middle level in the oven and preheat to 220°C/gas mark 7. Line a baking tray with parchment paper.

3. Bring the water, butter and salt to the boil in a small saucepan. Remove from the heat and stir in the flour all at once. Return the pan to the heat and beat the paste for about 20 seconds until the bottom of the pan is filmed.

4. Scrape the paste into a mixing bowl and stir for 1 minute to cool it down. Beat in the eggs, one at a time, then beat in the pepper, nutmeg, cheese and cooked bacon.

5. Trace a 25cm circle on the paper lining the prepared tin and turn it over. Use a pastry bag fitted with a 2.5cm opening and no tube to pipe large spheres of the paste close together on the traced circle.

6. Brush the pastry with the egg wash and scatter the pecans all over the surface.

7. Bake for 10 minutes, then reduce the temperature to 180°C/gas mark 4 and bake until well-risen, deeply coloured, and crisp, about 20 minutes more. A good *gougère* is still moist inside.

8. Cool the pastry on a rack and serve warm, or cool completely and reheat it at 180°C for 10 minutes before serving.

Makes one 23cm ring or 24 small puffs

55g thick-cut bacon, cut into 0.5cm dice

75ml water, milk, or a combination

45g unsalted butter, cubed

½ teaspoon fine sea salt

65g unbleached plain flour

2 medium eggs, at room temperature

¼ teaspoon freshly ground black pepper

Large pinch of freshly grated nutmeg

115g coarsely grated Swiss Gruyère cheese

Egg wash: 1 egg whisked with a pinch of salt

60g pecan pieces, coarsely chopped

VARIATIONS

Substitute walnuts or pistachios for the pecans. Or for a traditional *gougère*, omit the bacon and pecans.

To make small *gougères*, pipe like the *petits choux* on page 204, using a 13mm plain tube (Size 6, Ateco #806), and resume at step 6 above, baking for only about 5 minutes after reducing the temperature; taste one to check doneness.

AFTERWORD

This pastry book has marked several important milestones in my life and my career. My first book, *Nick Malgieri's Perfect Pastry*, was published in 1989, exactly twenty-five years before the appearance of this book. While there are a few similarities between the two books, the present one is 90 per cent new material, the result of many years spent teaching and writing about baking and desserts.

While this book was in the editing process, about a year before publication, I had the joyful experience of visiting with some friends I had met exactly forty years prior, when I arrived in Switzerland to work at my first job after culinary school. My friend and mentor, Albert Kumin, who was my pastry teacher at the Culinary Institute of America, had urged me to work in Switzerland if I was serious about becoming a pastry chef. The start of that process was a foundation for many opportunities to learn first hand about pastries, desserts, chocolates, breads, and a whole world of baking and desserts that continues to fascinate me.

I've been fortunate that through my work over the years, I've been able to indulge my passion to learn more and more about my craft and share it with readers like you.

Today, because of all the computer technology within everyone's easy reach, I can even provide video tutorials for some of the more complex parts of this book: look for them at my website, www.nickmalgieri.com.

It's my hope that you use this book to learn new techniques and recipes and that you delight yourself as well as your family and friends with the results.

And remember, bake something!

BIBLIOGRAPHY

Bachmann, Walter. *Swiss Bakery and Confectionery.* London: Maclaren & Sons Limited, 1949.

Calvel, Raymond, *Le Goût du Pain.* Paris: Éditions Jérôme Villette, 1990.

Darenne, E., and E. Duval. *Traité de Pâtisserie Moderne* (rev. ed.). Paris: Flammarion, 1974.

Fance, Wilfred James. *The New International Confectioner.* London and Coulsdon, England: Virtue & Company, 1981.

Ferber, Christine. *Mes Tartes Sucrées et Salées.* Paris: Payot, 1998.

Gouffé, Jules. *Le Livre de Pâtisserie.* Paris: Hachette, 1873.

Grigson, Jane. *Jane Grigson's Fruit Book.* New York: Atheneum, 1982.

Kaltenbach, Marianne. *Aus Schweizer Küchen.* Bern, Switzerland: Hallwag, 1977.

Lacam, Pierre. *Memorial Historique et Géographique de la Pâtisserie.* Paris: Chez l'Auteur, 1895.

Mayer, Eduard. *Wiener Süßspeisen.* Linz, Austria: Trauner Verlag, 1968.

Nutt, Frederick. *The Complete Confectioner; or, the Whole Art of Confectionary Made Easy.* London: L. Harrison & J.C. Leigh, 1815.

Polshenke, Paul. *Gebäck aus Deutschen Landen.* Alfeld, Germany: Gildeverlag, 1949.

Schumacher, Karl. *Wiener Süßspeisen.* Linz: Trauner Verlag, 1990.

Skrach, Hans. *Die Wiener Konditorei.* Vienna, Austria: Verlag Für Jugend und Volk, 1949.

Spriano, Carlos. *Mi Cocina.* Buenos Aires: Sociedad Impresora Americana, 1939.

Thuries, Yves. *Le Livre de Recettes d'un Compagnon du Tour de France* (3 vols.). Cordes-sur-Ciel, France: Société Éditar, 1980.

Vogt, Ernst, et al. *Der Schweizer Bäcker-Konditor* (3 vols.). Thun, Switzerland: Ott Verlag, 1944.

Witzelsberger, Richard. *Das Österreichesche Mehlspeisen Kochbuch.* Vienna: Verlag Kremayr & Scheriau, 1979.

INDEX

ACKNOWLEDGEMENTS

Enormous thanks to all my colleagues and friends whose kindness and support contributed to this book:

Phyllis Wender, my agent, and her team Susie Cohen and Allison Cohen;

At Kyle Books: Kyle Cathie, owner; Anja Schmidt, US publisher; Ron Longe, publicist; and Judith Hannam and Vicki Murrell in the London office;

Natalie Danford, my 24/7 writing advisor;

Our production team: Dirk Kaufman, designer; Romulo Yanes, photographer; Paul Grimes, food stylist; PJ Mehaffey, prop stylist; Ana Deboo, copyeditor and Liana Krissoff, proofreader;

For recipe testing: Kyra Effren, Jeff Yoskowitz, and Sandy Gluck;

At the Institute of Culinary Education: Rick Smilow, owner; Andrea Tutunjian, Director of education; and director of purchasing Shawona Jones and all her staff;

For sharing recipes and their experience with various recipes and processes: Rhonda Caplan, Lesley Chesterman, Philippe Conticini, Rachel Fletcher and Stephen Fagg, Gunther Heiland, Albert Kumin, Sandy Leonard, Ben Mims, Nancy Nicholas, Ann Nurse, Brian Pansari, Hermann Reiner, Roberto Santibañez and Marco Diaz, Chef Somsak, Michelle Tampakis, Barbara Bianco Tutunjian, and Jeff Yoskowitz;

In Austria: Hans Diglas, Erik Goeller, and Astrid Pockfuss of Vienna Tourism;

In Switzerland: Aurelia Carlen of Zurich Tourism, Brian Jaeger, Ivo Jud, Fredi Nussbaum, Kerrin Rousset, Michaela Ruoss of the Switzerland Tourism New York office, and Claudia Schmid;

In Turkey: Aylin Öney Tan, Cenk Sönmeszoy, Seraç Deniz Akgüneş, Sitare Baras, Cem Erol, Nadir Güllü, Ömer Güllü, Murat Güney, Filiz Hösükoğlu, Mary İšin, Dinçer Oruçoğlu, Mustafa Özgüler, and Ahmed Sevim.